The Encyclopedia of
CLASSICAL
MYTHOLOGY

PRENTICE-HALL, INC. ENGLEWOOD CLIFFS, N.J.
A SPECTRUM BOOK

This book was originally entitled ELSEVIERS MYTHOLOGISCHE ENCYCLO-
PEDIE (Copyright by Elsevier—Amsterdam). It was translated from the Dutch by
D. R. Welsh. The author, *Dr. A. R. A. Van Aken,* studied classical literature at the
University of Utrecht. A pupil of the famous archaeologist Wilhelm Vollgraf, he
received his doctorate *cum laude* with a thesis on Roman domestic architecture.
He has contributed a number of articles, mainly on archaeological subjects, to in-
ternational journals and is presently a member of the board of directors of a *lyceum*
in Hilversum.

Preface

In this encyclopedia reference has been made, whenever it seems useful, to such classical writings as those by Homer, Ovid, Virgil, Livy, and (more rarely) Catullus and Tacitus, although completeness in this respect should not be expected.

An asterisk (*) often appears after a name to show that the reader may find other useful information under that name. The absence of an asterisk, however, should not be taken to mean that no further information may be found under other entries. For example, frequently used names of personages (Zeus, Heracles, Apollo, Priam, and so on) and most place names (Troy, Olympus, Mt. Ida, Latium, and so on) appear without asterisks, except when particularly emphasized.

The reader should also be aware that many terms other than proper names appear in the encyclopedia. He will find, for example, entries for the words *coin, temple, oracle, metope, thyrsus, ambrosia,* and *ether;* as well as for such compounds as *Homeric laughter, Eleusinian mysteries, Wooden Horse, Calydonian hunt,* and *Golden Fleece.*

Except where the text refers definitely to Roman beliefs or Roman works of art, the Greek names of deities, rather than the Roman, have been used (e.g., *Aphrodite* rather than *Venus*). As a rule, however, the names are given in the Latin spelling (e.g., *Aegisthus* rather than *Aigisthos*)—their most familiar form—the only exceptions being names better known in an English form or the original Greek form (e.g., cities or islands such as Knossos, Delos). Maps of the regions, cities, and mountains of ancient Greece, as well as of the islands of the ancient Aegean, will be found at the end of the text.

Abbreviations

Etr. = Etruscan

Gr. = Greek

Hellen. = Hellenistic

Lat. = Latin

Rom. = Roman

Herod. = Herodotus

Hom. = Homer

Il. = *Iliad*

Od. = *Odyssey*

Liv. = Livy

Ov. = Ovid's *Metamorphoses*

Virg. = Virgil's *Aeneid*

a.t.o. = according to others

a.t.s. = according to some

prob. = probably

ins.: *insula* = block of houses

reg.: *regio* = city district

Vatic. = Vatican

S. = south

W. = west

N. = north

E. = east

A

ABAS. 1. Son of Lynceus* and Hypermnestra*; king of Argos. A.t.s. he founded Abae in Phocis. 2. Companion of Diomedes*, changed into a swan by Aphrodite* for behaving arrogantly toward her (Ov. xiv, 505f.). 3. Companion of Perseus* (Ov. v, 126). 4. Name of two friends of Aeneas*, one a Trojan, the other an Etruscan (Virg. i, 121; x, 427).

ACAMUS [Gr. Akamas]. Son of Theseus* and Phaedra*. He took part in the campaign against Troy and was among those smuggled into the city in the Wooden Horse* (Virg. ii, 262).

ACARNAN [Gr. Akarnan]. Son of Alcmaeon*. When his father was killed, he fled to the S. of Epirus and ruled over the country which came to be called Acarnia after him.

ACASTUS [Gr. Akastos]. King of Iolcus and eldest son of Pelias*. He was one of the Argonauts*. His wife Astydamea* became enamored of Peleus*, but when her love was not returned she maligned him to her husband. Acastus then tried to kill Peleus but was foiled by the intervention of Hermes*.

ACCA LARENTIA. Wife of the shepherd Faustulus*, who raised Romulus* and Remus*. The annual Larentalia festival in Rome (Dec. 23) was perhaps connected with her.

ACESTES. Founder of Segesta in Sicily. He helped Aeneas when the latter landed in Sicily (Virg. i, 550; v, 36, 61, 73).

ACHAEMENIDES. A Greek left behind by Ulysses* among the Cyclopes* in Sicily and later rescued by Aeneas* (Virg. iii, 614; Ov. xiv, 158f.).

ACHAEUS [Gr. Achaios]. Grandson of Erechtheus* and ancestor of the Achaeans.

ACHATES. Most faithful of the companions of Aeneas* (Virg. i, 188, 312; vi, 34, 158).

ACHELOUS [Gr. Acheloios]. The long- est river in Greece (now the Aspropotamos), on the border of Acarnania and Aetolia. The god of this river, reputed to be one of the sons of Oceanus* and Thetis*, fought with Heracles* for Deianira*; although he assumed various forms, he was defeated (Ov. viii, 547f.; ix, 1f.).

Iconography. Represented as an old man with horns, as a dragon with a human head, and most often as a bull with a man's face and long beard—the conventional way of depicting river gods (cf. the coins of Gela in Sicily). His fight with Heracles is the subject of a wood carving (Doric-Archaic) of the school of the Cretan masters Dipoenus and Scyllis (c. 7th century B.C.).

ACHERON. River in Epirus, which flows underground for part of its course, and hence was regarded by the Greeks as one of the rivers of the lower world. The shades of the dead were ferried across the Acheron by Charon* (Virg. vi, 107).

ACHILLES [Gr. Achileus]. Son of Peleus* and Thetis*. To make him invulnerable his mother rubbed him with ambrosia* in the daytime and laid him in the fire at night; a.t.o. she held him by the heel and dipped him in the Styx*. Consequently he was invulnerable except for his heel (Achilles tendon) and it was there that he eventually received a mortal wound. Given the choice between a long but obscure life and a short but glorious one, he opted for the latter and became the bravest of the heroes of the siege of Troy*, where he led his Myrmidons* into battle. Another tradition tells how his mother, wishing to prevent his departure for Troy, hid him at the court of King Lycomedes* on Skyros. Here Odysseus discovered his identity by means of a trick. During the siege of Troy he was insulted by Agamemnon*, who disputed possession of the slave girl

1

Briseis* with him. In his resentment he withdrew from the siege and did not take up arms again until his friend, Patroclus*, was killed by Hector*. Determined to avenge his friend's death, Achilles engaged Hector in battle and killed him, but was himself killed shortly afterward by Paris* with the help of Apollo (Ov. xii, 580f.). His place was taken by his son Neoptolemus*, who assisted in the capture of Troy. The main theme of Homer's *Iliad* is Achilles' hatred of Agamemnon, his return to the siege, and his revenge on Hector (Hom. Il. i, 121f.; xviii, 22f., 231f., 316f., xxii, 395f.). Even in ancient times a Phrygian burial mound near Cape Sigeum was regarded as Achilles' grave.

Iconography. Many scenes from Achilles' life have been depicted, particularly in Greek vase paintings—e.g., his meeting with Troilus: the famous François krater by Clitias and Ergotimus (c. 570 B.C.) at Florence; playing at dice with Ajax: amphora by Execias (c. 530) in the Vatic. Museum; binding the wounds of his friend Patroclus: plate by Sosias (c. 500 B.C.) at Berlin; Achilles and Penthesilea: Attic plate (c. 460 B.C.) at Munich, and many vase paintings representing scenes from the Trojan War. Among the funerary paintings at Tarquinia there is a fresco in the Tomba dei Tori showing Achilles, hidden behind a fountain monument, awaiting the unsuspecting Troilus. Some of the frescoes at Pompeii show the hero fighting with Agamemnon (Temple of Apollo), taking leave of Briseis (Casa del Poeta Tragico), and amidst King Lycomedes' daughters on Skyros (Casa dei Dioscuri). There was one famous sculpture, Scopas' Achilles and Troilus, made for the Temple of Athena at Tegea (c. 380 B.C.), but most of it has been lost. The Middle Ages produced few representations of the hero; Rubens' famous Achilles series dates from c. 1620; in the 19th century, Leighton and other historical painters did paintings of him.

ACIDALIA. Another name for Venus*, originally the name of a spring in Boeotia where she was accustomed to bathe (Virg. i, 720).

ACIS [Gr. Akis]. Son of Faunus* who loved Galatea* and was slain with a rock by his rival, the Cyclops Polyphemus*. His blood was changed into a river of the same name in Sicily (Ov. xiii, 750f.).

ACOETES [Gr. Akoites]. Helmsman of a Greek ship whose crew tried to abduct the god Dionysus*, who had assumed the form of a handsome boy. Acoetes recognized the deity and opposed the plot, and when Dionysus revealed his identity and punished the sailors by changing them into dolphins, Acoetus was spared and appointed priest of Naxos (Ov. iii, 696).

ACONTIUS [Gr. Akontios]. An inhabitant of Ceos who became enamored of Cydippe, daughter of a prominent Athenian. Prevented by difference in social rank from asking her hand in marriage, he tricked her into taking an oath which compelled her to agree to marry him.

ACRISIUS [Gr. Akrisios]. King of Argos, father of Danaë*. When it was foretold that his daughter's son would slay him, he placed Danaë in a subterranean prison. Nevertheless, Zeus* came to her in the form of a golden shower, and she bore him a son, Perseus*. Both mother and child were thrown into the sea by Acrisius but were miraculously saved. Later, Perseus unintentionally killed his grandfather with a discus (Ov. iv, 613).

ACROPOLIS [Gr. Akropolis = high city]. A fortified rock or hill found in several Greek cities—e.g. Athens, Argos, Mycenae, and Tiryns. Originally this fortress served as a place of refuge in times of danger. Later it became the site where outstanding buildings and temples were erected. The best known acropolis is that at Athens. A royal citadel in Mycenaean times, it became in the fifth century a sacred temple area, reserved for the main sanctuaries of the city, especially those dedicated to Athena. During the Persian Invasion in 480 B.C. the acropolis was completely destroyed. Rebuilding took place under Pericles, and the Parthenon, Erechtheum, Propylaea, and Temple of Athena Nike were among the edifices erected.

ACTAEON [Gr. Aktaion]. Grandson of Cadmus*. An ardent huntsman, he once by chance saw Artemis* bathing. The outraged goddess changed him into a stag and he was torn to pieces by his own hounds (Ov. iii, 193f.).

Iconography. Actaeon being attacked by his hounds is represented on many Greek vases—e.g., on a krater (c. 450 B.C.) at Boston. The same scene occurs on a metope of the Temple of Hera at Selinus (Sicily), dating from the first half of the 5th century B.C.; on a late Etruscan urn from Volterra (3rd-2nd century); and in Titian's famous painting.

ACTOR [Gr. Aktor]. King of Opus in Locris, father of Menoetius* and Astyoche*.

ADMETE. Daughter of Eurystheus*, from whom Heracles wrested the girdle of Hippolyta*, the queen of the Amazons*. This was one of the Twelve Labors of Heracles.

ADMETUS [Gr. Admetos]. King of Pherae in Thessaly. Apollo, on his banishment from Olympus*, spent nine years in Admetus' service as a shepherd. The god promised Admetus the gift of eternal life if, when the time came for him to die, someone else would accept death in his stead. Admetus wooed Alcestis*, but her father, King Pelias*, refused his consent unless Admetus came to fetch his bride in a carriage drawn by wild boars and lions, which he did with Apollo's help. When Admetus' dying hour grew near, Alcestis gave her life for him; but Heracles*, who was staying with them at the time, brought her back from Hades and restored her to her beloved husband. Euripides chose this as the theme of his tragedy, *Alcestis.*

Iconography. A Roman relief shows Admetus and Alcestis before King Pelias, who is seated on his throne. A sarcophagus (2nd century B.C.) from Ostia, now in the Vatican Museum, depicts the death of Alcestis, and also a scene in which Heracles brings her back from the lower world.

ADONIS [Phoen. *adon* = lord]. 1. Phoenician god of dying and renascent nature. The source of the cult is the Phoenician seaport of Byblos (now Jebeil) at the mouth of the Adonis river. 2. In Greek mythology, a youth of extraordinary beauty, loved by Aphrodite*. After he was killed by a boar while hunting he was allowed, as a favor to Aphrodite from Zeus, to leave the lower world to visit her during the spring and summer of every year (Ov. x, 519f.). Sorrow at his death and joy at his resurrection were occasions of tumultuous celebration at Alexandria and other places (see description by Theocritus).

Iconography. The oldest representations of Adonis are on Etruscan mirrors and on vases—e.g., Aphrodite and Persephone* by the bier of Adonis on an Apulian vase. There is also a statue of Adonis from Capua (4th century B.C.) ascribed to the Greek sculptor Euphranor. Adonis is frequently represented on murals—e.g., at Pompeii (Casa di Adone)—and on Roman sarcophagi. From a much later period, Adonis setting out for the hunt and Aphrodite's grief at the death of her beloved have been depicted by Titian and Rubens. Adonis is also the subject of sculptures by De Rossi, De Vries, Canova, and Thorwaldsen.

ADRASTUS [Gr. Adrastos]. 1. King of Argos. He married his daughters to Tydeus* and Polynices*, both of whom were expelled from Thebes. In order to restore them he led the expedition known as the Seven against Thebes*, of which all the leaders except Adrastus were slain. He later died of grief upon the loss of his son Aegialeus*, and was venerated as a demigod in various Greek cities, e.g. Sicyon. 2. Son of Gordias*, king of Phrygia. He killed his brother accidentally and fled to Lydia, where he enjoyed the hospitality of King Croesus. He unintentionally slew Croesus' son also, whereupon he took his own life (Herod. i, 34-35).

AEA [Gr. Aia]. See AEAEA.

AEACUS [Gr. Aiakos]. Son of Zeus and Aegina, king of the island of Aegina, and father of Telemon* and Peleus*. When his country was ravaged by a plague, he beseeched Zeus to repopulate it, which Zeus did by turning ants into men. These men, known as Myrmidons* (ant-people), served under Achilles in the Greek expedi-

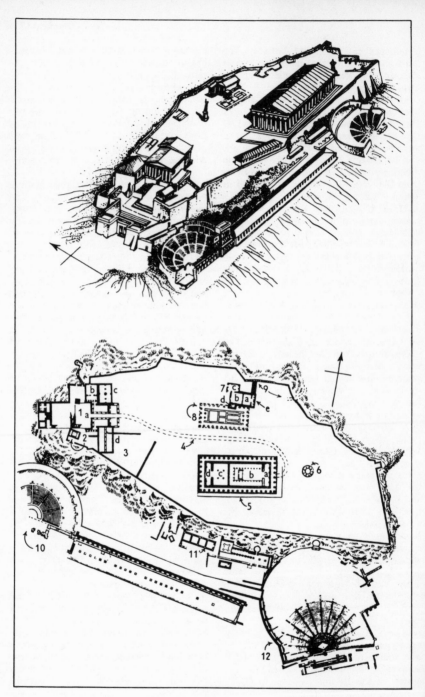

tion against Troy. After his death, Zeus made Aeacus a judge in the underworld, along with Minos* and Rhadamanthys*. He is the ancestor of Ajax* and Achilles*.

AEAEA [Gr. Aiaia]. 1. The island of the sorceress Circe*, situated somewhere in the western Mediterranean (Hom. Od. x, 135); believed by the Romans to be the promontory of Circei (now San Felice di Circeo) in Latium. 2. The land of the Golden Fleece*, somewhere in the east, usually identified with Colchis* (Georgia).

AEDON. Daughter of Pandareus*, married to Zethus*, king of Thebes. When she tried to kill the eldest son of her sister-in-law Niobe*, of whose large family she was jealous, she slew her own child Itylus* instead. She was then changed into a nightingale by Zeus (Hom. Od. xix, 518f.). The story of Procne* and Philomela* is related to this myth.

AEËTES [Gr. Aietes]. Son of Helius* and king of Colchis, during whose reign

---

THE ACROPOLIS OF ATHENS:
KEY TO GROUND PLAN

1 - Propylaea (monumental entrance):
   a - roofed entryway
   b - pinakotheke (picture gallery)
   c, d - unfinished wings
2 - temple of Athena Nike
3 - sacred area of Artemis
4 - Sacred Way (processional path)
5 - Parthenon [Gr. = the virgin's place]
   a - pronaos (front portico)
   b - cella, containing 40-foot statue, the *Athena Parthenos*
   c - inner chamber (treasury)
   d - opisthodome (rear portico)
6 - Roman temple of Augustus
7 - Erechtheum
   a - cella of Athena
   b - western cella
   c - northern portico
   d - southern portico, the Porch of the Caryatids
   e - eastern portico
8 - Pandroseum (sacred area dedicated to Pandrosus)
9 - fragments of the original wall
10 - Odeum (roofed theatre) of Herodes Atticus
11 - Sanctuary of Asclepius
12 - Theatre of Dionysus

Phrixus* brought the Golden Fleece* to Colchis, whence it was removed later by the Argonauts*.

AEGAEON [Gr. Aigaion], one of the Centimani*, giants with a hundred arms, sons of Uranus* and Gaea*.

AEGEUS [Gr. Aigeus]. King of Athens, father of Theseus*. The Panathenaea (see ATHENA) is said to have been founded by him. He slew Androgeus*, son of Minos*, the king of Crete, and thenceforth had to send seven youths and seven maidens to Crete every ninth year as a sacrifice to the Minotaur*. When Theseus had slain this monster, he forgot to replace the black sails of his ship by white, as he had arranged to do as a sign of his victory. Aegeus, seeing the black sails, assumed that his son had been killed by the Minotaur and threw himself into the sea, which received its name, the Aegean, from this event.

AEGIALE [Gr. Aigiale]. Daughter of Adrastus* and Amphithea, and wife of Diomedes*.

AEGIALEUS [Gr. Aigialeus]. Son of Adrastus*. When the sons of the heroes who had perished on the expedition of the Seven against Thebes took up arms to avenge their fathers, they were joined by Aegialeus. This punitive expedition against Thebes is known as the war of the Epigoni*. The city was taken but Aegialeus lost his life.

AEGIMIUS [Gr. Aigimios]. Mythical ancestor of the Dorians, who became involved in a war with the Lapithae*. He called on Heracles for help, and on gaining the victory offered a third of his land as a reward. When Heracles magnanimously refused, Aegimius adopted Heracles' son Hyllus* as his own, to show his gratitude. The names of the three Doric phyles, Pamphylii, Dymanes, and Hylles, are derived from Hyllus and the names of Aegimius' other two sons, Pamphylus and Dymas.

AEGIS [Gr. Aigis]. Originally described as the fear-inspiring weapon of Zeus*, but also, and later almost exclusively, as an attribute of his daughter Athena*. It is usually conceived of as a kind of cloak made of goatskin, fringed with serpents covered with scales, and with the Gorgon's* head in the center. The aegis could also be used as a shield. *Iconography.* In older Greek art the aegis hangs down over both shoulders and covers the entire breast, e.g. as worn by Athena on the W. façade of the Temple of Aphaea in Aegina (early 5th century B.C.) It later became smaller, e.g. on a signet of Aspasius (Augustan Age).

AEGISTHUS [Gr. Aigisthos]. Son of Thyestes*. When his uncle Atreus* made an attempt on his life, Aegisthus slew him and assumed power over Mycenae. He was expelled by Atreus' son Agamemnon*. Upon Agamemnon's departure for Troy, Aegisthus seduced his wife Clytaemnestra*, and together they killed Agamemnon on his return. Orestes*, son of Agamemnon, later took revenge on both murderers.

AEGLE [Gr. Aigle]. Mother of the three Graces* or Charites*.

AEGYPTUS [Gr. Aiguptos]. Son of Belus (1)*, and twin brother of Danaus*. He had fifty sons, of whom all but one were slain by Danaus' daughters (see DANAIDES). He ruled over Egypt, which took its name from him.

AËLLO. One of the Harpies* (Ov. xiii, 710).

AENEADAE. Companions of Aeneas* on his wanderings. In Virg. used also in the general sense of "Trojans."

AENEAS [Gr. Aineias]. Trojan hero, son of Aphrodite* and Anchises*, married to Creusa (2)*. He fled with his father and small son Ascanius* from burning Troy, was joined by a band of fugitives (see AENEADAE), and, in obedience to the command of the gods, set sail with the Penates* of Troy for Latium, which he reached after many wanderings and delays [see map, "The Wanderings of Aeneas"]. Landing finally in Latium, he successfully founded a settlement, but only after much hard fighting, in which his main opponent was Turnus*, king of the Rufuli. Aeneas married Lavinia*, daughter of Latinus* and Amata*, the rulers of Laurentum*, and became the progenitor of the people of resurrected Troy, i.e. Rome. In particular he was an ancestor of the imperial Julian family. Virg. sings of his deeds in the epic of Aeneas: the *Aeneid.*

Iconography. Often represented on early Greek vases, sometimes in Phrygian dress but usually in Greek clothing and bearing Greek arms, e.g. fighting for the body of Achilles (Chalcidian amphora, c. 550 B.C.); at the fall of Troy (Attic hydria by the Cleophrades painter, c. 485 B.C., now at Naples); the "classic" representation of Aeneas, showing the hero fleeing from Troy with his father on his back and holding his son by the hand (Virg. ii, 707f.), found on vases, coins, seals and terra cottas. Also in wall paintings at Pompeii (house on the Via dell' Abbondanza) and Herculaneum (in caricature with animals' heads); Aeneas wounded, in the Casa di Sirico at Pompeii. Also on Roman reliefs dating from the Empire, e.g. Petronia Grata's tombstone, and the famous peace altar of Emperor Augustus, Ara Pacis Augustae.

AEOLIA. Mythical island where King Aeolus (2)* watched over the winds.

AEOLUS [Gr. Aiolos]. 1. Son of Hellen* and legendary ancestor of the Aeolians. 2. Son of Hippotes* or, a.t.o., Poseidon*. He was king of the winds, which he kept shut up on the island of Aeolia* (Hom. Od. x, 2f.; Virg. i, 52).

AËROPE. Wife of Atreus*. She committed adultery with his brother Thyestes*, to whom she presented the golden ram which would enable him to become the lawful ruler of Mycenae. This Atreus was able to prevent.

AESACUS [Gr. Aisakos]. Son of Priam* and Alexirrhoë*. He fell in love with the nymph Hesperia*, who, in escaping from his attentions, was fatally bitten by an adder. In despair Aesacus threw himself into the sea but was changed into a diving bird by Tethys* (Ov. xi, 759f.).

AESCULAPIUS. See ASCLEPIUS.

AESON [Gr. Aison]. Son of Cretheus* and Tyro*, father of Jason*, and king of Iolcus. He was dethroned by his half brother Pelias*.

AETHALIDES [Gr. Aithalides]. Son of Hermes*; herald of the Argonauts*.

AETHER [Gr. Aither]. The pure upper air which is the abode of the gods, as

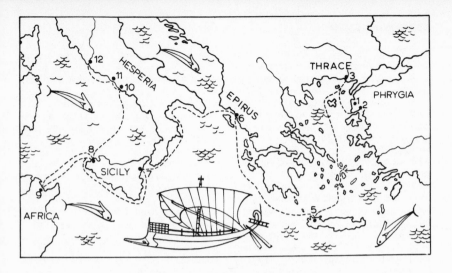

THE WANDERINGS OF AENEAS

When Troy (1) fell after ten years of fighting, the Trojan hero Aeneas, after offering desperate resistance to the conquering Greeks, fled from the city. Obeying divine orders, he took the Penates of Troy to safety and embarked with his aged father Anchises, his small son Ascanius, and a number of fugitives. His wife, Creusa, had died in the confusion of the flight. The fleet of the Trojan exiles set sail from the harbor of Antandros (2) in search of a new homeland. They arrived in Thrace, where Aeneas founded a city, Aeneadae (3), but a terrifying apparition, the shade of the murdered Trojan prince Polydorus, caused them to resume their wandering. Landing on Delos (4), they consulted the oracle of Apollo, which ordered them to visit the original home of the Dardanians. Old Anchises wrongly thought that this meant Crete, and when Aeneas founded a settlement there which he named Pergamum (5) a horrible plague broke out, making it clear to him that he had not reached his final destination. The Penates of Troy appeared to him in his sleep and named Italy as the land that Apollo had meant in his oracular pronouncement. After a perilous voyage through the Ionian Sea, the Trojans landed at Buthrotum (6) in Epirus, where they met Priam's son Helenus, who lived there with his wife Andromache. The latter, Hector's widow, had been taken from Troy as a slave, but had been rescued by Helenus. From Helenus Aeneas obtained further advice on his proposed voyage to Italy before his fleet once more set sail. They sailed along the south coast of Italy, carefully avoiding contact with the Greek settlements there, and arrived safely in Sicily, in the vicinity of Mt. Etna (7). There a Greek called Achaemenides, who had been left behind by his compatriots, asked the Trojans for protection. The appearance of the Cyclops Polyphemus caused Aeneas and his men to depart hurriedly and continue their voyage along the south coast of Sicily to the port of Drepanum (now Trapani) (8). Here they received a hospitable welcome from Acestes, a Trojan by descent. During their stay Anchises died and was buried on Mt. Eryx. When they tried to continue their voyage to Italy, a storm drove them back in the direction of the African coast—a setback contrived by the goddess Juno, who nursed a long-standing hatred of the Trojans. The battered remains of Aeneas' fleet were driven ashore near Carthage (9), a recent settlement of the Phoenicians, where Queen Dido received Aeneas and his company with great hospitality. It was in vain that Dido, who had been smitten by Juno with a hopeless love for the Trojan hero, tried to persuade him to renounce his divine undertaking and share her throne. On Jupiter's orders the Trojan fleet once more put to sea, leaving the ill-starred Dido to take her own life. Arriving back in Sicily, they held solemn ceremonies at the tomb of Anchises. They sailed on to Italy and landed near Cumae (10), where Aeneas visited the renowned Sibylla and was escorted into the underworld by her. After calling at Caieta (now Gaeta) (11), the Trojans finally reached the mouth of the Tiber and hence their promised land, Latium. After a long and bitter struggle against the Rutulian natives and their king Turnus, Aeneas established a permanent foothold in Italy. His son Ascanius (or Iulus) later founded Alba Longa, the city from which Rome (12) was colonized.

opposed to the *aer* or lower air that mortals breathe. Sometimes represented as the son of Erebus (darkness) and Nyx (night), it is one of the elements of the cosmos, stated in the Orphica* to be the cosmic soul from which all life springs. AETHON. 1. One of the horses of the sun god (Ov. ii, 153). 2. In Virg., the horse of Pallas (Virg. xi, 89).

AETHRA [Gr. Aithra]. Wife of Aegeus* and mother of Theseus*.

AETNA [now Etna]. Volcano in Sicily under which Zeus buried Typhon* in the course of his battle against the Giants*; this explained the volcanic activity. Etna was also thought to be the smithy of the Roman fire god, Vulcan,* where he and the Cyclopes* forged shafts of lightning for Jupiter.

AETOLUS [Gr. Aitolos]. Son of Endymion*, originally king of Elis, later resident in the territory that was called Aetolia after him.

AGAMEDES. Son of the Boeotian king Erginus*. With his brother Trophonius (2)* he built the temple of Apollo at Delphi; the two men then prayed to the god to grant them whatever favor was best for man. Shortly afterward they were both found dead in the temple. According to another tradition they built a treasury for King Hyrieus of Boeotia. However, they also made a secret passage to the room for themselves and stole the treasures kept there. When Agamedes was caught in a trap set in the treasury by the king, Trophonius cut off and removed his brother's head to make identification impossible. This tale is the same as the story of Rhampsinitos (Herod. ii, 121).

AGAMEMNON. Son of Atreus*, king of Mycenae. When Atreus was slain by Thyestes*, Agamemnon and his brother Menelaus* fled to Sparta, where they married King Tyndareus'* daughters, Clytaemnestra* and Helen*. Agamemnon later succeeded in dethroning Thyestes and ruled Mycenae while his brother became king of Sparta. After the abduction of Helen*, Menelaus' wife, Agamemnon undertook the leadership of a Greek punitive expedition against Troy.

The assembly point was the harbor of Aulis*, where, while hunting, Agamemnon had the misfortune to kill a stag sacred to Artemis*. When a calm caused by the goddess prevented the Greek fleet from leaving Aulis, a command was conveyed to Agamemnon by the seer Calchas* that he should sacrifice his daughter Iphigenia to the goddess. During the siege of Troy a quarrel between Agamemnon and Achilles* nearly proved fatal for the Greeks. On his return home after the fall of Troy, Agamemnon was treacherously murdered by his wife Clytaemnestra and her lover Aegisthus*. Agamemnon's son Orestes*, later avenged the death of his father. The story of Agamemnon was used by the tragedian Aeschylus as material for his trilogy *Oresteia*. Agamemnon is one of the main figures in Homer's *Iliad*.

Iconography. Agamemnon is represented as a royal, bearded figure, e.g. on a Greek relief from Samothrace, on Greek vases: carrying Briseis off (Attic scyphus, c. 490 B.C., now at Paris, and at the destruction of Troy (Attic hydria c. 490 B.C., at Naples). The Pompeian fresco showing the sacrifice of Iphigenia (Casa del Poeta Tragico) is well known. Agamemnon's death is frequently depicted on Etruscan cinerary urns.

AGANIPPE. Daughter of the river god Termessus; nymph of the fountain Aganippe near Thespiae, at the foot of Mt. Helicon*. The winged horse Pegasus* was said to have caused the spring to flow with a blow of his hoof; the water of the fountain gave inspiration to poets.

AGAVE [Gr. Agaue]. Daughter of Cadmus*, mother of Pentheus*. In a frenzy brought on by Bacchic rites she tore her own son to pieces (Ov. iii, 725).

AGDISTIS. A monster, half male, half female, fathered by Zeus*.

AGELAUS [Gr. Agelaos], one of Penelope's* suitors (Hom. Od. xxiii, 131, 212, 247).

AGENOR. 1. King of Phoenicia (Virg. i, 338), son of Poseidon*; father of Cadmus* and Europa*. 2. Son of the Trojan Antenor* (Hom. Il. xxi, 545f.).

AGIS. Son of Eurysthenes and ancestor of several Spartan kings of the same name.

AGLAEA [Gr. Aglaia]. See GRACES.

AGLAURUS or **AGRAULUS** [Gr. Aglauros]. Daughter of Cecrops* and sister of Herse* and Pandrosus*. Once, when Athens was being sorely tried by a long war, Aglaurus threw herself from the Acropolis after an oracle had said that the city would be saved by this sacrifice. On entering military service young Athenians took an oath of allegiance to their country in her temple. A.t.o. the goddess entrusted to Cecrops' three daughters a chest concealing the young hero Erichthonius (2)*, which they were forbidden to open. When, nevertheless, Aglarus and Herse opened the chest, the sight of the boy drove them insane and they jumped from the Acropolis (Ov. ii, 739f.).

AGRAULUS [Gr. Agraulos]. See AGLAURUS.

AGRIUS [Gr. Agrios]. Son of the Calydonian ruler Parthaon* and brother of Oeneus*. The latter was dethroned by Agrius' sons, who then placed their father on the throne of Calydon. Diomedes* later restored Oeneus to power.

AGRON. Inhabitant of Cos who, with his two sisters, professed contempt for all the gods except Gaea*. They were punished by being changed into birds.

AIUS LOCUTIUS. When the Gauls were pushing toward Rome in 390 B.C., a certain M. Caedicius heard a mysterious voice issuing from a grove on the Forum several nights before the disastrous battle of the Allia. The voice warned of approaching danger and advised strengthening the walls. Caedicius' story was not believed by the authorities, and a few days later the Gauls entered Rome with little resistance. After the enemy withdrew, the Romans erected near the Temple of Vesta in the Forum an altar in honor of the mysterious deity with the warning voice, who was named Aius Locutius or Loquens (Liv. v. 32, 10).

AJAX [Gr. Aias]. 1. Ajax the Lesser, son of Oïleus*, king of Locris. One of the bravest heroes at the siege of Troy, he was surpassed in swiftness only by Achilles. At the fall of Troy he abducted Cassandra* from the sanctuary of Athena; by way of punishment he lost his life in a shipwreck on the voyage home (Virg. i, 41). He is called the Lesser to distinguish him from Telamon's son. 2. Ajax the Great, son of Telamon*, king of Salamis. He and Achilles were probably the most distinguished of the Greek heroes at Troy. He held up the Trojans singlehanded when they had come dangerously close to the Greek camp and were attempting to set fire to the ships (Hom. Il. xv, 415f.). Upon Achilles' death he claimed the latter's armor, but Odysseus*, with the support of Athena*, successfully contested its possession with him; in anger, Ajax fell on his sword. A.t.o. he went mad and effected great slaughter among the cattle, thinking he was fighting Odysseus and the Atrides*. On recovering his sanity he committed suicide in shame and despair (theme of Sophocles' tragedy, *Ajax*).
Iconography. Ajax is represented mainly on Greek vases: e.g. carrying Achilles' body (François krater, c. 570 B.C., at Florence) or fighting for Achilles' body (amphora, c. 550 B.C.). His duel with Hector was painted on a bowl by Douris (c. 490 B.C., at Paris), and Execias shows him playing dice with Achilles (amphora, c. 535 B.C., Vatic. Museum).

ALBA LONGA. prob. modern Castel Gandolfo, S.E. of Rome, center of the old Latin League and traditionally founded by Ascanius* (Iulus), the son of Aeneas*. Romulus* and Remus* were descended from the kings of Alba, which was consequently considered the parent city of Rome. Alba was destroyed by Tullus Hostilius, third king of Rome, c. 650 B.C. (Virg. i, 271; Liv. i, 22-30).

ALBUNEA. Roman fountain nymph of a sulfur spring near Tibur (now Tivoli).

ALCAEUS [Gr. Alkaios]. Son of Perseus* and Andromeda*; king of Tiryns and father of Amphitryon*.

ALCATHOUS [Gr. Alkathoös]. Son of Pelops* and Hippodamea*. Megareus, king of Megara, gave him the hand of his daughter and made him his successor in return for great services. With Apollo's* help Alcathous rebuilt the walls of Megara.

ALCESTIS [Gr. Alkestis]. Daughter of Pelias* and wife of Admetus*. She chose of her own free will to die for him (theme of Euripides' play *Alcestis*). She is a classic example of love and conjugal fidelity. *Iconography*. Alcestis is represented as a bride in the company of her servants on a piece of painted earthenware from Eretria which was used as a knee protector when spinning (end of 5th century B.C.). On a richly sculptured column of the Temple of Artemis—rebuilt after the fire of 356 B.C.—at Ephesus, Alcestis stands between the winged god of death and Hermes. This work is by Scopas or Praxiteles (4th century B.C.).

ALCIMEDE [Gr. Alkimede]. Mother of Jason*.

ALCINOUS [Gr. Alkinoös]. King of the Phaeacians*, father of Nausicaä*. He entertained Odysseus (Hom. Od. vi, vii, viii). The Argonauts* also received a cordial welcome from him on their return voyage.

ALCIPPE [Gr. Alkippe]. Daughter of Ares* and Agraulus* (see HALIRRHOTIUS).

ALCMAEON [Gr. Alkmaion]. Son of Amphiaraus* and Eriphyle*. The latter persuaded her husband to take part in the expedition of the Seven against Thebes*. Amphiaraus, knowing that this would mean his death, instructed his son to avenge him if he perished. Alcmaeon joined the expedition of the Epigoni and, having survived the war unscathed, killed his mother in obedience to his father's order. Pursued by the avenging Furies* he went from place to place, finally seeking peace in the land of King Phegeus*, who gave him his daughter in marriage. Still the Furies did not cease to pursue him until an oracle told him that peace awaited him where the sun had not shone when he slew his mother. This was the mouth of the river Achelous, where land had recently been formed by silt deposits. There Alcmaeon married Callirhoë (2)*,

the daughter of the river god, who asked him to fetch the necklace and garment with which Eriphyle had induced him to take part in the expedition of the Epigoni, and which he had left with Phegeus. Alcmaeon told Phegeus that he wanted to consecrate them to Apollo, but Phegeus, discovering Alcmaeon's deceit, had him killed by his sons.

ALCMENE [Gr. Alkmene]. Daughter of Electryon* and wife of Amphitryon*. While her husband was abroad, she was seduced by Zeus, who had assumed the appearance of Amphitryon. Hera's* hatred then pursued her, and she suffered under her husband's suspicion until Zeus intervened and presented her with twin sons, one by himself—Heracles*—and the other by Amphitryon—Iphicles*. (Ov. ix, 281ff.). *Iconography*. On an archaic relief (c. 600 B.C.) from Sparta, Zeus is shown trying to seduce Alcmene. A statue of Alcmene by Calamis was well known in antiquity but has since been lost. Many representations of Alcmene can be seen on Greek and Roman vases.

ALCYONE [Gr. Alkuone]. Daughter of Aeolus*, the god of the winds. Her husband was Ceyx*, and their marriage was said to have been very happy. When Ceyx was shipwrecked and drowned, she threw herself into the sea in despair. Both were then changed into kingfishers (Ov. xi, 410f.).

ALCYONEUS [Gr. Alkuoneos]. One of the Giants*, rendered harmless by Heracles* on one of his expeditions.

ALECTO or **ALLECTO**. One of the Furies* (Virg. vii, 324, 341, 415, 476).

ALECTRYON [Gr. Alektruon = cock]. A youth whom Ares*, on a visit to Aphrodite*, placed on guard at the door. Alectryon, however, fell asleep, and the love play was observed by Helius*. By way of punishment Alectryon was changed into a cock, which since then has always crowed to announce the rising of the sun.

ALETES. Son of Aegisthus*. He usurped power over Myceneae while Orestes* was away at Tauris*, but was slain by Orestes on his return.

ALEXANDER [Gr. Alexandros]. See PARIS.

ALOADAE or ALOIDAE. Two giants, Otus and Ephialtes, sons of Iphimedea and Aloëus*. When they tried to invade the heavens by piling Ossa*, Pelion*, and Olympus* one on top of the other, Apollo struck them down with his arrows. They had even dared to hold the god Ares* prisoner for thirteen months until he was freed by Hermes (Hom. Il. v, 385; Od. xi, 308). According to another legend, they were not hostile to men, but spread civilization and founded several cities.

ALOËUS. Son of Poseidon* and Ca nace*; husband of Iphimedea and father of Otus and Ephialtes, who were named Aloadae* after him.

ALOPE. Daughter of Cercyon*. She bore Hippothoön* to Poseidon*. When Cercyon discovered this, he had her buried alive, but the god changed her into the fountain of Alope near Eleusis*.

ALPHESIBOEA [Gr. Alphesiboia]. Daughter of Phegeus* and wife of Alcmaeon*.

ALPHEUS [Gr. Alpheios]. Largest river in the Peloponnesus. The river god of the same name was enamored of the nymph Arethusa*.

ALTES. Father of the lovely Laothoë, one of the wives of King Priam* (Hom. Il. xxi, 86; xxii, 51).

ALTHAEA [Gr. Althaia]. Wife of Oeneus* and mother of Meleager*. At the birth of her child the Furies prophesied to Althaea that Meleager would die when the log of wood that lay in the fireplace was consumed. Althaea thenceforth guarded the log carefully. Later, when her son had slain two of her brothers in a quarrel, she threw the wood on the fire in her wrath and Meleager died immediately (Ov. viii, 445ff.).

AMALTHEA [Gr. Amaltheia]. The goat that suckled Zeus* in Crete. Zeus changed one of her horns into the "horn of plenty," filled to overflowing with everything she desired. A.t.o. Amalthea was a nymph who fed Zeus with goat's milk and honey.

AMARYNCEUS [Gr. Amarunkeus]. Thessalian prince who supported Augias* in his fight against Heracles*.

AMATA. Wife of Latinus*, king of Laurentum*, and mother of Lavinia*, whose betrothed Turnus* seconded Amata in her resistance to Aeneas*. When she saw that Turnus must lose the battle against the Trojans, she committed suicide (Virg. vii, 343; xii, 56, 593f).

AMAZONS. A race of warrior women in Pontus (Asia Minor). Their capital is said to have been Themiscyra. They tolerated no males in their society, except to keep the race alive. They figure in many mythological stories of antiquity; e.g., one of the labors of Heracles* was to seize the girdle of the Amazon queen, Hippolyta*. Also famous is the support they gave the Trojans after Hector's death; in their brave fight against the Greek besiegers of Troy, their queen, Penthesilea*, died by the hand of Achilles*. Homer relates how the Amazons invaded Lycia but were defeated by Bellerophon* (Hom. Il. vi, 186f.). The belief that they had their right breasts amputated to enable them to draw the bow more skillfully arose from the Greek explanation of their name: without breast (mazos = breast).
Iconography. The fight of the Amazons against the Greeks was a favorite theme in Greek art; on vases they were often represented wearing Scythian dress—a cap and trousers. Micon (475 B.C.) painted an Amazon battle in the Stoa Poikile at Athens; at Munich there is a famous kylix (broad, shallow drinking cup) showing the death of Penthesilea (460 B.C.). The Amazons can also be seen on temple friezes and metopes, e.g. on the Temple of Apollo at Bassae (5th century B.C.), the heroum at Gyölbashi (5th century B.C.), and the Mausoleum at Halicarnassus (4th century B.C.). Four celebrated sculptors—Phidias, Polycletus, Cresilas, and Phradmon—vied with each other in making an Amazon for the Temple of Diana at Ephesus (c. 430 B.C.); all four sculptured a wounded Amazon. In medieval, Renaissance, and Baroque art, Amazons were often represented, especially the death of Penthesilea, e.g. by Rubens, Giulio Romano, and Jordaens.

AMBARVALIA [= procession round the

fields]. A Roman festival, held in the spring, originally in honor of Mars* as god of spring, but later in honor of Dea Dia*, the goddess of fertility. The group of priests called the Fratres Arvales walked in procession through the fields, and many ancient ceremonies took place; e.g. ears of corn were consecrated, statues of gods were crowned with wreaths, a sacrifice was offered to the powers of the underworld, and a hymn was sung.

AMBROSIA. The fabled food of the Greek and Roman gods.

AMMON or AMON. Egyptian deity, identified with Zeus* by the Greeks and with Jupiter* by the Romans. The oracle of Ammon at the Siwa oasis in Libya was well known in the Greek world; when Alexander the Great visited it, he was greeted by the priests as the son of Ammon.

AMOR or CUPID. Roman name for the Greek god Eros*, the god of love. Various deities are named as his parents, but Aphrodite*—Venus* to the Romans—was generally regarded as his mother. In Virg. Amor plays an important part in the love story of Dido* and Aeneas* (Virg. i, 658).
Iconography. In antiquity Amor was represented as a boy, often winged, armed with a bow and arrow. He was the subject of works by the sculptors Praxiteles, Scopas, and Lysippus (4th century B.C.), and several centuries later he appears together with Psyche. Hellenism represented him as a small child; amoretti are an important feature of Hellenistic and Roman painting, e.g. in the Casa dei Vettii at Pompeii. There is also the well-known fresco in the Casa di Amore Punito (i.e. Cupid punished) at Pompeii. The playful little amoretti also occur frequently in Renaissance and Baroque painting and book illustration, e.g. Boccaccio's Decameron.

AMPELOS [Gr. = vine]. A satyr and member of Dionysus'* retinue.

AMPHIARAUS [Gr. Amphiaraos], son of Oecles* and Hypermnestra*, husband of Eriphyle*. One of the Argonauts*, he possessed the gift of prophecy and sec-

ond sight. Consequently, knowing that to take part in the expedition of the Seven against Thebes* would mean his death, he at first refused to join it. His wife, Eriphyle, having, nevertheless, induced him to go, he charged his son Alcmaeon* to avenge his death. At the siege of Troy, Zeus rescued him from the hands of his enemies by opening up the earth and causing the hero to disappear. His oracle at Oropus in N.W. Attica was well known; visitors to it sacrificed a black ram and slept on the animal's skin. The god then appeared to them in their dreams.
Iconography. At Berlin there is a famous Corinthian krater (6th century B.C.) on which Amphiaraus' departure for Thebes is represented: the hero is mounting his chariot, sword in hand, while a soothsayer, foreseeing the tragic outcome, sits in an attitude of mourning.

AMPHILOCHUS [Gr. Amphilochos]. Son of Amphiaraus* and Eriphyle*, brother of Alcmaeon*. Took part in the expedition of the Epigoni* and the siege of Troy. A famous soothsayer, he founded various oracles, including that of Mallos in Cilicia, and, together with the soothsayer Mopsus*, that of Apollo at Coliphon.

AMPHINOMUS [Gr. Amphinomos]. Son of Nisus*; one of Penelope's suitors (Hom. Od. xviii, 395, 412; xx, 244; xxii, 89).

AMPHION. Son of Zeus* and Antiope*; king of Thebes and husband of Niobe*. When he and his brother Zethus* built the walls of Thebes, he played the lyre so beautifully that the stones came together of their own accord.
Iconography. The two brothers are represented on, for example, an Etruscan mirror (6th century B.C.). There is a famous Hellenistic statuary group, known as the Farnese Bull, showing Amphion and Zethus taking revenge on Dirce*; it is the work of the Rhodian artists Apollonius and Tauriscus (c. 150 B.C.).

AMPHITRITE. A Nereid*. She was loved by Poseidon*, from whom she fled to Atlas*, who hid her. Poseidon's dolphin traced her and brought her to the god,

who made her his wife. She was considered the goddess of the sea. Triton* was her son.
Iconography. Amphitrite can be seen on Greek vases with her husband, riding in a chariot drawn by sea horses or other creatures of the sea, or seated upon one of these creatures, surrounded by Tritons. She is dressed as a queen, her flowing hair enclosed in a net, and sometimes a crab's claws at her temples. On the Theseus bowl at Paris (early 5th century) she is represented as youthful, clad in a short, transparent garment, and handing Theseus a wreath. A magnificent, large-scale mural mosaic showing Neptune and Amphitrite can be seen in the house named after this work at Heculaneum (ins. V, 1-2); from a later age there is Rubens' painting.

AMPHITRYON [Gr. Amphitruon]. Son of Alceaeus* and husband of Alcmene*. Forced on account of bloodguilt to flee from Tiryns, his father's kingdom, he was received by Creon*, king of Thebes. While he was fighting the Taphians, Zeus* visited his wife, becoming the father of Heracles (see ALCMENE).

AMULIUS. Brother of King Numitor* of Alba Longa*. He drove Numitor from the throne and killed his sons. To prevent Numitor's only daughter, Rhea Silvia*, from having offspring that might one day be a source of danger to him, he forced her to become a Vestal virgin and thus remain unmarried. When, nevertheless, she became mother of Romulus* and Remus*, he had the twins thrown into the Tiber and their mother shut up in a cell. Romulus and Remus later succeeded in killing Amulius and restoring their grandfather to the throne (Liv. i, 3-5).

AMYCUS [Gr. Amukos]. Son of Poseidon* and the nymph Melia*. He was king of the Bebryces, a mythical race in Bithynia, and an extremely skilled pugilist. When the Argonauts were passing through his territory, he was slain by Polydeuces*.

AMYMONE. Daughter of Danaus*. When she was attacked near a fountain by a Satyr and rescued by Poseidon*, she fell in love with the god and became mother of Nauplius* by him.

Iconography. Amymone is represented on vases and signet rings, usually with her attribute, the water jug. A fresco at Pompeii shows her with Poseidon (Casa della Regina Margherita).

AMYNTOR. King of the Dolopians, killed by Heracles when he refused the hero admission to his kingdom.

ANAXARETE. A maiden of Cyprus, beloved by the shepherd Iphis. She reacted so coldly to his passionate love that he killed himself. When even the sight of the dead man failed to move her, she was changed into a stone by Aphrodite (Ov. xiv, 698f.).

ANCHISES. Son of Capys* and son-in-law of King Ilus* of Troy. By him, Venus* became the mother of Aeneas*, who, when Troy fell, rescued him from the burning city and took him on his voyage to Latium*. Anchises, however, died in Sicily on the way to Latium (Virg. ii, 634, 687, 721, etc.).
Iconography. Anchises is shown as a frail old man, borne on Aeneas' shoulders, on a mural at Pompeii, in the Via dell' Abbondanza, reg. ix, ins. 13.5. See also AENEAS.

ANCUS MARCIUS or **MARTIUS.** Fourth king of Rome, c. 630 B.C. He subjugated part of Latium* and forced the populations of four cities to settle on the Aventine Hill at Rome. He is reputed to have founded the port of Ostia and to have built the Pons Sublicius, the wooden bridge across the Tiber (Liv. i, 32-34). He incorporated the Janiculum Hill into the city.

ANDROGEUS [Gr. Androgeos]. Son of Minos*, king of Crete, and Pasiphaë*. Having won all the prizes at the Panathenaea in Athens, he was slain by the jealous Aegeus*. The city was punished for this by being made to provide a number of its youths and maidens annually as a sacrifice to the Minotaur (Virg. vi, 20).

ANDROMACHE. The noble wife of Hector*. After the fall of Troy, Neoptolemus* took her with him as a slave to Epirus, where he married her. Upon his death, she became the wife of her brother-

in-law, Helenus*. The description of her farewell to Hector and that of her mourning his death are among the most famous passages in Homer's *Iliad*. Euripides also chose Andromache as the subject of one of his tragedies (Hom. Iliad, viii, 187; vi, 371f.; xii, 437 f.; Virg. ii, 456; iii, 297f.).
Iconography. Andromache is frequently represented on Greek vases; her farewell to Hector is illustrated on a Chalcidian amphora (c. 530 B.C.) at Würzburg: She is clad in a long garment, and her head is veiled.

ANDROMEDA. Daughter of Cepheus* and Cassiopea*. The latter boasted of being more beautiful than the Nereids*. The enraged Poseidon* sent a sea-monster to ravage Cepheus' land, and only by sacrificing Andromeda to the monster could the disaster be ended. She was chained to a rock, awaiting her fate, when she was rescued by Perseus*, who slew the monster. Having also slain his rival Phineus*, Perseus obtained Andromeda in marriage (Ov. iv, 670f.; v, 1f.).
Iconography. The earliest representation of Andromeda is on a Corinthian amphora (6th century B.C.). Of the murals showing Perseus and Andromeda, the best-known is the large tableau in the Casa dei Dioscuri at Pompeii, in which Perseus is leading Andromeda from the rock after his victory over the monster, this is prob. a copy of a work by the Attic painter Nicias (4th century B.C.). The subject has also been treated by Rubens.

ANGITIA. Ancient snake-goddess of the Marsi, a tribe in Central Italy (Virg. vii, 759).

ANIUS [Gr. Anios]. Son of Apollo; priest of Apollo on the island of Delos, which was dedicated to Apollo. Aeneas and his companions were hospitably received by Anius on their wanderings (Ov. xiii, 622f.; Virg. iii, 80).

ANNA. Daughter of Belus* and sister of Dido* (Virg. iv). On Dido's death she is said to have fled from Africa and landed in Latium*, where she was well received by Aeneas*. Dido's spirit warned her of the jealousy of Lavinia*, wife of Aeneas. Anna then threw herself into the Numicius and drowned. As a river nymph she was later venerated under the name of Anna Perenna. A.t.o., however, there is absolutely no connection between the latter and Dido's sister.

ANTAEUS [Gr. Antaios]. Son of Poseidon* and Gaea*; a huge giant who beat everyone at wrestling because he kept gaining new strength every time he touched his mother (Gaea = earth). Heracles* discovered the secret, lifted him off the ground, and strangled him (Ov. ix, 184).
Iconography. Heracles' fight with Antaeus is depicted on Greek vases. Particularly well known is the representation on the red-figured krater by Euphronius (5th century B.C.) at Paris. The fight is also featured on coins, particularly the scene in which the giant is lifted clear of the ground. From a later period there is Baldung's painting.

ANTEA [Gr. Anteia]. Daughter of Iobates; wife of King Proetus of Argos. When she fell in love with Bellerophon* and her love remained unrequited, she maligned Bellerophon to her husband, finally taking her own life in despair.

ANTENOR. Brother-in-law of Priam*; married to Theano. He steadily advocated meeting Greek demands for the return of Helen*. He was spared when Troy fell (Hom. Il. iii, 148, 203, 262; vii, 347). In Virgil he is the founder of Patavium (now Padua) (Virg. i, 242).

ANTEROS. The god of reciprocated love, brother of Eros*. When Eros was languishing in loneliness, Aphrodite, on the advice of Themis*, gave him Anteros as a playmate. After that Eros thrived, since love, if it is to prosper, must be returned. Anteros was also regarded as the avenger of slighted love.

ANTHESTERIA. One of the great Dionysian festivals, held at Athens February 11-13, in the Greek month of Anthesterion, to celebrate nature's awakening from her winter sleep. On the first day the casks of new wine were opened. The second was marked by a festive procession and a public meal, at which the wine was duly tasted. On the third, pots of cooked pulse were laid out as offerings to the shades of the dead.

ANTICLEA [Gr. Antikleia]. Daughter of Autolycus*; wife of Laertes* and mother of Odysseus*. She pined away with grief at her son's long absence (Hom. Od. xi, 85).

ANTIGONE. 1. Daughter of King Oedipus* of Thebes and his wife, Jocasta*. When her father, relentlessly pursued by fate, blinded himself and went into exile, she voluntarily followed him and shared his lot. Returning to Thebes on the death of Oedipus, she disregarded King Creon's* ban and buried her slain brother Polynices*. She was prepared, even at the cost of her life, to do her duty toward her dead brother and to obey divine law, for only burial could bring peace to the spirits of the dead. Antigone was shut up by Creon in a cave, where she took her own life, whereupon her lover, Creon's son Haemon*, also put an end to his life. Her character and actions form the theme of Sophocles' tragedy Antigone. 2. Daughter of the Trojan king, Laomedon*. She was so proud of her beautiful hair that she incurred Hera's* disfavor and was changed by the goddess into a stork (Ov. vi, 93). 3. Wife of Peleus*. The jealous Astydamea*, whose love for Peleus was not returned, told Antigone that her husband was unfaithful to her. Believing this slander, she committed suicide.

ANTILOCHUS [Gr. Antilochos]. Son of Nestor*. One of the bravest heroes at the siege of Troy, and after Patroclus the favorite friend of Achilles. He was slain by Memnon* while trying to rescue Nestor from great danger (Hom. Il. xxiii, 423, 541, 556; Od. iv, 188).

ANTINOUS [Gr. Antinoös]. The most insolent of Penelope's suitors. Having made an attempt on the life of Telemachus* and insulted Odysseus*, he was the first to be slain by the latter's avenging arrows (Hom. Od. iv, 628, 660, 773; xvii, 409; xxii, 8).

ANTIOPE. Daughter of Nycteus*, king of Thebes. She was seduced by Zeus and fled in shame to Epopeus*, king of Sicyon, who married her. Nycteus did not succeed in bringing her back, and on his deathbed he bade his brother Lycus* carry out that task. Lycus laid waste to

Sicyon, killed Epopeus, took Antiope prisoner, and gave her as a slave to his wife, Dirce*, by whom she was cruelly treated. She managed to escape and joined the two sons, Amphion* and Zethus*, she had had by Zeus. The twins avenged their mother by capturing Thebes and putting Dirce to a horrible death. Iconography. Antiope is shown on an Etruscan mirror with Zeus, who, in the form of a satyr, is embracing her; also on Greek vases, e.g. a red-figured scyphus (5th century B.C.). There was a statue of Antiope in the Temple of Aphrodite at Sicyon. In more recent times: Antiope sleeping, by Correggio.

ANTIPHATES. The cruel king of the Laestrygones*, who destroyed the fleet of Odysseus* so that only one ship was left (Hom. Od. x, 106, 114, 199).

ANTIPHUS [Gr. Antiphos]. Son of Priam*; slain by Agamemnon (Hom. Il. iv, 489).

ANTOR. In Virg., a companion of Hercules*, left behind on the latter's visit to Euander* in Italy (Virg. x, 779).

ANUBIS. Egyptian god of the dead, represented with the head of a jackal. Conceived of by the Greeks and Romans as a dog (Virg. viii, 698).

AOEDE [Gr. Aoide]. Name of the single Muse* that was originally venerated before the number of Muses was increased to the familiar nine.

AON. Greek hero, son of Poseidon*, specially honored in Boeotia.

APHAEA [Gr. Aphaia]. Greek goddess, venerated on Aegina, where she had a temple. Prob. came from Crete (see BRITOMARTIS).

APHAREUS. King of Messenia, father of Idas* and Lynceus*, who dared to measure their strength against that of the Dioscuri*.

APHRODITE. Greek goddess of fertility, sexual love, and beauty, daughter of Zeus* and Dione*. A later Greek tradition regards her as having been born from the foam of the sea (Gr. aphros = sea foam). Her cult is of eastern origin and appears connected with that of Astarte*-Ishtar. Aphrodite was regarded not only as the goddess of love and the power of growth, but also as the bringer of blessings in general and as the protectress of sailors in particular. Her cult was particularly widespread in seaports and on the islands. Cyprus was the main and earliest center of her worship, since it was off this island that she was believed to have risen from the sea. Other places where she was venerated include Cythera, Cos, Corinth, and Sicily, where her main sanctuary stood on the mountain of Eryx (now Erice). Neither men nor gods could resist her beauty. It is for this reason that Paris*, prince of Troy, awarded her the apple of Eris* even in preference to Hera.* The god Hephaestus* is named as her husband, but in other myths she is the wife of the war god Ares*. The legend of her love for Adonis* comes from Asia. Of the mortals who could boast of her favor the most important figure is Anchises*, by whom she was the mother of Aeneas*. The goddess plays a leading part in the story of Troy, for it was she who gave Paris possession of Helen*, thus becoming the cause of the Trojan war. In this struggle she supported the Trojans (Hom. Il. xx, 40) and in particular her son Aeneas (Hom. Il. v, 312f.). Her retinue includes the Graces* and the Horae*; the dove, the myrtle, and the pomegranate are sacred to her. The Italian spring goddess Venus* was identified with her, just as the Greek Eros* (= love), who was later regarded as her son, was identified with Amor by the Romans.

Iconography. Aphrodite is one of the most frequently depicted figures of the Greek pantheon. In archaic art and on Greek vases she is shown fully clothed, but in ancient sculpture she is entirely naked or with the upper part of her body bare. She appears richly dressed in, for instance, the Judgment of Paris scene on an Ionian-Etruscan amphora (c. 525 B.C.) at Munich, and in the Rape of Helen painted on an Attic scyphus by Hieron and Macron (c. 490 B.C.) at Boston. On a bowl by the painter Pistoxenos (c. 460 B.C.), she is represented hovering on a goose, with a blossoming branch in her hand. Apelles, the court painter of Alexander, painted an Aphrodite rising from

the sea for the sanctuary of Asclepius on Cos. This was one of the chief sights of the temple, but it has been lost. The numerous sculptures representing the goddess include the celebrated Aphrodite of Knidos by Praxiteles (4th century B.C.). Phidias made several statues of the goddess, all as draped figures. Scopas' Aphrodite rivaled that of Praxiteles in fame. Another favorite theme, particularly in Hellenistic times, is Aphrodite bathing, e.g. the statue by Doedalsas (3rd century B.C.) in the Louvre, and the Venus Capitolina (late 2nd century B.C.) at Rome. Also the Venus Medici, a copy of a Hellenistic sculpture, and the renowned Venus de Milo (late 2nd century B.C.) in the Louvre. A frequent subject of Pompeian murals is the love of Venus and Mars, e.g. in the Casa di Marco L. Frontone. On reliefs Venus is shown as ancestress of the Gens Julia, together with Emperor Augustus. Aphrodite-Venus also appears on innumerable coins (e.g. those of Knidos) and in terra cottas. The Middle Ages present her richly garbed as Frau Minne or Dame Amour. She figures particularly often in Renaissance and Baroque paintings (e.g. Botticelli and Rubens). For illustrations see VENUS.

APIS. The Egyptian bull god. He was the image of the soul of Osiris. His name is prob. related to Serapis*, a Hellenistic deity who was also venerated by the Romans. The Egyptian Apis was worshiped at Memphis in the form of a living bull, which had to have certain characteristics—black color, white triangular spot on the front of its head, etc. Upon his death Apis was buried in the Serapeum at Memphis (Herod. ii, 38; iii, 27-29, 33, 64).

Iconography. The god is represented as a bull with the sun's disk between his horns, sometimes also as a man with a bull's head.

APOLLO [Gr. Apollon]. One of the most important gods of antiquity. Son of Zeus* and Leto*; twin brother of Artemis*. He was born on the island of Delos, which ever after was sacred to him. A.t.s. he was originally the sun god; a.t.o. he was not so venerated before the 6th century, when he was particularly venerated by the Romans as Phoebus Apollo (*phoibos* = radiant). For the Greeks he was the god of goodness, beauty, and harmonious peace, the preserver of law and order, and the bringer of catharsis— purification of the guilt-ridden conscience. As an archer he punished the arrogant. He was the god of healing and father of Asclepius*. Another of his special tasks was, as deliverer of oracles, to reveal the will of the gods, especially at sacred Delphi*, although he also spoke to men through priests in many other places. Many cities in the ancient world regarded him as their founder, e.g. Troy*, whose walls he built singlehanded. He was also the god of music and poetry and leader of the Muses*, who gave inspiration to poets. His many functions are reflected in his honorary titles, which bear witness to his help to mankind in need: Smintheus*—destroyer of mice; Pythius*—killer of pythons; and Paean* —healer. In Italy he was early venerated by the Etruscans, and later by the Romans, especially after the victory at Actium, for which Augustus acknowledged his debt to Apollo by building a sanctuary in his honor on the Palatine (Virg. viii, 704). In Homer's *Iliad* he caused an epidemic in the Greek camp with his plague-scattering arrows, and this led to the disastrous quarrel between Agamemnon* and Achilles* (Hom. Il. i). An important theory about Apollo was developed by Nietzsche, who contrasted him with Dionysus*: Apollo, the god of wisdom and analytical thought, the constructor of personality, the god of reflection and understanding; Dionysus, the god of religious ecstasy.

Iconography. The god is represented on Greek vases of all periods. On ancient Greek pottery of the 7th century B.C. he is shown as a lyre player. He is also seen inspiring the Muses (Attic bowl, c. 450 B.C., at Boston), armed with a bow and accompanied by his sister (Attic vase, c. 490 B.C., at Munich), protecting Hector before Troy (bowl by Duris, c. 490 B.C., at London), and in countless other situations. Mysterious and somewhat demonic

is the Etruscan terra cotta statue, the Apollo of Veii (6th or 5th century B.C.). He is represented as a noble judge and protector on the west façade of the Temple of Zeus at Olympia (early 5th century B.C.). A familiar archaic statue of Apollo is that from Tenea (c. 525 B.C.). He is shown, as Alexikakos (repeller of evil) by, *interalia*, statues of c. 500 B.C. that exhibit the style of Phidias. The Apollos of the 4th century are more elegant and relaxed, e.g. the Sauroktonos (killer of lizards) after Praxiteles and the famous Apollo Belvedere at Rome, for earlier generations the ideal of Greek sculpture. The middle ages represent Apollo as an archer. In Renaissance art he is seen as leader of the Muses (Mantegna, Perugino); he is shown by Dürer as the sun god and by Raphael as the ideal of human beauty. In the 17th century the figure of Apollo was a favorite theme of garden statuary (De Vries, Duquesnoy).

APPIAS. Roman nymph. Two fountains in her honor flanked the entrance to the Temple of Venus Genitrix on the Forum of Caesar at Rome.

APSYRTUS [Gr. Apsurtos]. Young brother of Medea*. When, after obtaining possession of the Golden Fleece, Medea was fleeing with Jason*, she cut the boy into pieces to delay the pursuing King Aeëtes*. Aeëtes collected Apsyrtus' remains and buried them at Tomi (now Constanta). See ARGONAUTS.

ARACHNE. Lydian maiden who possessed such skill in the art of weaving that she challenged Athena* to a contest and defeated her. The enraged goddess changed her into a spider (Gr. *arachne*) (Ov. vi, 1f.).

Iconography. It is prob. the story of Arachne that is illustrated on the frieze of the Temple of Athena in the Forum of Nerva at Rome. From the Baroque period there is an etching by Stefano della Bella and a painting by Velasquez.

ARCAS [Gr. Arkas]. Son of Zeus* and the Arcadian nymph Callisto*. In jealousy Hera changed Callisto into a she-bear. When Arcas, out hunting, met Callisto and in ignorance was about to kill her, Zeus changed them into the constellations of the Great and Little Bear (Ov. ii, 466f.).

ARCESIUS [Gr. Arkessios or Arkeisios]. Father of Laertes*; king of Ithaca (Hom. Od. xiv, 182).

ARDEAS. Son of Odysseus* and Circe*; legendary founder of Ardea in Latium. A.t.o., however, this city was founded by Danaë.*

ARES. Greek god of war and bloodshed, son of Zeus* and Hera*. He was detested by all the gods, including his father, for his cruelty and aggressiveness. He was powerfully built, had a thunderous voice, and surpassed all other gods in fleetness. Deimos (= terror) and Phobos (= fear) accompanied him and are sometimes represented as his sons. Only the loveliness of his wife, Aphrodite, could move him. (Hom. Od. viii, 266f.). His cult was never general in Hellas and was probably introduced from Thrace, where he was held in greatest honor. He was identified with Mars* by the Romans, but Mars acquired greater significance than Ares. *Iconography.* On early Greek vases Ares is seen as a bearded old warrior with shield and helmet, usually accompanied by other gods, e.g. on an Attic amphora (c. 540 B.C.) in the Vatican Museum and on the famous François vase (c. 570 B.C.) at Florence. Later the god appears more youthful and less warlike, e.g. the Ares Ludovisi (4th century B.C.), a work by Lysippus or Leochares, which depicts a youthful figure, sitting in a relaxed attitude on a rock, his hands clasped around his upraised knee. Another well-known statue is the Roman Ares Borghese in the Louvre. A famous work of Etruscan art is the bronze Mars of Todi (4th century B.C.) in the Vatican museum, in which the god is wearing a helmet and armor. Several Pompeian murals depict the love of Mars and Venus, e.g. in the Casa di Marte e Venere and the Casa di Marco L. Frontone. Renaissance art has a preference for showing him as the lover of Venus, and Baroque art for showing him as the god of war, e.g. in Velasquez. In a later period there are sculptures of the god by Canova and Thorwaldsen.

ARETE. Wife of Alcinius*, mother of Nausicaä*. Odysseus* was hospitably received by her (Hom. Od. vii, 54, 66f., 141f., 233f.).

ARETHUSA [Gr. Arethousa]. A Nereid* for whom the river god Alpheus conceived a passionate love. She escaped from him and was changed by Artemis into a spring on the island of Ortygia, part of the city of Syracuse. Alpheus made his way beneath the sea and united his waters with those of the spring (Ov. v, 572f.; Virg. iii, 692f.). *Iconography.* The head of Arethusa frequently appears on coins of Syracuse, not only on the archaic tetradrachms and decadrachms (c. 510 B.C.), but also on those struck at the height of the city's prosperity in the 5th century B.C. Her hair is often held in a net and her head is usually surrounded by fish.

ARETUS [Gr. Aretos]. Son of Nestor*, king of Pylos (Hom. Od. iii, 414).

ARGEA [Gr. Argeia]. Daughter of Adrastus*; wife of Polynices*.

ARGO. Name of the fifty-oared ship on which the Argonauts* sailed to Aeaea*. Athena helped to build it, including a piece of wood from the speaking oak of Dodona*, so that the vessel could speak and prophesy. At the end of the expedition the ship was given a place among the stars.

ARGONAUTS. The Greek heroes who sailed to Colchis* in the Argo* under the leadership of Jason* in quest of the Golden Fleece*, which had been hung up in a sacred wood there and was guarded by Phrixus*. Jason, deprived of his kingdom by his uncle, Pelias*, was promised the throne on condition that he brought back the Golden Fleece, a task which Pelias presumed to be impossible. Among the fifty Greek heroes who came to Jason's aid and embarked on the Argo were Amphiaraus*, Heracles*, Orpheus*, Theseus*, and the Dioscuri*. When the Argonauts reached Colchis after many adventures, King Aeëtes* agreed to surrender the Fleece on the condition that Jason harness a pair of fire-breathing bulls to a plow, plow a field, sow dragons' teeth in the furrows, and slay the men that came forth from them. After this he still had to fight the dragon that guarded the Golden Fleece. With the aid of the sorceress Medea*, daughter of Aeëtes, Jason successfully completed his various tasks and obtained the Fleece. Although the Fleece was in his possession, the return voyage was not without difficulty (see APSYRTUS); only after many more wanderings and adventures did the Argonauts reach Iolcus, their point of departure. *Iconography.* Of the representations of the Argonaut legend on Greek vases, the best-known is on a krater from Orvieto (c. 460 B.C.), on which the Argonauts are seen awaiting the moment of departure. This was prob. based on a painting by Polygnotus. From the 4th century we have a beautifully engraved toilet box, now at Rome, showing various scenes from the expedition of the Argonauts. In the Renaissance, the expedition is frequently represented on Italian cassoni. There is also a well-known painting by Piero di Cosimo (c. 1487).

ARGUS [Gr. Argos]. A giant with a hundred eyes, ordered by Hera to watch Io, whom she had changed into a cow. He was charmed to sleep and slain by Hermes, and Hera transferred his eyes to the peacock's tail (Ov. i, 625f.). *Iconography.* Argus the watchman is seen on many Greek vases, e.g. an amphora from Clazomenae (6th century B.C.), now at Munich. On murals he is shown in the Macellum at Pompeii and in the Casa di Livia on the Palatine at Rome. Rubens painted the metamorphosis of Argus into a peacock.

ARIADNE. Daughter of King Minos* of Crete and Pasiphaë*. When Theseus had killed the Minotaur, Ariadne helped him to escape from the labyrynth by giving him a ball of string to mark his path. She fled from Crete with Theseus, but while asleep she was abandoned by him on Naxos, where Dionysus found her and made her his wife (Ov. viii, 168f.).

From that time on she accompanied the god, although a.t.o. she became one of the Olympians. *Iconography.* The famous François vase (c. 570 B.C.) at Florence shows Theseus abandoning Ariadne on Naxos. The same scene occurs as a mural in the Casa del Poeta Tragico at Pompeii. In the Villa dei Misteri in Pompeii Ariadne is represented with the god Dionysus on the famous frieze in the "sala dell' grande affresco." The best-known statue of Ariadne is the Hellenistic one in the Vatican: Ariadne on a couch. From a later period we have Dannecker's statue of Ariadne mounted on a panther.

ARION. 1. Singer and lyric poet of Methymna on Lesbos, who spent a long time at the court of Periander of Corinth. When he sailed from there to Italy, the crew, covetous of his riches, planned to kill him. Arion, observing the danger, asked as a final favor to be allowed to sing a song. He went up to the prow, sang his most beautiful song, and threw himself into the sea. A dolphin, attracted by the lovely song, took him on its back and brought him safely to Cape Taenarum, on the southern tip of the Peloponnesus. From there he returned to Corinth, where, some time later, the crew of the ship reported that Arion had remained in Italy. They were ignominiously exposed by the sudden appearance of the poet (Herod. i, 23-24). 2. The lightning-swift and immortal horse of Adrastus*.

ARISBE. 1. Daughter of Teucer (1)* and wife of Dardanus*. 2. Wife of Priam* before his marriage with Hecuba.*

ARISTAEUS [Gr. Aristaios]. Old Greek god, son of Uranus* or Apollo*. He was regarded as the patron of agriculture, cattle breeding, and hunting.

ARISTODEMUS [Gr. Aristodemos]. King of Sparta, a descendant of Heracles*, and father of Eurysthenes and Procles.

ARISTOMACHUS [Gr. Aristomachus]. Great-grandson of Heracles*; and father of Cresphontes*. He made a vain attempt to conquer the Peloponnesus; his sons eventually succeeded.

ARSINOË. 1. Nurse of Orestes*, the

son of Agamemnon*. 2. Mother a.t.s. of Asclepius* by Apollo*.

ARTEMIS. Greek goddess of the hunt, daughter of Zeus* and Leto*, and twin sister of Apollo*. Her oldest role, viz. that of goddess of wild animals, is probably of pre-Greek origin. An excellent huntress, she used to hunt, accompanied by her nymphs, in the mountains and woods of Arcadia and Lacedaemon. She was in many ways the female counterpart of her brother Apollo: she punished lawbreakers, killing some of them with her arrows, e.g. the proud Niobe*. Immune to love, she remained the virgin goddess and was in particular the protectress of chastity (see ACTAEON). Women in labor also enjoyed her protection (see ILITHYIA). Just as her brother was venerated as the sun god, she was regarded as the moon goddess. In some districts her cult was of a very special kind. In Sparta, for instance, her title was Artemis Orthia, and she was more feared for her punishments than loved for her blessings; her cult was crude, and she was offered human victims. In the East she was regarded as a fertility goddess, and as such she was venerated in her famous sanctuary at Ephesus. On Aegina she was bracketed with Aphaea*. The Romans identified her with the Italian goddess Diana*.

Iconography. In archaic art Artemis is represented as the ruler of the animals; as such she is shown enthroned among the animals on a Corinthian alabastrum (7th century B.C.) of Delos. Sometimes she is the moon goddess with a half-moon in her hair or, as on a coin of Pagae, with a torch in her hand. From an early date the goddess is also represented as a huntress, as on a vase from Melos (7th century B.C.), now at Athens, where she is seen armed with a bow and quiver of arrows, holding a stag by the antlers with her right hand. The frieze of the Parthenon shows her enthroned among other gods. A statue of Artemis from Pompeii shows her attired in a long Ionic robe; this statue is a copy of a 5th-century Greek original. Also well-known is the Diana of Gabii in the

Louvre (suggesting Praxiteles, 4th century B.C.). In this the goddess stands in a relaxed attitude, fixing her robe on her shoulder with one hand. The Diana of Versailles in the Louvre is probably by Leochares (4th century B.C.; the statue shows the goddess as a nimble huntress, with kilted dress, accompanied by a deer. The Diana of Ephesus is a goddess of fertility, with many breasts. Artemis can also be seen on several frescoes at Pompeii, including one with Actaeon. From more modern times there are paintings by Correggio, Rubens, Boucher, and Corot, and statues by Goujon, Houdon, Milles, and Falquières.

ASCALAPHUS [Gr. Askalaphos]. 1. King of Orchomenus, son of Ares and Astyoche (1)*. He took part in the expedition of the Argonauts and died later at Troy (Hom. Il. xiii, 518). 2. Son of Acheron* and Orphne*. He betrayed Persephone* when she ate the forbidden fruit of the pomegranate in the lower world. As punishment, Ascalaphus was changed into an owl (Ov. v, 534f.).

ASCANIUS. Son of Aeneas* and Creusa*. He fled with his father from burning Troy* to Latium* where, under his other name of Iulus*, he became the founder of Alba Longa* and ancestor of the Roman people, especially of the Gens Julia (Virg. i, 267, 644; ii, 710).

ASCLEPIUS [Gr. Asklepios]. Greek god of healing, son of Apollo* and Coronis*. The earliest Greek literature speaks of him not as a god but as a Thessalian hero. In Homer he is the ruler of Trikke in Thessaly, father of Podalirius* and Machaon*, who were physicians in the Greek army at Troy (Hom. Il. ii, 731; iv, 194). He was entrusted by his father Apollo to Chiron*, who brought him up and taught him medicine, to which he was so responsive that he could not only cure the sick but also bring the dead back to life. This enraged Zeus*, who killed him with his lightning. Later, Asclepius was venerated as a healing god in Greece, and his cult spread from Epidaurus*, where his principal sanctuary stood. The sick were laid in the temple, and while they slept the god appeared to them and cured them, or told them of the right medicine in a vision. Around the temple there rose a group of buildings, including the magnificient theater which is now the best-preserved of antiquity. Also venerated within the domain were serpents, especially sacred to the deity because they were symbols of the constantly renewed forces of life. From practical experience with the many patients who sought healing at Epidaurus, the priests of the temple eventually learned the art of diagnosis and medical prescription, so that Epidaurus and other places of Asclepian worship, particularly the island of Cos, became centers around which Greek medical science developed. When a plague was ravaging Rome and the country around it c. 280 B.C., a mission was sent, after consultation of the Sibylline Books*, to Epidaurus to bring Asclepius to Rome. The god came to Rome in the form of his sacred animal, the serpent, and chose as his abode the island of the Tiber. He was venerated by the Romans under the name Aesculapius (Ov. xv, 622f.).

Iconography. The god is represented as a kind, aged man with a beard. His attributes are a staff and a serpent. In art he figures chiefly in sculpture, and famous sculptors such as Alcamenes and Scopas are known to have made statues of him. There are copies of Alcamenes' work at Berlin and Naples. They show the god standing, a cloak thrown over his left shoulder and his right arm and shoulder bare. He is leaning on a rod with a snake coiled round it, and his abundant hair and full beard make his head resemble somewhat that of Zeus. Asclepius is also found on many votive reliefs and coins. Of the statue in the temple at Epidaurus made by Thrasymedes (4th century B.C.) of gold and ivory, nothing has survived. In the Middle Ages drawings of Asclepius were sometimes used in medical books, and he occasionally figured as an apothecary in Renaissance manuscripts.

ASIA. Greek sea nymph, daughter of Oceanus and Tethys*. A.t.o. she was the mother of Prometheus'* wife (Herod. iv, 45).

ASOPUS [Gr. Asopos]. God of the river of the same name in Boeotia, son of Oceanus* and Tethys*.

ASSARACUS [Gr. Assarakos]. Son of Tros*, king of Troy. Grandfather of Anchises* (Virg. vi, 650).

ASTARTE. Phoenician goddess of fertility. Her cult was very widespread in the East and shows affinity with the Babylonian cult of Ishtar and the Greek veneration of Aphrodite*.

Iconography. In Syrian art Astarte is frequently represented with two curled ram's horns on her head.

ASTERIA. Daughter of the Titan Coeus* and Phoebe*. When she was abducted by Zeus*, she threw herself into the sea and was changed into the island of the same name.

ASTERION. King of Crete, husband of Europa*. He brought up as his own the children, Minos* and Rhadamanthys*, that Europa had had by Zeus, and on his death he appointed Minos to succeed him.

ASTRABACUS [Gr. Astrabakos]. Ancient Laconian hero, ancestor of the Spartan king Demaratus who participated in the Persian wars.

ASTRAEA [Gr. Astraia]. Daughter of Zeus* and Themis*, or of Astraeus* and Eos*. During the Golden Age her abode was with mankind, but when evil took a firmer grip on man she disappeared from the earth. Since then she has shone in the sky as the constellation of Virgo.

ASTRAEUS [Gr. Astraios]. One of the Titans*, married to Eos* (dawn). He is the father of the four winds: Boreas* (north), Zephyrus* (west), Eurus* (southeast), and Notus* (south).

ASTYANAX. Son of Hector* and Andromache*, actually called Scamandrius. At the fall of Troy he was cast from the walls by the enemy (Hom. Il. vi, 403, 466f.; Virg. ii, 457).

Iconography. Astyanax appeared on the murals painted by Polygnotus (5th century B.C.) in the Lesche at Delphi, an inner court surrounded by colonnades, which depicted the destruction of Troy.

Astyanax, and particularly his death, is represented on various Greek vases, e.g. an amphora from Lydos (middle of 6th century B.C.), which shows him hanging helplessly upside down, with Neoptolemus holding him by one leg. The same scene occurs on a bowl now at Paris, by the painter Brygus (5th century B.C.). Priam with the bloodcovered corpse of Astyanax on his lap can be seen on an Attic hydria by the Cleophrades painter (c. 485 B.C.) at Naples.

ASTYDAMEA [Gr. Astudameia]. Wife of Acastus*. She fell in love with Peleus*, but when he rejected her she maligned him to her husband.

ASTYMEDUSA [Gr. Astumedousa]. See OEDIPUS.

ASTYOCHE. 1. Daughter of Actor*, mother of Ascalaphus*. 2. Daughter of Laomedon*, wife of Telephus*.

ATALANTA. Daughter of the Arcadian king Iasus and Clymene*. Exposed by her father in infancy, she was suckled by a she-bear and grew up among hunting people, thus becoming a courageous huntress, excelling particularly in swiftness of foot. When, on the Calydonian hunt*, she was the first to hit the wild boar, Meleager* awarded her the animal's skin for a prize and took her as his wife. A.t.o., however, Atalanta was the daughter of Schoeneus, a Boeotian king, and had sworn never to marry unless the suitor first defeated her in a race. Any who lost were to die. Milanion, or a.t.o. Hippomenes*, managed to defeat her by dropping at her feet during the race the three golden apples that Aphrodite had given him. Atalanta was unable to resist the temptation to pick up the apples, and thus lost the race and her heart (Ov. x, 560f.). Later, when Atalanta and her husband had the misfortune to desecrate a wood that was sacred to Cybele*, they were changed by the goddess into lions (Ov. x, 686f.).

Iconography. Atalanta is represented on Greek vases as a participant in the Calydonian hunt, e.g. on the François vase (c. 570 B.C.). She is also seen as huntress in the statuary group on the tympanum

of the Temple of Athena at Tegea (prob. by Scopas, middle of 4th century B.C.). She is frequently shown with Meleager on sarcophagi and murals (e.g. at Casa di Meleagro in Pompeii). From more recent times she appears in a painting by Guido Reni.

ATE. Greek goddess of infatuation (*ate* = blindness), daughter of Zeus* or Eris*. She led men to do evil and thus plunged them in misery (Hom. Il. ix, 504f.; xix, 91f., 126f.).

ATHAMAS. King of Orchomenus, son of Aeolus*. He repudiated his first wife, the goddess Nephele*, to marry Ino*, the daughter of Cadmus*. In addition to Nephele's children, Phrixus* and Helle*, he had two sons by Ino, Learchus* and Melicertes*. When his land was ravaged by a drought, Ino persuaded him to sacrifice her stepchildren, but they were saved by Nephele. Hera, incensed at Ino for having reared Dionysus, struck Athamas with madness, causing him to attack his own sons and slay Learchus. Ino managed to save her own life and that of her son Melicertes, but in their flight they plunged into the sea, becoming sea gods. The guilt-stricken Athamas fled to Phthiotis and there married Themisto* (Ov. iv, 416f.).

ATHENA or ATHENE. Greek goddess of the arts and sciences, as well as the womanly crafts, daughter of Zeus* and Metis*. Zeus, fearing that the child Metis was expecting would dethrone him, swallowed Metis and himself gave birth to the child. Hephaestus* cleft his head with an ax, whereupon Athena emerged fully armed from the opening. She was the protectress of everything that distinguishes civilized society. She maintained justice and law, and the people's assembly met under her protection. She taught man to use fire and the plow and to harness the horse to the cart. On the other hand, she was also the patroness of war operations. She was the invincible goddess who led armies into the field, who gave victory, who protected many legendary heroes such as Achilles*, Diomedes*, etc. The shrewd Odysseus* in particular was dear to her, and Homer describes her as the special divine protectress of Telemachus*, son of Odysseus. As the goddess of war she bore a helmet, shield, lance, and the fear-inspiring aegis*, but as the goddess of peace she brought blessings and taught mankind many useful things. Spinning and weaving were particularly dear to her, and at the festival of the Panathenaea, held every four years, the Athenian maidens offered her a richly embroidered peplos (robe of state). Athena was also the bringer of health. She was regarded with great reverence all over Greece, particularly in Attica, which she had acquired as her personal possession. Zeus had promised Attica to the god who gave the most useful gift. Poseidon produced a horse and Athena an olive tree, for which she was awarded Attica without dispute. From that time on the olive tree was especially sacred to her, along with the owl, the cock, and the serpent. She was a virgin goddess and Pallas (girl) or Parthenos (maiden) was an epithet added to her name. Her chief sanctuary was the Parthenon (temple of the maiden) at Athens, which, as the main citadel in Attica, was particularly sacred to her and still bears her name. In honor of Athena Polias (of the city), the national festival of the Panathenaea was celebrated every second or fourth year by the citizens of Athens. The Roman Minerva was identified with her.

Iconography. No goddess is represented more often in ancient art than Athena-Minerva. She is invariably shown as a "virago," a soldierly woman, armed with helmet, spear, and frequently with a shield, her breast and shoulders covered by the aegis. She is a subject that recurs in all periods of Greek vase painting, very often as the arbiter of a fight or as a participant. The prize amphorae of the Panathenaic games occupy a special place among Greek vases; they always represent Athena in a fighting attitude between two pillars, one crowned with a cock and the other with a Nike. The vases are always of the black-figure type and

range in date from 550 to 300 B.C. The most famous statues of the goddess include the Athena Parthenos (c. 438) in the Parthenon and the Athena Promachos and Athena Lemnia, both on the Acropolis (c. 447 B.C.) (all three have been lost, but the Lemnia is known from copies, including a head at Bologna), the Athena and Marsyas group (school of Myron), and the Athena on the tympanum of the temple at Aegina. The best-known Roman statues of the goddess are the Athena Albani, the Athena Farnese, and the Athena Velletri. Athena is also seen on reliefs, for example as the protectress of Perseus on an archaic metope of Selinus (early 6th century B.C.), and as a helper of Heracles on a metope of the Temple of Zeus at Olympia (5th century B.C.). The fascinating relief known as Athene at the Boundary Stone is ascribed to Myron; it shows the goddess as a youthful figure, leaning in reflective posture on her lance. From about 650 B.C., the coins of her city bear the head of the goddess, with her owl on the reverse side. Her likeness also occurs on seals, e.g. the seal of Aspasius (Augustan Age). Finally, there is the representation of the goddess on the silver platter of Augsburg (Hellenistic), which shows Athena seated, a helmet on her head and her left hand grasping her shield.

ATHOS. One of the Giants* who tried to storm the heavens. He hurled a mountain at Zeus*, but the god caused it to drop on the spot off the coast of Macedonia where the sacred Mount Athos now stands.

ATLANTIDES. A name for the Hyades* and Pleiades*, daughters of Atlas*.

ATLANTIS. The mythical island of Atlas, situated according to ancient tradition, to the W. of the Pillars of Hercules (the two promontories at the eastern end of the Strait of Gibraltar). It gave its name to the Atlantic Ocean. It was said to have been hit by an earthquake and engulfed in the sea as a punishment for the wickedness of its inhabitants. In his *Critias,* Plato gives a detailed description of the island, including its position, its fauna and flora, and its political conditions. His fantasy has led to the publication of a great many writings, including romances, which appear from time to time today.

ATLAS. One of the Titans*, son of Iapetus*. As punishment for his invasion of the heavens, he was condemned to carry the heavens, or the pillars on which they rested. He was the father of the Hyades* and Pleiades*. He was identified even in antiquity with the Atlas Mountains in N. Africa, having been changed into a mountain by Perseus* by means of the Gorgon's head (Ov. iv, 632.).

Iconography. Atlas occurs on various Greek vases. The best-known representation of him is on the metope of the Temple of Zeus at Olympia, where Heracles has taken over his task for a moment and Atlas is offering Heracles the apples of the Hesperides* (early 5th century B.C.). He is also seen bearing the world on his shoulders on a marble statue at Naples.

ATREUS. Son of Pelops* and Hippodamea*, father of Agamemnon* and Menelaus*. With his brother Thyestes* he murdered their stepbrother Chrysippus* and was banished by Pelops. Atreus sought refuge in Mycenae at the court of King Sthenelus*, whom he later succeeded. When Thyestes, consumed with jealousy, seduced Atreus' wife, Aerope*, Atreus expelled him from the land. Thyestes then tried to murder Atreus, making use of Plisthenes*, a son of Atreus. When the attempt failed and Plisthenes was slain by his father, Atreus pretended to desire a reconciliation and invited Thyestes to a banquet at which he served the latter's two sons as food. On discovering the atrocity, Thyestes cursed Atreus and his descendants and left the country, which was then visited by all kinds of disasters. Atreus was finally murdered by Aegisthus, the son of Thyestes. The horrible deeds of Atreus and Thyestes are the fulfillment of the destiny and curse pronounced upon their ancestor Tantalus*.

ATRIDES. The two sons of Atreus:* Agamemnon* and Menelaus*.

ATROPUS [Gr. Atropos = the inavertible], one of the three Fates*.

ATTIS. Deity of growth and fertility in Asia Minor, also venerated by the Greeks. His cult, however, remained more Asiatic than Greek and was associated with that of Cybele*. In its expression of excessive grief and ecstatic joy, his worship resembled that of Adonis*. Attis is said to have been loved by Cybele and, when he rejected her love, to have been driven to madness by the goddess, so that he emasculated himself. Some of his followers did likewise.

Iconography. The god is represented chiefly on Roman coins and on tombstones. He is shown as a youth in a tightly fitting garment, with a Phrygian cap and a shepherd's crook.

AUGE. Daughter of the king of Tegea. She became mother of Telephus* by Heracles and hid her child in the sacred wood of Athena. When the goddess consequently sent a famine over the land, the king exposed the child and sold Auge as a slave. She ended up in Mysia, where she married King Teuthras. In a miraculous manner Telephus later succeeded Teuthras on the throne.

AUGEAS or AUGIAS [Gr. Augeias]. King of Elis. He had 3,000 cattle in his stables, which had not been cleaned for thirty years. Nevertheless, Heracles succeeded in carrying out King Eurystheus' * order to remove all the filth in one day by diverting the Alpheus* and Peneus rivers through the stables and washing away the dung, much to the displeasure of Augeas, who had promised him onetenth of his herd if he completed the task in one day. When he refused to keep his promise, Heracles engaged him in combat and slew him. Legend has it that the hero instituted the Olympic Games* on this occasion.

Iconography. The cleaning of the Augean stables is illustrated on one of the metopes of the Temple of Zeus at Olympia (c. 460 B.C.).

AULIS. Seaport in Boeotia where the

Greek fleet collected for the expedition against Troy. It was also the scene of the sacrifice of Iphigenia*.

AURORA. See Eos.

AUTOLYCUS [Gr. Autolukos]. Son of Hermes* and Chione*, and maternal grandfather of Odysseus*. The most cunning and skillful deceiver in antiquity, he dwelt on Parnassus* and conducted raiding expeditions from there. Since he possessed the gift of making himself invisible or changing form, he was assured of success in his undertakings

AUTOMEDON. Son of Diores* and charioteer of Achilles* (Hom. Il. xvi, 145f.; xvii, 429f.).

AUTONOË. Daughter of Cadmus* and Harmonia*; mother of Actaeon* and sister of Agave*.

AUXESIA. Greek goddess of the crops, probably an epithet for Demeter*. Often venerated along with Damia*.

AVERNUS. Roman name for the underworld (see HADES).

AVERNUS LACUS [Lago d'Averno]. Crater lake near the Gulf of Naples, surrounded in ancient times by dark cypress woods reputed to be the entrance to the underworld. In Virg. the Sibyl * lives in a cave to the S. of the lake (Virg. iii, 442; vi, 118).

AZAN. Son of Arcas* and Erato*. Azania, a part of Arcadia, was named after him.

B

BACCHANALIA. Secret feasts held by the Romans in honor of Bacchus*, introduced to Rome from the Greek cities in southern Italy. Because of the debauchery and crime which accompanied them, the Senate decided in 186 B.C. to ban them.

BACCHANTES. Women who accompanied the god Dionysus* on his processions. In a state of ecstatic madness and wearing animals' skins, they roamed through fields and woods. Hence their other name, Maenads* (raving). Women who celebrated the Dionysian feasts with clamor and frenzy were also known as Bacchantes, Maenads, or Thyiads*.
Iconography. In both Greek vase painting and sculpture, the Bacchante is represented with her hair hanging loose, dancing in ecstasy, and holding a staff (thyrsus) with vine tendrils or ivy wound around it, e.g. the dancing Maenads on a bowl by Hieron and Macron at Berlin, and the Maenad with thyrsus and panther on a bowl by Brygus (5th century B.C.) at Munich. Famous among ancient sculptures was the Maenad of Scopas (4th century B.C.). In later ages, too, Bacchantes are frequently shown in paintings, e.g. by Rubens and Poussin.

BACCHUS. Latin form of the Greek Bakchos, another name for Dionysus*.

BAIUS [Gr. Baios]. Odysseus'* helmsman. Reputed to have been buried at the site of the city named Baiae (now Baia) after him, on the Gulf of Naples.

BALIUS. The immortal horse of Achilles*, a wedding gift from the god Poseidon* to Achilles' father, Peleus* (Hom. Il. xvi, 149; xix, 400).

BATTUS [Gr. Battos]. 1. Son of Polymnestus of Thera. Acting on the advice of the Delphic oracle, he settled in Libya and founded Cyrene (Catullus vii). 2. Shepherd of Neleus, who witnessed the theft of Apollo's* cattle by Hermes*. When he broke his promise to keep silent about the matter, Hermes changed him into a stone (Ov. ii, 688f.).

BAUCIS. See PHILEMON.

BERBRYCES. A mythical people of Bithynia, which in ancient times was called Berbrycia after them.

BELLEROPHON or BELLEROPHONTES. Son of the Corinthian king Glaucus*. When he killed an opponent in a contest, he fled to King Proetus of Argos. Defamed by the latter's wife, he was sent to King Iobates* of Lycia, who gave him the task of destroying the Chimaera* and doing battle against the Amazons. With the aid of Athena, who sent him the winged horse Pegasus*, Bellerophon managed to slay the monster. He was also successful against the Amazons*. Made presumptuous by his good fortune, he tried to climb Olympus* but was prevented by the shafts of Zeus*. Pegasus threw his rider and returned to Olympus.
Iconography. The hero, seated on Pegasus, fighting the Chimaera, is represented on a Corinthian scyphus (9th century B.C.) at Aegina and on many other vases. He can also be seen on a terra cotta relief from Melos and on Corinthian coins. Bellerophon is shown in relief on the inner wall of the Heroum at Gyölbashi (late 5th century B.C.). From a more modern period is the relief in the Palazzo Spada, Rome.

BELLONA. Roman goddess of war, who accompanied Mars* into battle and was considered to be his wife, sister, or daughter. Her sanctuary in Rome was on the Capitoline Hill (destroyed by fire in 48 B.C.).
Iconography. She was represented in Roman art as a marching woman, armed with a helmet, spear, and torch. She was

later painted by Rembrandt as a Roman matron in armor.

BELUS [Gr. Belus], 1. Son of Poseidon* and father by Anchinoë of Aegyptus* and Danaus*. 2. King of Sidon and father of Dido* (Virg. i, 621, 729). 3. Latin name for Baal, a Semitic god.

BENDIS. Thracian goddess, also venerated in Greece, especially Athens. She was identified with Artemis*, and her cult was associated with orgiastic debauches.

BIANOR. Son of Heracles*; legendary founder of Mantua.

BIAS. Brother of Melampus*, with whose help he obtained the hand of Neleus'* daughter, Pero. With Melampus he ruled over Tiryns.

BITON. See CLEOBIS.

BONA DEA. Roman goddess of fertility and purity, was a.t.s. the daughter of Faunus*, against whom she successfully defended her chastity. Her mysteries were celebrated early in December, not in her sanctuary on the Aventine at Rome but in the house of one of the highest magistrates, and only women were allowed to attend. The magistrate's wife and other distinguished matrons performed the ceremonies after all the men had left the house and all representations of male persons and animals had been removed from sight. The Bona Dea was regarded as a healing deity; in the garden of her temple on the Aventine Hill curative herbs were administered to the sick. *Iconography.* Roman statuettes show her seated in dignity on a throne, with a cornucopia in her hand and with a serpent as the symbol of healing. Her image is also found on coins.

BOREADES. Zetes* and Calais*, the children of Boreas and Orithyia*. They took part in many exploits, including the expedition of the Argonauts*.

BOREAS. Greek god of the north wind, son of Astraeus* and Eos*. He carried off and married Orithyia*, daughter of Erechtheus*, and was thus closely related to the Athenians. When, during the Persian wars, Xerxes' fleet was approaching, the Athenians prayed to Boreas, who destroyed part of the fleet with a gale. Under the name of Aquilo he was revered by the Romans (Ov. vi, 675f.). *Iconography.* Boreas is represented as an old man with a thick beard, a loose mantle, and wings on his shoulders, e.g. on the Tower of the Winds at Athens (1st century B.C). A Rubens painting shows the god eloping with Orithyia.

BOSPORUS. See Io.

BRANCHIDES. See BRANCHUS.

BRANCHUS. Legendary founder of the Temple of Apollo at Didyma (Asia Minor). He was the ancestor of the priestly family of Branchides, who administered the temple and the oracle associated with it. When they handed over part of the temple's treasures to Xerxes during his campaign against Greece, they feared the revenge of the Greeks and moved to Bactriana (now part of Afghanistan), where their descendants were punished for the crime by Alexander the Great.

BRIAREUS. Another name for Aegaeon, one of the Centimani*.

BRISEIS. Daughter of Briseus, priest at Lyrnessus (Asia Minor). When the city was captured by the Greeks, she was carried off as a slave by Achilles*. She was forcibly taken from him by Agamemnon, an incident which led Achilles to avenge the insult as described in the *Iliad* (Hom. Il. i, 184f.). *Iconography.* A fresco in the Casa del Poeta Tragico at Pompeii shows Achilles ordering the grief-stricken Briseis to be led off to Agamemnon.

BRITOMARTIS. Cretan nymph, daughter of Zeus. She was loved by King Minos* of Crete, who pursued her until she threw herself into the sea. A.t.o. she fled to Aegina and hid in the sacred wood of Artemis*, where she was given the name of Aphaea*. She was frequently identified by the Greeks with Aphaea or Artemis.

BRIZO. Greek goddess, protectress of seafarers, worshiped on Delos, particularly by women.

BUBASTIS [Gr. Boubastis]. Egyptian goddess, daughter of Osiris* and Isis*; identified by the Greeks with Artemis*. The center of her cult was the city of the same name on the Nile delta.

BUSIRIS [Gr. Bousiris]. King of Egypt who was notorious for his cruel treatment of Greeks. He was slain by Heracles. *Iconography*. There is a famous painting on a hydria from Caere (c. 550 B.C.), now in Vienna, which shows, in a naïve and humorous way, Heracles as a powerful, curly-haired prize fighter, defeating six Egyptians and Negroes simultaneously while others seek safety on and behind an altar. Busiris himself lies manacled on the step of the altar.

BUTES [Gr. Boutes]. 1. Son of Pandion* and Zeuxippe* and priest of Athena and Poseidon. After his death he was honored as a hero by the Athenians. 2. Sicilian king who was loved by Aphrodite* and by whom she became mother of Eryx*. 3. Son of Boreas* who violated one of Dionysus' Bacchantes* and was punished with madness by the god.

BUTO. Egyptian goddess, foster mother of Isis'* two children. She was identified with Leto* by the Greeks.

BUZYGES [Gr. Bouzuges], an Attic hero, identified by some with Triptolemus*. He taught man to harness the ox to the plough.

BYBLIS [Gr. Bublis]. Daughter of Miletus, founder of Milete. She fell in love with her brother Caunus, who fled from her. Pursuing him through various regions of Asia Minor, she died of exhaustion and grief, and was changed into a spring. (Ov. ix, 450f.).

BYZAS. Son of Poseidon* and legendary founder of Byzantium.

C

CABEIRI or CABIRI. Deities whose cult was introduced into the Greek world from the East in Hellenistic and Roman times. They were probably fertility demons, but later also protectors from danger. Their cult was a mystic one about which little is known except that they were venerated on the islands of Samothrace. Lemnos, and Imbros, and in Boeotia, and were identified with the Dioscuri*, with the Corybantes*, and, by the Romans, with the Penates*.

CACA. Old Italian goddess of the hearth, but regarded from an early date as the sister of the villainous Cacus*, whose hiding place she is said to have revealed to Hercules out of affection for the hero.

CACUS. An old Roman god, son of Vulcan*. He was a fire-breathing, rapacious giant who dwelt in a cave in the Aventine Hill at Rome. When Hercules* was passing the spot with Geryon's* herds, Cacus stole some of the animals and drove them backward to his cave to put the owner off the trail. Guided either by Caca* or the lowing of the cattle, Hercules forced his way into the cave and slew Cacus (Virg. viii, 205, 231, 259). Roman veneration for Hercules (i.e. Heracles) originates in this legend (Liv. i, 7).

CADMUS [Gr. Kadmos]. Son of Agenor*, king of Tyre. When Cadmus' sister Europa* was abducted by Zeus*, he was ordered by his father to find her. The oracle of Delphi, however, told him to abandon his search and to follow a cow; at every place where the cow lay down he was to found a city. In this way Cadmus came to found Thebes. With Athena's* help he slew a dragon that was terrorizing the land round Thebes and had also killed his companions. On the goddess' advice he sowed the dragon's teeth, and from them sprang up armed men who fought with one another until only five were left. These five, called Sparti (Gr. *spartos*

= sown), became the forefathers of the Thebans. Cadmus married Harmonia*, daughter of the god Ares*, reigned long and happily over Thebes, and later emigrated with his wife to Illyria. Before their death they were changed into serpents and sent to the Elysian Fields*. Cadmus was venerated by the Greeks partly because he was supposed to have introduced the alphabet (Ov, iii, 1f.).
Iconography. Cadmus is rarely represented in ancient art. Only on a few Greek vases and an Etruscan mirror is the hero seen, at the point of slaying the dragon.

CADUCEUS. A herald's rod, particularly that carried by Hermes* as messenger of the gods. It is an olive branch with bands around it. The caduceus of Hermes is entwined by two serpents whose heads face each other on either side of the rod, near the top. The caduceus was also a magic wand with which the god could put people to sleep or awaken them.

CAECULUS. An ancient Italian hero, son of Vulcan*. He is said to have founded Praeneste (now Palestrina).

CAENEUS [Gr. Kaineus]. A Greek hero, born as a female (Caenis*). He was invulnerable, and took part in the expedition of the Argonauts* and the Calydonian* hunt. In a fight with the Centaurs* he was buried under tree trunks because they could not kill him; but in the form of a bird he flew out from the mound of logs (Ov. xii, 168f.). (See CAENIS.)

CAENIS [Gr. Kainis]. Daughter of Elatus, beloved by Poseidon and changed into a man, Caeneus*, by him.

CAIETA. Nurse of Aeneas*. Buried at the port of the same name in Latium (now Gaeta) (Virg. vii, 2).

CALAIS [Gr. Kalaïs]. Son of Boreas* and brother of Zetes*. Zetes and Calais played an important part in the expedition of the Argonauts, as when they rescued their king Phineus* from the Harpies*.

CALCHAS [Gr. Kalchas]. Son of Thestor*, a soothsayer with the Greek army besieging Troy. He ordered Iphigenia* to be sacrificed and Chryseis* to be given back to her father, and foretold that the Trojan War would be a long one. When he was outshone at Colophon by the seer Mopsus*, he died of a broken heart (Hom. Il. i, 69f., 384f.; ii, 300; Virg. ii, 122f.).

Iconography. On an Etruscan mirror (5th-4th century B.C.) in the Vatic. Museum, Calchas is shown as a powerful, bearded demon, standing at a sacrificial table, inspecting a liver.

CALLIOPE [Gr. Kalliope]. Eldest of the nine Muses*, the Muse of epic poetry. A.t.s., Orpheus* was her son.

Iconography. She is shown playing a flute on the François krater (c. 570 B.C.). A Hellenistic statue in the Vatican represents her sitting at a desk with a stylus.

CALLIRRHOE [Gr. Kallirrhoë]. 1. Daughter of Oceanus* and mother of Echidna*. 2. Daughter of Achelous*; married to Alcmaeon*. 3. Maiden of Calydon* who spurned the love of a priest of Dionysus, whereupon the god threatened all the women of Calydon with madness. When an oracle ordered the priest to sacrifice Callirrhoë, he committed suicide in despair and the maiden threw herself into a fountain, which afterwards bore her name (Callirrhoë, = fair-flowing).

CALLISTO [Gr. Kallisto]. Nymph of Artemis'* retinue, and daughter of the Arcadian king Lycaon*. She later became the mother, by Zeus*, of Arcas*, for which the irate Hera* changed her into a she-bear. Zeus placed her in the heavens as the Great Bear (Ov. ii, 409f.).

Iconography. An Arcadian coin (4th century B.C.) shows Callisto's punishment being administered. On a silver vase (3rd century B.C.), Zeus in the form of Artemis visits the unsuspecting nymph. The same theme has been treated by Titian, Rubens, Poussin, and Boucher.

CALYDON. Ancient city of Aetolia.

CALYDONIAN HUNT. When Oeneus*, king of Calydon*, offended Artemis* by

failing to offer her a sacrifice, the goddess sent a wild boar to ravage the land and terrify the people. Meleager* summoned the bravest of the Greeks to hunt the monster; the hunters included Theseus*, Telamon*, Peleus*, Jason*, Atalanta*, etc. Meleager himself slew the boar and received its hide as his prize (Ov. viii, 260f.).

Iconography. The hunt is illustrated on, inter alia, the François krater (c. 570 B.C.). Also famous was the work of Scopas (4th century B.C.), who sculptured the hunting scene for the east façade of the Temple of Athena at Tegea.

CALYPSO [Gr. Kalupso]. Greek nymph on the mythical island of Ogygia,* who hospitably received Odysseus after his shipwreck and kept him with her for seven years. Despite her promise to make him immortal, she was unable to make him forget his wife and homeland. Through Hermes*, Zeus ordered her to let Odysseus go. By Odysseus she was the mother of Nausithous* and Nausinous* (Hom. Od. vii, 244f.).

Iconography. Calypso and Hermes are found on a single Greek vase and on an Etruscan mirror; they can also be seen on a mural at Pompeii.

CAMENAE or CASMENAE. Ancient Italic fountain nymphs, later identified with the Muses*. At Rome they were venerated in a sacred wood near the Porta Capena.

CAMILLA. Daughter of the Volscian king Metabus. She was killed fighting alongside Turnus* in his war against Aeneas* (Virg. vii, 803; xi, 432, 498, 535, 648, 796).

CAMILLUS. Marcus Furius Camillus, legendary Roman hero, who was said to have taken Veii in 396 B.C. Banished on false accusations, he was named dictator when the Gallic hordes captured Rome in 390 B.C. He defeated the withdrawing Gauls and took back the gold they had received as ransom. He was elected dictator three more times and vanquished the Etruscans, the Volsci, and other enemies of Rome. He died of the plague in 365 B.C. (Liv. v).

CAMPE [Gr. Kampe]. Monster who

guarded the Cyclopes* in the lower world.

CANACE [Gr. Kanake]. Daughter of Aeolus* and Enarete*, loved by Poseidon*. When she became enamored of her own brother Macar*, she was slain by her father.

CAPANEUS [Gr. Kapaneus]. Son of Hipponous. While taking part in the expedition of the Seven against Thebes*, he was struck by one of Zeus'* thunderbolts as punishment for an arrogant utterance.

CAPITOL. One of the two peaks of the Capitoline*, the most important of the seven hills of Rome. Also called the Capitol was the main sanctuary of the city, the temple of Jupiter Capitolinus or Jupiter Optimus Maximus (= most excellent and most powerful), which stood on this hill. Not only Jupiter but also Juno* and Minerva* were worshiped in this temple. The sanctuary was dedicated in 509 B.C., destroyed by fire in 83 B.C., and restored to use in 69 B.C. It was again destroyed in A.D. 69, the year of the three emperors, and rebuilt by Vespasian in A.D. 75. It was destroyed a third time in A.D. 80, but by A.D. 82 a new temple was dedicated by Domitian, a part of the podium of which still survives. The temple was unusual in design, having three cellae (square rooms) grouped together, containing the statues of Jupiter, Juno, and Minerva, the Capitoline triad. In imitation, many other cities of the Roman Empire had their own Capitol, which always occupied a site on the Forum at the center of the city. The Sibylline Books were kept in the crypts of the Capitol.

CAPITOLINE HILL or MONS CAPITOLINUS. Hill in Rome. It has two peaks, the Capitol and the Arx. On the former stood the temple of Jupiter Capitolinus, also sacred to Juno and Minerva (see CAPITOL); on the Arx (= citadel) stood the temple of Juno Moneta. The site of the first sanctuary is now occupied by the Museo Capitolino, and that of the second by the church of S. Maria in Ara Coeli. Between the two peaks lay the Tabularium or public archives, upon the ancient substructure of which the Palazzo Senatorio now stands. In addition to the great Temple of Jupiter, many smaller temples, statues, and civic buildings were situated on the Capitol.

CAPYS. 1. Grandfather of Aeneas*. 2. A Trojan, the legendary founder of Capua (Virg. x, 145).

CARDEA. See CARNA.

CARMENTA or CARMENTIS. Roman goddess of birth, one of the Camenae*, and mother of Evander*. Her temple, to which it was forbidden to bring leather, stood near the Roman Porta Carmentalis. Her festival, the Carmentalia (held on Jan. 11 and 15), was celebrated chiefly by women.

CARNA or CARDEA. Roman goddess, guardian of physical welfare. Cardea was the guardian of door-hinges, and hence of home and family life, and probably for that reason identified with Carna.

CASSANDRA [Gr. Kassandra]. Daughter of Priam* and Hecuba*. She was loved by Apollo*, who granted her the gift of prophecy and who, when she spurned his love, decreed that none of her prophecies should be believed. Consequently, when she warned the Trojans against the Wooden Horse* and foretold the fall of Troy, her people failed to respond. When Troy was taken she sought refuge in the Temple of Athena, where she was ravished and carried off by Ajax, son of Oïleus*. She became part of the spoils of Agamemnon*, and after his tragic end she was murdered by Clytaemnestra* (Hom. Il. xiii, 366; Od. xi, 421f.; Virg. ii, 246, 404).

Iconography. Greek vases illustrating the destruction of Troy sometimes show the rape of Cassandra. On an Attic hydria by the Cleophrades painter (c. 485 B.C.) at Naples, Agamemnon is seen pulling a naked Cassandra away from the statue of Athena she is clutching. At Pompeii a wall painting in an exedra of the atrium of the Casa del Menandro shows Cassandra vainly warning the Trojans about the Wooden Horse; on another she is pursued by Ajax.

CASSIOPE or CASSIOPEA [Gr. Kassiopeia], wife of Cepheus*. When she offended Poseidon* by boasting that her own beauty was superior to that of the Nereids*, her innocent daughter Andromeda* was punished. Upon her death, Cassiopea was placed among the stars.

CASSOTIS [Gr. Kassotis]. Greek nymph of the sacred temple fountain at Delphi.

CASTALIA [Gr. Kastalia]. A Greek nymph loved by Apollo* who, to escape the god, jumped into the fountain of Castalia at Delphi, at the foot of Parnassus. The fountain water was considered holy, being used for purifications in the Delphic temple. It also gave inspiration to poets.

CASTOR. See Dioscuri.

CATAMITUS. Latin name for Ganymede*.

CATILLUS. Brother of the river god Tiburtus* and co-founder of Tibur (Now Tivoli).

CAUCASUS. A chain of mountains north of Armenia, regarded in the Greek world as one of the limits of the earth. Here Prometheus* was chained to a rock at Zeus' command.

CAUNUS. See Byblis.

CEBRIONES [Gr. Kebriones]. Son of Priam* and a slave woman. He was Hector's* charioteer and was slain by Patroclus* (Hom. Il. viii, 318f.; xi, 521f.; xvi, 727f.).

CECROPS [Gr. Kekrops]. First king of Attica and founder of the Acropolis at Athens, bringing civilization and order to his land. He judged a contest between Poseidon* and Athena* for the possession of Attica. He was sometimes regarded as being half man and half serpent, having been born of the earth. *Iconography.* Aside from a few Greek vases, e.g. a bowl by the Codrus painter (5th century B.C.) at Berlin, the best-known representation of Cecrops is the badly damaged group on the metope of the W. façade of the Parthenon. On the bowl the hero is shown as a bearded man, the lower half of whose body ends in the curling tail of a serpent. The damaged figures on the Parthenon metope are thought to represent Cecrops and his daughter but are scarcely recognizable as such.

CEDALION [Gr. Kedalion]. Servant of Hephaestus*.

CELAENO [Gr. Kelaino]. 1. One of the Harpies* (Virg. iii, 211, 245). 2. One of the Pleiades*.

CELEUS [Gr. Keleus]. King of Eleusis*, and father of Triptolemus* and Demophon*. He entertained Demeter* hospitably and became the first priest of her sanctuary in his city.

CENTAURS. A barbaric mountain race of semi-human creatures with horses' bodies and men's heads, who dwelt in Thessaly, where there were many horses. They were noted for their misbehavior at the marriage feast of Pirithous*, king of the Lapithae*, where they assaulted the bride and other wedding guests, causing a bloody fight. It is not known whether the Lapithae wiped them out or drove them from Thessaly. Chiron* and Nessus* are among the best known Centaurs (Ov. xii, 210f.). *Iconography.* Even in archaic art the Centaurs are represented as half men and half horses, e.g. on a bronze relief from Olympia (7th century B.C.) and on proto-Corinthian lecythae (8th-7th centuries B.C.). With Phidias' metopes at the Parthenon (c. 440 B.C.) the type reaches its most perfect form. The battle of the Centaurs is illustrated on various temples: the W. frieze of the Temple of Hephaestus in Athens (formerly the Theseum), the Temple of Apollo at Bassae, and the Temple of Zeus at Olympia (sculptor Alcamenes); also on reliefs from the sepulchral monument at Gyölbashi (5th century B.C.) and the Mausoleum of Halicarnassus (c. 350 B.C.). There are countless Greek vases with representations of the Centaurs, e.g. the François krater (c. 570 B.C.) and an amphora from Clazomenae (6th century B.C.), now at Munich, showing Centaurs hunting. Further, there are statues of Centaurs: the Borghese Centaur in the Louvre and the two Centaurs of the Villa Hadriani near Tivoli. Also in Hadrian's villa is the Marefoschi mosaic, which shows Centaurs fighting with panthers.

CENTIMANI. Three hundred-armed giants, Aegaeon*, Cottus*, and Gyges*, sons of Uranus* and Gaea*. Zeus rescued them from Tartarus*, where they had been confined by their father, and used their services in his fight against the Titans*. Also called HECATONCHIRES.

CEPHALUS [Gr. Kephalos]. son of Hermes* and Herse*. He was married to Procris*, a daughter of Erechtheus*. Eos* abducted him while out hunting but was unable to shake his love for Procris. But when Procris, jealous, spied upon him on a subsequent chase, he killed her, mistaking her for an animal. For this Cephalus was banished. Later, he helped Amphitryon* in a war and was rewarded with the island of Cephallenia. *Iconography.* Some Greek vases show Cephalus as a huntsman; others illustrate the story of Cephalus and Procris. The abduction of Cephalus by Eos adorns an Etruscan mirror. From modern times there are paintings by Piero di Cosimo, Guido Reni, and others.

CEPHEUS [Gr. Kepheus]. Son of Belus (1)*, king of Ethiopia and father of Andromeda*. He was changed into a constellation on his death.

CEPHISSUS [Gr. Kephissos]. God of the river of the same name in Phocis and Boeotia. He was the father of Narcissus*.

CERBERUS [Gr. Kerberos]. Three-headed dog, son of Typhon* and Echidna*, who guarded the entrance to the infernal regions to prevent anyone from returning from them. Only an occasional favored mortal, e.g., Orpheus*, managed to lull him to sleep. The last labor of Heracles* consisted in bringing Cerberus to the upper regions. *Iconography.* The monster is represented with three or more heads, a serpent's tail, and sometimes a lion's claws. He is often shown with Heracles on Greek vases, e.g. a hydria from Caere (middle of 6th century B.C.) and an amphora by the Andocides painter, both at Paris. He is also represented on a few temple sculptures, on cameos, and on coins.

CERCOPES [Gr. Kerkopes]. Forest spirits who continually practiced deception. They stole Heracles' weapons from him and were punished by being tied to a pole with their heads downward. Their home, according to the Greeks, was near Thermopylae or on Euboea. *Iconography.* One of the metopes of Tem-

ple C at Selinus shows Heracles carrying them on his rod. The same scene is also found on several archaic amphorae.

CERCYON [Gr. Kerkuon]. Son of Poseidon* or Hephaestus*. He dwelt near Eleusis* and compelled all strangers to wrestle with him. The task of slaying him fell to the hero Theseus*.

CEREALIA. See CERES.

CERES. Roman goddess of agriculture, originally venerated along with Tellus* but identified at an early date with the Greek Demeter*. The first temple to Ceres-Demeter was consecrated in 493 B.C. after a crop failure and famine. It was built in the Greek style, Greek women performed the temple ceremonies, and all myths relating to Demeter were transferred to Ceres. In fact, Emperor Claudius (A.D. 41-54) attempted to bring the Eleusinian mysteries* to Rome. Ceres was essentially the goddess of the plebeians; her temple stood near the Circus Maximus in the plebeian district of Rome. The annual festival of Cerealia (April 12-19) was in her honor.

CERYX [Gr. Kerux]. Son of Hermes* and Pandrosus*; founder of the Athenian family of priests called the Ceryces.

CETO [Gr. Keto. Daughter of Pontus* and Gaea*. With her brother and husband Phorcys, she is the personification of the dangers and terrors of the sea. She was regarded as the mother of the Gorgons* and other monsters.

CEYX [Gr. Keux]. King of Thracis, son of Hesperus* and Philonis, and husband of Alcyone*. Upon his tragic death he was changed into a kingfisher (see ALCYONE).

CHAOS. In Greek philosophy, the infinite void from which everything originated. Another school of thought considered Chaos not as a vacuum but as a shapeless mass. From Chaos came Gaea* the earth, Tartarus* the underworld, and Eros* or Love, which gave form and shape to the universe.

CHARITES or GRACES [Lat. Gratiae]. Goddesses of beauty, grace, and mirth. The Greeks regarded them as daughters either of Zeus* and Eurynome*, Helius* and Aegle*, or Dionysus* and Aphrodite*. Originally only two Charites were venerated in Athens and Sparta, but usually three are named: Aglaea (= brilliance), Euphrosyne (= mirth), and Thalia (= bloom). They were companions of the Muses*, or of Apollo*, Dionysus, and Aphrodite. From Orchomenus in Boeotia their cult spread over the whole of Greece.

Iconography. In archaic art the Graces are represented as separate figures, clad in long garments, e.g. on a late archaic relief from Thasos. After Scopas and Praxiteles, nudity became the fashion and the 90-100 copies known to us of Hellenistic and Roman sculptures show the Graces nude and as a group, their arms intertwined. Later times produced Botticelli's Primavera and the sculptures of Canova and Thorwaldsen.

CHARON. Son of Erebus* and Nyx*, the grimy ferryman who received the shades of the dead from Hermes* and rowed them across the Styx* in a dilapidated boat. Charon's fee was one obolus (a small coin) placed in the mouth of a corpse at burial. Only if a dead person had been buried or cremated was he ferried across the Styx; otherwise his ghost continued to wander along the shores of the river. The figure of Charon is probably Etruscan in origin.

Iconography. Charon is represented in Greek art as a grim, bearded man. He occurs particularly on Greek funerary vases or lecythae, but also on a few reliefs and cameos. The best-known representations are in Etruscan tomb paintings, e.g. in the François Tomba at Vulci, which show Charu (Etr.) as a hideous figure with a crooked nose, carrying his attribute, a double hammer, in his hand. In the Tomba dell' Orco at Tarquinia he is even more repulsive as a winged demon with serpents instead of hair. Here, too, he wields the double hammer.

CHARYBDIS. Sea monster, daughter of Poseidon* and Gaea*. Her cave was near the Straits of Messina, and thrice daily she gulped down the waters of the sea, along with any ships that were passing, and spewed them out again. Op-

posite Charybdis dwelt the monster Scylla*, no less dangerous. Odysseus, for one, had an anxious time when his ship sailed between Scylla and Charybdis (Hom. Od. xii, 101f., 235f., 428f.). Aeneas also had to face these monsters (Virg. iii, 420).

CHIMAERA [Gr. Chimaira]. A monster, daughter of Typhon* and Echidna*, which ravaged Lycia until it was slain by Bellerophon with Athena's help. The forepart of the Chimaera's body was that of a lion, its middle that of a goat, and its rear that of a dragon. It is sometimes shown with several heads.

Iconography. The Chimaera is often used as a decorative figure on Greek vases. In a few cases the fight with Bellerophon is shown. The bronze Chimaera of Arezzo is renowned (Etruscan, c. 450 B.C.).

CHIONE. 1. Daughter of Boreas* and Orithyia*; mother of Eumolphus*. 2. The beautiful daughter of Daedalion, with whom even the gods fell in love. When she boasted of her beauty, she was slain by Artemis*.

CHIRON [Gr. Cheiron]. A Centaur*, son of Cronus* and Philyra*. He excelled in wisdom and knowledge, especially of medicine, in which Apollo* had personally instructed him. Chiron in turn was the teacher of many Greek heroes, including Jason*, Theseus*, and Achilles*. He was immortal, but when struck by a poisoned arrow from Heracles' bow, he passed immortality on to Prometheus* in order to obtain release from his pain. He was placed among the stars and named Sagittarius.

Iconography. The most famous representation of Chiron is on a mural in the so-called Basilica at Herculaneum, where he is shown with Achilles.

CHLOË [= young green]. Epithet for Demeter*.

CHLORIS. 1. Greek goddess of flowers, married to Zephyrus*. Her Roman name was Flora*. 2. Daughter of Amphion* and Niobe*. She and her brother Amyclas were spared when Apollo* and Artemis* revenged themselves on Niobe's children. 3. Daughter of Neleus*. 4.

Daughter of Tiresias*.

CHRONOS [= time]. Greek personification of time.
Iconography. He is shown as an old man, e.g. on the dedicatory relief of Archelaus from Priene, representing the apotheosis of Homer (2nd century B.C.).

CHRYSAOR. Son of Medusa*. He sprang from her body when Perseus* cut off her head.

CHRYSEIS. Daughter of Chryses*, the priest of Apollo. After the fall of Troy* Agamemnon* obtained her as his slave. When her father tried to buy her back and was opprobriously insulted by Agamemnon, Apollo caused an outbreak of the plague in the Greek camp, which did not cease until Chryseis was given back to her father. The disgruntled Agamemnon then demanded Achilles' slave Briseis*, and this led to a fateful conflict between the two heroes (Hom. Il. i, 111, 143).
Iconography. Chryseis is occasionally found on Greek vases in scenes from the Trojan War, e.g. on an Attic scyphus by Hieron and Macron (c. 490 B.C.) in the Louvre.

CHRYSES. Priest of Apollo from Chryse, a town near Troy; father of Chryseis.*

CHRYSIPPUS [Gr. Chrusippos]. Son of Pelops* and Axioche who was basely murdered by his stepbrothers Atreus* and Thyestes*.

CHRYSOTHEMIS. Daughter of Agamemnon* and Clytaemnestra*. Unlike her proud, inflexible sister Electra*, she resigned herself to her degenerate mother's adultery.

CILIX [Gr. Kilix]. Son of Agenor*. Dispatched by his father in search of his sister Europa*, he settled in Cilicia, which takes its name from him.

CIMMERIANS or CIMMERII. A people living in southern Russia who were compelled to flee to Asia Minor in the 8th century B.C. In Homer, they are a mythical nation living on the edge of the earth in darkness and mist.

CINCINNATUS. Lucius Quinctius Cincinnatus, Roman consul and many times dictator. During a war against the Aequi,

Cincinnatus was proclaimed dictator while plowing like a simple peasant. He successfully relieved the consul Mincius, who had been surrounded, and put an end to the critical war situation (458 B.C.). He then returned to his farm, whence he was once more recalled to save his country. For the Romans he remained a national figure, the paragon of Roman simplicity and reliability (Liv. iii, 26f.).

CINYRUS [Gr. Kinuras]. King of Cyprus; son of Apollo*, and father of Adonis*.

CIRCE [Gr. Kirke]. Greek sorceress, daughter of the sun god Helius* and Perse*. Circe lived on the mythical island of Aeaea*. When Odysseus* landed there, she changed his companions into swine by means of a magic potion. Thanks to an herb obtained for him by Hermes, Odysseus himself remained immune to her sorcery. Nevertheless, he stayed with her for a year and made her mother of Telegonus* (Hom. Od. x, 135f., 467; vii, 20).
Iconography. She is represented on various Greek vases, e.g. a Boeotian scyphus (c. 400 B.C.) at London, which shows her handing her magic potion to Odysseus. On one of the famous Odyssey landscapes (45-25 B.C.) in Rome, Odysseus is asking Circe to change his crew back into human beings. In later times, Circe figures on a painting by Dossi.

CITHAERON [Gr. Kithairon]. A mountain range in Greece on the frontier between Boeotia, Attica, and Megaris. The cult of Dionysus was, for the most part, practiced here, and many myths had these bare mountains for their background (e.g. Actaeon*, Niobe*, Pentheus*, and Oedipus*).

CLEOBIS [Gr. Kleobis] and BITON. Sons of Cydippe*, a priestess of Hera* at Argos. When she had to drive to the temple on a feast day of the goddess and the oxen which were to pull her chariot failed to turn up, her sons pulled the chariot to the temple, a distance of 45 stadia (5 miles). The grateful mother thereupon asked the goddess to grant her children the best gift that can be bestowed on mortals. Hera caused them to die in their sleep in her temple (Herod. i, 31).

Iconography. Two archaic sculptures (7th century B.C.) by Polymedes of Argos were found at Delphi. They represent Cleobis and Biton and were, according to Herodotus, erected in Delphi by the inhabitants of Argos.

CLEOMEDES [Gr. Kleomedes]. A famous Greek wrestler who, after a victory in the Olympic* games, was denied the prize because he had killed his opponent. Enraged by this decision, he added more victims to his list, finally fleeing to the Temple of Athena, whence he was taken up into the heavens.

CLETA [Gr. Kleta]. In Spartan mythology, one of the Charites*.

CLIO [Gr. Kleio]. The Muse of history. *Iconography.* She is shown with a scroll in her hand (see MUSES).

CLITUS [Gr. Kleitos]. Son of Mantius and grandson of Melampus*. He was abducted by Eos*.

CLOTHO [Gr. Klotho]. One of the three Moirai*.

CLYMENE [Gr. Klumene]. 1. Sea nymph, mother by Iapetus* of Atlas*, Menoetius*, Prometheus*, and Epimetheus*. 2. Wife of Helius* and mother of Phaëthon*. 3. Mother of Atalanta*. 4. Granddaughter of King Minos* of Crete and mother of Palamedes*.

CLYMENUS [Gr. Klumenos]. King of Boeotia, father-in-law of Nestor*.

CLYSONYMUS [Gr. Klusonumos]. Friend of Patroclus* and slain by him in a quarrel.

CLYTAEMNESTRA [Gr. Klutaimnestra]. Daughter of Tyndareus* and Leda*; wife of Agamemnon*, during whose absence at the Trojan War she committed adultery with Aegisthus*. She and her lover murdered Agamemnon on his return, and ruled Mycenae and Argos until her son Orestes* avenged the death of his father by killing her.

CLYTIE [Gr. Klutie]. Nereid* loved by the sun god Apollo. When he became enamored of Leucothoë*, the jealous Clytie betrayed the love affair to Leucothoë's father, who in his rage buried his daughter alive. Deserted by the grieving sun god, Clytie pined away and was changed into a sunflower (Ov. iv, 206f.).

CLYTIUS [Gr. Klutios]. One of the Giants*.

COCALUS [Gr. Kokalos]. A king in Sicily who gave Daedalus* hospitality and protection when he fled from Crete (Ov. viii, 261).

COCLES. See HORATIUS COCLES.

COCYTUS [Gr. Kokutos]. One of the rivers that enclosed the underworld. The others were the Styx*, the Acheron*, and the Pyriphlegethon*.

COEUS [Gr. Koios]. One of the Titans*.

COINS. Greek coins date back as far as the 7th century B.C., and Roman coins probably to the 3rd century B.C. Their importance for mythology lies in the fact that coins of the Greek cities very frequently bear an impression of the local guardian deity and Imperial Roman coins with an emperor's head on one side often show a deity on the reverse.

COLCHIS [Gr. Kolchis]. Region on the E. coast of the Black Sea (now Georgia). It was here that the Golden Fleece*, the objective of the Argonauts*, was guarded by an ever-wakeful dragon.

COLUMNAE HERCULIS. See PILLARS OF HERCULES.

COMAETHO [Gr. Komaitho]. Taphian princess, enamored of Amphitryon*. When the latter waged war against the Taphians, she cut off the golden lock of hair that made her father immortal. Although she thus made Amphitryon's victory possible, he did not condone her treachery, but killed her.

CONCORDIA. Roman goddess of harmony. Her chief temple was on the Forum Romanum and was founded in 367 B.C., when reconciliation was brought about between the patricians and the plebs by the Licinian and Sexten laws, which decreed that one of the two consuls must be a plebeian. The temple was also often used as a place of assembly for the Senate.

CONSENTES DII. The twelve principal Roman gods, namely Jupiter* and Juno*, Neptune* and Minerva*, Apollo* and

Diana*, Mars* and Venus*, Vulcan* and Vesta*, and Mercury* and Ceres*. Their statues were set up in the Forum Romanum in the partly restored "porticus Deorum Consentium" (4th century B.C.).

CONSUS. Ancient Italic god of the safely garnered harvest (condere = to store). His temple stood on the Aventine Hill at Rome. His festival was a harvest feast (Aug. 21), at which mule races took place, the mule being sacred to Consus.

COPREUS [Gr. Kopreus]. Son of Pelops*. He served at the court of Eurystheus*, who used him as a herald to announce his orders to Heracles*.

CORIOLANUS. Cnaeus Marcius Coriolanus, legendary hero of the earliest Roman times. Received his surname after the capture of Corioli, a Volscian city. Banished from Rome for political reasons, he fled to the Volscians and marched with them against his native city. In distress Rome sent various envoys to Coriolanus to beg him to abandon the siege; only the pleas of his mother and wife induced him to do so (Liv. ii, 39-40).

COROEBUS [Gr. Koroibus]. Son of the Phrygian king Mygdon*. For love of Cassandra* he came to Priam's assistance during the siege of Troy* (Virg. ii, 341, 424).

CORONIS [Gr. Koronis]. Princess of Thessaly, mother of Asclepius* by Apollo*. She deceived the god even before the birth of their child; ravens told Apollo what had happened and she was killed by him or, a.t.o., Artemis*. But before the body was consumed on the funeral pyre, Apollo saved the child Asclepius. Since then the feathers of ravens, previously white, have been black (Ov. ii, 542f.).

CORONUS [Gr. Koronos]. Son of the Lapithian king Caeneus*. He was among those slain by Heracles* in his battle against the Lapithae*.

CORYBANTES. Priests of the Phrygian goddess Cybele*. They worshipped the goddess in wild ritual dances which degenerated into uncontrollable frenzies, in which they sometimes mutilated themselves. The cult spread all over Greece and later to Rome, where the priests were called Galli.

CORYCIDES NYMPHAE. "Nymphs of the Corycian cave" on Parnassus* near Delphi. Also an epithet for the Muses* (Ov. i, 320).

CORYTHUS [Gr. Koruthus]. Son of Paris* and Oenone*. To put an end to the idyl of Paris and Helen*, Oenone sent her son to Helen. Paris failed to recognize Corythus and killed him.

COTTUS [Gr. Kottos]. One of the Centimani*.

COTTYTO. Thracian goddess, also worshipped at Athens. Her cult included a kind of baptism.

CRANAUS [Gr. Kranaos]. Successor of Cecrops* as king of Attica.

CREON [Gr. Kreon]. 1. Son of Menoecus* and brother of Jocasta*, ruler of Thebes from the death of Laius* until Oedipus* ascended the throne. He forbade the burial of Polynices'* body and sentenced Antigone* to death for disobeying his command. 2. King of Corinth and father of Creusa (1)*, who married Jason*.

CRESPHONTES [Gr. Kresphontes]. One of the three sons of Aristomachus*, descendants of Heracles* who conquered the Peloponnesus. He obtained Messenia as his share.

CRETHEUS [Gr. Kretheus]. King of Epirus, son of Aeolus* and Enarete*, and father of Aeson*.

CREUSA [Gr. Kreousa]. 1. Daughter of the Corinthian king Creon (2)*; when Jason* and Medea* were staying in Corinth, Jason repudiated his wife and married Creusa. The embittered Medea took a horrible revenge by giving the young bride a poisonous garment which, as soon as Creusa put it on, clung to her body and burned her to death. 2. Daughter of Priam*; wife of Aeneas*. During the night of Troy's fall she died while fleeing from the city. She was the mother of Ascanius* (Virg. ii, 562, 738, 772). 3. Daughter of Erechtheus*; mother of Achaeus* and Ion*. 4. Daughter of Oceanus* and Gaea*.

CRIUS [Gr. Kreios]. One of the Titans*.

CRONUS [Gr. Kronos]. The youngest of the Titans*, son of Uranus and Gaea*. Aided by his mother, he attacked and dethroned Uranus. The subsequent reign of Cronus and his wife Rhea* over the world was a Golden Age. To ensure that he in his turn would not be deposed by his children, he swallowed them all immediately after birth. Only the infant Zeus* was saved by his mother, who gave Cronus not the child but a stone wrapped in clothes, which he immediately swallowed. When Zeus grew up, he rebelled against his father and forced him to disgorge the children he had swallowed. Zeus' subsequent battle against the Titans who remained faithful to Cronus ended in their defeat, and Zeus cast them into Tartarus. The Romans identified Cronus with Saturn*. At Athens the "Kronia"—a Cronus festival—was celebrated in memory of the Golden Age; the corresponding festival of the Romans was the Saturnalia*.

CUPID [*cupido* = desire]. See AMOR.

CURETES. Priests of the goddess Cybele* on Crete (see CORYBANTES). When Zeus was taken to Crete by his mother Rhea* (= Cybele) to preserve him from his father's gluttony (see CRONUS), the noise of their Pyrrhic dances made the crying of young Zeus inaudible to his father. The original Curetes were probably Cretan demons.

CURTIUS. Marcus Curtius, Roman hero. According to legend, the earth in the Forum at Rome suddenly opened up, forming a chasm which the oracle said could only be filled up with Rome's most precious possession. The city's future was at stake. Curtius offered himself as a sacrifice to the underworld by jumping mounted and fully armed into the chasm, which then closed over him (Liv. vii, 6). See LACUS CURTIUS.

Iconography. Curtius' brave deed is illustrated on various reliefs, e.g. that found near the Lacus Curtius in the Forum (125 B.C.). Frequently shown on later reliefs and façade paintings (e.g. Pordenone).

CYANEAE INSULAE. See SYMPLEGADES.

CYBELE or CYBEBE [Gr. Kubele]. Phrygian goddess, honored as the Great Mother of all life in nature and as mistress of the animals. Attis* was her lover. Her worship spread from Asia Minor to Greece where she was identified with Rhea*. Its ceremonies, conducted by priests who were called Corybantes* or, on Crete, Curetes*, were accompanied by ecstatic dancing and tumultuous excitement. The Rhea–Cybele–Magna Mater cult was introduced into Rome at the time of the reverses in the Second Punic War (205 B.C.); by order of the Sibylline Books* a statue made of meteoritic stone from Pessinus (Asia Minor) was brought to the Palatine Hill. There a temple was built for Cybele, and there the Ludi Megalenses were held annually in her honor (Liv. xxix, 10-11).

Iconography. The goddess is represented in statues and on reliefs and coins, sitting on a throne flanked by lions or riding in a chariot drawn by lions. Usually she wears a turreted crown and carries a scepter, laurel branch, or cornucopia in her hand. A remarkable altar relief at Rome shows Cybele's arrival in that city; the ship bearing the statue of the goddess is pulled by Claudia Quinta, a Roman woman wrongly suspected of leading a loose life and using this means—so the legend says—to prove her innocence with the aid of the goddess.

CYCHREUS [Gr. Kuchreus]. Son of Poseidon*. He was the patron of the island of Salamis, which he rid of a dragon and thus made habitable again.

CYCLOPES. In Greek mythology, giants with only one eye and that in the forehead. Sometimes regarded as sons of Uranus* and Gaea*, who were cast into Tartarus*, but liberated by Zeus*. They helped Zeus in his war against the Titans*, and forged his thunderbolts. As smiths they served Hephaestus* or Vulcan* in his workshop under Aetna*. They were also thought of as builders of walls made of huge blocks of stone, like the fortification walls of Tiryns. In Homer the Cyclopes are a lawless race who de-

vour human beings. A familiar figure from the Odyssey is the Cyclops Polyphemus*, who swallowed up several of Odysseus' companions and was blinded by Odysseus.
Iconography. Cyclopes are shown as one-eyed giants on, *interalia*, an Etruscan wall-painting and on Greek vases, e.g. a Chalcidian amphora (c. 530 B.C.) at London, but equally often with two eyes, e.g. on a Laconian kylix (c. 550 B.C.) at Paris and a Roman sarcophagus in the Capitoline Museum at Rome. Polyphemus as a shepherd is shown on a wall decoration in the Casa di Amando Sacerdote (3rd style: c. A.D. 25) at Pompeii.
CYCNUS [Gr. Kuknos]. 1. Son of Sthenelus (4)*, and king of Liguria. He was so grief-stricken by the death of Phaëthon*, his very close friend, that the gods in compassion changed him into a swan (Ov. ii, 367f.). 2. Son of Poseidon* and king of Colonae in the Troad. Misled by his second wife, he tried to kill his son Tenes*. The attempt failed, and both father and son later supported the Trojans in their resistance to the Greeks. He was slain by Achilles* and changed into a swan (Ov. xii, 64f.). 3. Son of Ares*, a powerful giant who was slain by Heracles*. 4. Son of Apollo*. A fine hunter, but so extremely difficult to get on with that everyone deserted him and his only friend finally killed him. He was changed into a swan by the god.
CYDIPPE [Gr. Kudippe]. Athenian beauty loved by Acontius*.
CYLLENE [Gr. Kullene]. Mountain in the Peloponnesus, on the border between Achaea and Arcady, the birthplace of Hermes*.
CYNOSURA [Gr. Kunosoura]. Nymph of Mt. Ida on Crete. Nurse of Zeus*, later given a place among the stars.
CYNTHUS [Gr. Kunthos]. Mountain on Delos*, birthplace of Apollo* and Artemis.*
CYPARISSUS [Gr. Kuparissos]. Son of Telephus*. When he accidentally killed a deer given to him by Apollo*, he was inconsolable, and the god changed him into a cypress—the tree of mourning in antiquity (Ov. x, 86f.).
Iconography. A mural decoration in the Casa dei Vettii at Pompeii shows Cyparissus being changed into the tree of the same name.
CYTHEREA [Gr. Kuthereia]. Epithet of Aphrodite*, from the island of Cythera, where she was especially revered (Hom. Od. viii, 288; Virg. i, 257).

D

DACTYLS. Mountain demons, located by the Greeks on Mt. Ida in Asia Minor, or on Crete. They were reputed to be the first workers of metal. Sometimes identified with the Curetes* or Corybantes*.

DAEDALION [Gr. Daidalion]. Father of Chione (2)*. In his grief at her death he threw himself from Mt. Parnassus and was changed into a hawk by Apollo (Ov. xi, 291f.).

DAEDALUS [Gr. Daidalos]. Greek hero, personification of artistic handwork and a famous architect and inventor. He was condemned to death at Athens for murdering his nephew and pupil. He fled to Crete, where he was the guest of Minos* and built the Labyrinth*. Suspected of having assisted Theseus* to escape, Daedalus felt in danger from Minos. He made wings for himself and his son Icarus* and they set off for the mainland. Icarus flew too close to the sun, and the wax attaching his wings to his body melted. He fell and was drowned in the sea later named after him (Icarian Sea). Daedalus is said to have reached Italy, where various monuments, including the Temple of Apollo at Cumae, were attributed to him (Ov. viii, 183f.).
Iconography. Daedalus and Icarus are frequently represented on Greek vases, and Pompeian wall paintings (e.g. Casa del Menandro). The making of the wings figures on a Roman relief at Rome. Renaissance art produced Breughel's painting showing the fall of Icarus. There are also Brill's painting and the statuary group by Canova.

DAMASTES. See PROCRUSTES.

DAMIA. Greek goddess of the crops, probably identical with Persephone*.

DANAË. Daughter of Acrisius* and mother of Perseus* by Zeus* (Ov. iv, 611).
Iconography. The Danaë legend is illustrated on Greek cameos and red-figure vases and on Pompeian mural paintings, e.g. in the Casa dei Vettii and the Casa della Regina Margherita. In Renaissance and Baroque art: paintings by Titian, Correggio and prob. Rembrandt, etc.

DANAIDS. The fifty daughters of Danaus*, king of Libya. When Danaus' twin brother Aegyptus* tried to force the girls to marry his fifty sons, Danaus fled with his daughters to Argos. Aegyptus' sons followed them, and Danaus finally consented to the marriage. On the wedding night, however, the Danaids obeyed the bidding of their father and slew their husbands. Only Hypermnestra* spared her bridegroom Lynceus*. For this crime the Danaids were condemned to fill a bottomless vessel with water for all eternity in Hades*.
Iconography. On a black-figure krater (6th century) the Danaids are shown as winged women pouring water into a bottomless vessel. A Roman relief shows them without wings and wearing sleeveless garments. The punishment scene is illustrated as a wall painting in the house of the Odyssey landscapes at Rome (c. 40 B.C.).

DANAUS [Gr. Danaos]. Son of Belus (1)* and Anchinoë. King of Libya and father of fifty daughters—the Danaids*. He quarreled with his twin brother Aegyptus* and fled to Argos, where he became king. His rule was a blessing for the land. When the Danaids, at their father's suggestion, killed their husbands, only Lynceus* being spared, Danaus was murdered by the latter.

DAPHNE [= laurel]. Greek nymph, daughter of the river god Peneus. She was loved by Apollo* but fled from him appealing for help to the gods, who changed her into a laurel (Ov. i, 452f.). Since then the laurel has been sacred to Apollo.

40

Iconography. The metamorphosis is the subject of a Roman mural in the Casa dei Vettii at Pompeii. There is also the famous Apollo and Daphne group by Bernini.

DAPHNIS. Son of Hermes* and a fountain nymph. Renowned as a shepherd and flute player; reputed to be the inventor of pastoral poetry. When he broke his vow of fidelity to a nymph, he was punished with blindness.

DARDANUS [Gr. Dardanos]. Son of Zeus* and Electra (3)*, mythical ancestor of the Trojans and founder of the city of Dardania, later called Troy (Virg. viii, 134).

DAUNUS. In Virg., father of Turnus* (Virg. x, 616).

DEA DIA. Roman goddess of the crops, identical with Ceres*. The ministers of her religion were the group of priests known as the Fratres Arvales, who celebrated the festival of Ambarvalia* in her honor in May.

DEIANIRA [Gr. Deianeira]. Lovely daughter of the Aetolian king Oeneus* and wife of Heracles*. Overcome by her beauty the centaur Nessus* tried to abduct her but was slain by Heracles. To obtain revenge Nessus gave his blood to Deianira as a magic means of making sure of her husband's love. When, later on, she used it to anoint Heracles' garment, it caused the hero to die a painful death (Ov. ix, 98f.).

Iconography. Many Greek vases show Deianira being rescued by Heracles from the clutches of Nessus. She is seen sitting on the centaur's back, standing beside him, or fleeing from him. At a much later period: the abduction of Deianira by Nessus, painted by Guido Reni.

DEIDAMIA [Gr. Deidameia], Daughter of Lycomedes*; mother of Neoptolemus* by Achilles*.

DEIONEUS. 1. (or Deion) Son of Aeolus*. He became king of Phocis. 2. Father-in-law of Ixion*, by whom he was treacherously killed when he demanded the bridal gifts.

DEIPHOBE. In Virgil, a priestess of the temple of Apollo at Cumae (Virg. vi, 36).

DEIPHOBUS [Gr. Deiphobos]. Son of Priam* and Hecabe*. He married Helen* after the death of Paris*. At the fall of Troy he was slain by Menelaus* (Virg. vi, 509, 523).

Iconography. A Roman relief from Aricia (c. 100 B.C.) shows Deiphobus sinking under the blow from Menelaus' dagger.

DEIPYLE. Daughter of Adrastus* and wife of Tydeus*.

DELIA. See THESEUS.

DELOS. One of the Cyclades. Reputed birthplace of Apollo* and Artemis*. The island, previously afloat, was anchored by Zeus to provide a place where Leto* could bring her twins into the world. Delos was one of the most sacred places in the Greek world. No burial or birth was allowed to take place there. The treasury of the Attic-Delian Confederation was kept on Delos, under the protection of Apollo, until Pericles transferred it to Athens in 454 B.C. The island is now wild and deserted, but very important as an archaeological site.

DELPHI [Gr. Delphoi]. Very ancient holy town in Phocis, on the S. slope of Parnassus*. A chthonian goddess was probably venerated here as early as the Mycenaean period. Apollo* slew the dragon Python that made the vicinity of Delphi (old name: Pytho) unsafe; after this the Delphic sanctuary became the center of the worship of Apollo Pythias—the Python-killer. Even in ancient times the city was famous for its oracle, where private persons and kings came for advice, which was given by a priestess called Pythia*. Seated on a tripod above a cleft in the ground from which overpowering vapors issued, she went into a trance and uttered incoherent sounds. These were interpreted by the priests of the sanctuary and given to the pilgrim as his answer. The Delphic priest thus exerted great influence on the political and social life of the Greek tribes. The Temple of Apollo also housed the Omphalos*, a sacred stone regarded as the center of the world. In its heyday the sanctuary was endowed with numerous treasuries, votive offerings, statues (including the famous Charioteer), a theater and a stadium, where every four years the Pythian games were held in

THE SACRED TEMPLE AREA AT DELPHI

Delphi lies on a slope of Mt. Parnassus and comprises a walled area of 210 x 150 yards. Its backdrop is the rocky masses of the Phaedriades. All that now remains of the Temple of Apollo are the foundations and parts of several columns. This Doric temple was built in the 4th century B.C., two previous temples having been destroyed in 525 and 373 B.C. Some 20 treasuries lined the Sacred Way, which zigzags uphill through the domain. Excavation started in 1840 and was undertaken on a large scale in 1863.

Plan

1 - The agora or market, dating from the Roman period

2 - New main entrance to the temple area and start of the Sacred Way; the old entrance was at the S.E. corner (near 12)

3 - Bull, an offering from Corcyra (now Corfu)

4 - The "base of Marathon," an offering from Athens to commemorate Miltiades' victory at Marathon

5 - Offering dedicated by the Lacedaemonians to commemorate Lysander's victory at Aegospotami

6 - Arcadian offering

7 - Argive offering: statues of the Epigoni

8 - Argive offering: statues of the Argive kings

9 - Sicyonian treasury, a small temple built of brown tuff

10 - Siphnian treasury; important sculptures surviving from this building are the friezes and fronton, which date from the second half of the 6th century B.C. and are preserved in the Delphi Museum.

11 - Syracusan treasury

12 - Theban treasury

13 - Cnidian treasury

14 - Athenian treasury, the only one that is almost perfectly preserved; it is a

honor of Apollo, with musical, poetical and sporting contests. From c. 650 B.C. on, the temple domain was administered by the Amphictyones, who, with others, rebuilt the temple after it had been destroyed by an earthquake in 373 B.C. After the Roman conquest the influence of Delphi waned. Sulla and Emperor Nero in particular pillaged the sanctuary, and later the Christian emperors did likewise. Constantinople was embellished with treasures removed from the temple at Delphi. On the site of the destroyed sanctuary was built the village of Kastri, which the French archaeologists who had started digging in the 19th century demolished to make it possible to restore the ancient remains.

DEMETER. Greek goddess of grain and agriculture. She taught man to sow and plow, thus enabling him to abandon his nomadic way of life. She was thus also the goddess of ordered society, sometimes identified with Gaea* and Rhea* as a fertility goddess. She was the daughter of Cronus* and mother of Persephone* (Kore) by Zeus*. When her daughter was seized by Hades* and carried off to the infernal regions, she persuaded Zeus to allow the girl to spend nine months of each year on earth. For the three winter months she remained in the underworld.

The death and renewal of nature thus came to be associated with Demeter. She and Persephone were especially venerated in the mysteries of Eleusis*, where the goddess was said to have been hospitably entertained by the king when she sought her abducted daughter. In gratitude she taught the king's son Triptolemus* to plow and sow. The Thesmophoria was a festival held in her honor, particularly by women. She was identified with Ceres* by the Romans.

Iconography. In ancient art Demeter is represented, especially on statues, as a clothed, dignified woman. From the 5th century B.C. date the Demeter of Cherchel and two statues at the Vatican and Capitol at Rome which probably represent the goddess. There are also the famous enthroned Demeter of Knidos (mid-4th century B.C.) and the relief from Eleusis showing Demeter with Kore and the boy Triptolemus (circle of Phidias, middle of 5th century B.C.). A mural at Pompeii shows the goddess seated on a throne, surrounded by ears of grain, with a torch in her right hand and a sheaf of grain in her left.

DEMODOCUS [Gr. Demodokos]. The blind bard at the court of King Alcinous* (Hom. Od. viii, 44, 62f., 266f., 471f.).

DEMOPHON. The young son of Metan-

Doric sanctuary measuring 33 x 23 ft. and dating back to the 6th century B.C.; the foundations are of tuff, the superstructure of Attic marble

15 - Bouleuterion or council chamber
16 - Sacred Way, about 16½ ft. wide, paved with limestone and marble
17 - Polygonal wall
18 - Colonnade of the Athenians with marble Ionic columns; alongside stood a copy of the Nike of Paeonius, the famous statue from Olympus.
19 - Corinthian treasury
20 - Stairway
21 - Aemilius Paulus memorial
22 - Great Altar dedicated by the Chians
23 - Tripod, an offering by Plataeae
24 - Victory chariot, an offering by Rhodes
25 - Temple of Apollo; in it was the "adyton," the holy room where Pythia delivered the oracle and to which laymen were not admitted;

earthquakes, etc. have so altered the terrain that its exact location has not been found.
26 - Sanctuary of Akanthos
27 - Offering of the Deinomenids: statues of Gelon and Hieron, tyrants of Syracuse
28 - Offering of Krateros; this included a statuary group by Lysippus and Leochares, showing Alexander the Great on a lion-hunt, but nothing of this work of art has survived; the famous bronze statue of the Charioteer was found very close to this monument.
29 - Theater
30 - "Skene" or theater stage
31 - Sanctuary of Dionysus
32 - Portico of the theater and the spring called Cassotis
33 - Colonnade of King Attalus
34 - Road leading to the Stadium higher up the mountain slope

ira*, queen of Eleusis. Demeter* brought the child up like a deity, laying him in the fire every night. When Metanira, unaware of all this, caught sight of the goddess at her strange occupation and was unable to suppress her alarm, Demeter abandoned her efforts with Demophon, who thus had to go through life as an ordinary mortal.

DEO. Mystical name for Demeter*.

DERCETIS or DERCETO [Gr. Derketis]. Mother of Semiramis; legendary founder of Babylon. She exposed her child and threw herself into a lake, whereupon she was changed into a mermaid. Honored as a goddess in Syria.

DEUCALION [Gr. Deukalion]. Son of Prometheus*. Only he and his wife Pyrrha* were spared when Zeus wiped out the impious human race with a flood. On the advice of Prometheus he had built a ship which he beached safely on Mt. Parnassus* when the waters subsided. The oracle ordered them to throw the bones of their mother behind them. Deucalion finally realized that this meant the stones of Mother Earth. The stones thrown by Deucalion changed into men, those thrown by Pyrrha into women (Ov. i, 313f.).

DEVERRA. Roman goddess, patroness of midwives.

DIANA. Italian moon goddess, later identified with Artemis*. She was particularly venerated by the lower classes of the people and was reputed to be the protectress of slaves. She was also patroness of the Latin League and in that function had a famous temple at Aricia near Lake Nemi and another on the Aventine Hill at Rome.

Iconography. Diana is represented as a huntress in a kilted skirt, carrying a quiver and accompanied by a doe (See ARTEMIS).

DIDO. Another name of Elissa, a sister of Pygmalion*, king of Tyre. When Pygmalion caused her husband Sichaeus to be murdered, she and a number of followers fled and landed in N. Africa, where, according to legend, she founded Carthage. She finally killed herself on a funeral pyre to escape the threats of the Numidian king Iarbas, or—as recounted

by the poet Virgil—in despair at the infidelity of Aeneas*, with whom she was in love but who deserted her by divine command.

Iconography. In antiquity Dido is represented on only a few mural decorations. In a later age her love story is illustrated in manuscripts. Her death is the subject of a painting by Rubens, an etching by Diamantini, and a statue by Cayot.

DI INDIGETES. This term is usually defined as meaning original, native Roman gods, in contradistinction to the Di Novensiles, the gods introduced from elsewhere. Another conception, however, does not regard the two terms as opposites but considers Di Novensiles and Di Indigetes as "designations for all the divine powers that were venerated by the Romans' ancestors and did not bear individual names."

DIKE [= law]. Greek personification of Justice, regarded as a daughter of Zeus* and Themis*; she was one of the Horae*.

DIKTE [Lat. Dicte mons]. Mountain in Crete where Zeus* was born.

DI MANES. The spirits of the dead— considered by the Romans as gods— whose dwelling place was the lower world. The festivals in honor of the dead were the Parentalia and Feralia, held in February.

DI NOVENSILES. See DI INDIGETES.

DIOMEDES. 1. Son of Tydeus* and Deipyle*. He took part in the expedition of the Epigoni*. Later he succeeded his grandfather Adrastus* as king of Argos and marched with the Greeks against Troy. There he distinguished himself by extraordinary bravery and, with Athena's help, even succeeded in wounding Ares* and Aphrodite* (Hom. Il. v, 330f., 850f.). Together with Odysseus he stole the Palladium* from beleaguered Troy. Disappointed in his wife Aegiale*, who had been unfaithful to him, he left Argos and landed in southern Italy, where he is said to have founded various cities, e.g. Brindisi and Arpi. He was venerated there as a hero (Hom. Il., particularly Book v; Virg. i, 97, 471; ii, 164; x, 28). 2. Thracian king with the barbarous custom of feeding strangers who visited him to his horses. Heracles punished him by meting out the same fate to him.

Iconography. Diomedes (1) is seen on many Greek vases in scenes from the *Iliad,* e.g. a Chalcidian amphora, where he is shown as a wounded warrior whose hand is being bound up by Sthenelus.

DIONE. One of the wives of Zeus*, especially worshiped as such at Dodona* and regarded there as the mother of Aphrodite*.

DIONYSIA. Festival in honor of the god Dionysus*, held in Athens and Attica in December and March. The lesser Dionysia in December was celebrated in the country with much merrymaking. The festival victim was a he-goat, and the festivities included a game for young people which consisted in trying to remain standing on the smoothed and inflated skin of the goat. The Great Dionysia was the chief festival of Dionysus and lasted several days. One of the ceremonies consisted in carrying the oldest statue of the god in the procession with much pomp. There were also performances of tragedies and comedies.

DIONYSUS [Gr. Dionysos]. Greek god of wine, also called Bakchos (Lat. Bacchus). Son of Zeus* and Semele*. When his mother died before his birth, the child was carried by Zeus in his thigh for several months; after his birth he was given to nymphs to rear. When he was grown up, Dionysus went around planting vines and teaching viniculture to men, escorted by Satyrs, his most faithful companion was Silenus*. The god and his gift were gratefully welcomed everywhere; the few who resisted were punished with madness (Lycurgus*) or death (Pentheus*). Like Demeter*, he was regarded as a bringer of civilization, and he was even honored with her in the Eleusinian* mysteries. The cult of Dionysus originated in Thrace. It was ecstatic in character and was celebrated particularly by women (Bacchantes*) at night in the mountains. From c. 1000 B.C. on, the religion quickly spread over northern Greece and Boeotia, where Thebes became its center. On Parnassus*, too, Maenads* or Bacchantes*, clad in animals' skins and flourishing the thyrsus to cries and music, celebrated their nocturnal orgiastic festivals. As god of wine Dionysus is also the bringer of enthusiasm, the patron of the fine arts. Dithyrambic poetry, tragedy, and comedy owe their origin to the Dionysian religion. Among the main festivals that were celebrated in honor of the god were the greater and lesser Dionysia*, the Lenaea*, and the Anthesteria*. At Delphi* Dionysus was accorded a place alongside Apollo* as the oracular god, and just as Apollo was venerated as the purifying god of Light, so Dionysus was worshiped as the Liberator; both gods were regarded as saviors of those in mental distress. Dionysus was identified with Zagreus* in the Orphic* and with Iacchus* in the Eleusinian mysteries. The ecstatic character of his religion linked the cult of Dionysus with that of Cybele* and Sabazius* in Asia Minor. By the Romans, he was indentified with Liber*. Ivy and the grapevine were sacred to him, and the thyrsus was his attribute.

Iconography. In the countless representations of Dionysus on Greek vases the god is shown as an old, bearded man. Among the better-known is a bowl by Execias (c. 540 B.C.), now at Munich, on which the god is sailing over the sea in a rickety boat, with dolphins all around and a vine growing from the boat. An amphora by Amasis (c. 550 B.C.) at Paris shows Dionysus with long hair and a beard, his head crowned with a vine, and a krater in his right hand; two Maenads dance before him. In earlier Greek sculpture, too, the god is presented as a dignified figure, e.g. the Sardanapalus statue in the Vatic. Museum. From the 4th century on, the god is given a more youthful figure with almost girl-like features, e.g. a nude Dionysus in the Louvre. He is even shown as a small child, e.g. holding Hermes by the hand (Praxiteles, 4th century B.C.) and in the arms of Silenus (Hellenistic statue in the Louvre). At Leyden there is a head of Dionysus, probably of the school of Scopas (4th century B.C.). Dionysus occurs countless times on frescoes, mosaics, cameos, and coins (e.g. Naxos). In later times he is the theme of works by Michelangelo, Titian, Rubens, Van Dyck, Jordaens, Poussin, and many others.

DIORES. 1. Son of Amarynceus*. 2. Father of Automedon*.

DIOSCURI [Gr. Dioskouroi = sons of Zeus]. The twin brothers Castor and Polydeuces (Lat. Pollux), sons of Zeus* and Leda*. Later Castor was thought to be the son of the mortal Tyndareus*, to whom Leda was married. Thus Castor was mortal and Polydeuces immortal. When Castor died in the fight against the sons of Aphareus*, Zeus granted Polydeuces' prayer that his brother should not be separated from him, on condition that both of them spent alternate days in the underworld and on Olympus*. The Dioscuri took part in the expedition of the Argonauts* and in the Calydonian* Hunt. They also abducted the daughters of King Leucippus*, who were betrothed to Aphareus' sons. Their cult is native to Sparta but spread all over Greece and later to Italy. The Dioscuri were, in particular, the protectors of seamen and were generally reputed to be charitable gods who brought blessings. They had many sanctuaries, especially in the Peloponnesus, e.g. at Sparta and Mantinea. The Olympic Games*, too, were under their protection. Their temple at Rome was in the Forum Romanum.

Iconography. In art the Dioscuri are represented as young heroes. Archaic art shows them naked, beardless, and without attributes, e.g. on an archaic metope of the Treasury of the Siphnians at Delphi. On Greek vases of the 6th and 5th centuries they are often seen on horseback, lightly clad in a mantle or chiton, e.g. on an amphora by Execias (c. 550 B.C.) in the Vatic. Museum. A favorite theme is the rape of the Leucippides, e.g. on an amphora by Meidias (c. 400 B.C.) at London. A relief in Tivoli, dating from the 5th century, shows Castor taming horses; a young man naked under a flapping mantle, he is holding a rearing horse in check. The twins are also seen as riders on Roman sarcophagi, on Etruscan mirrors, and on coins. Also familiar are the 13-ft.-high statues of the Dioscuri outside

the Quirinal at Rome (Hellenistic or Roman).

DI PENATES. Roman guardian deities of the household, orginally of the storeroom. Their cult is connected with that of Vesta* and the Lares*. They were honored at the hearth and received their portion of each meal. The Roman state also had its Penates, which had been removed from burning Troy by Aeneas and brought via Lavinium and Alba Longa to Rome. They were placed in the Temple of Vesta on the Forum Romanum.

DIRAE [= the frightful ones]. Poetical Latin name of the Furies (see ERINYES).

DIRCE [Gr. Dirke]. Wife of Lycus*. She maltreated the Theban princess Antiope*, who was her slave. Antiope's sons took revenge on Dirce by tying her to the horns of an enraged bull.

Iconography. Dirce's punishment is the subject of the celebrated statuary group called the Farnese Bull, a work by Apollonius and Tauriscus of Tralles (c. 150 B.C.). A wall decoration in the Casa dei Vettii shows the same scene.

DIS. See HADES.

DICORDIA. Roman goddess of discord. She formed part of the retinue of Mars* and Bellona* (Virg. viii, 702).

DODONA. City in Epirus (northern Greece), seat of the oldest oracle in Hellas. Priestesses and priests interpreted the will of Zeus* from the rustling of the leaves of the sacred oaks.

DOLON. A Trojan, son of Eumedes. While on his way to the Greek camp outside Troy to act as a spy, he was taken prisoner and killed by Diomedes (1)* and Odysseus* (Hom. Il. x, 314f.).

DORIS. Wife of Nereus*, mother of the Nereids*.

DORUS [Gr. Doros]. Legendary ancestor of the Dorians, regarded as a son of Apollo or Poseidon.

DRUIDS. Magicians among the Celts in ancient Gaul and Britain. They formed an influential and prominent section of the community. They prophesied the future, dispensed justice, and maintained a learning that was a mixture of astronomy, medicine, and jurisprudence. Because of their political influence they were suppressed by the Romans, and Emperor Claudius forbade their religion.

DRYADS. Nymphs of trees or woods.

DRYAS. Son of the Thracian king Lycurgus*. Slain by his father when the latter was stricken with madness by the god Dionysus*.

DRYOPE. Greek nymph loved by Apollo*; mother of Amphissus. Once, when she was about to pluck a lotus for her child, it proved to be the nymph Lotis, who had been changed into a flower. Dryope herself was thereupon changed into a lotus (Ov. ix, 329f.).

DYMAS. A Phrygian, father of Hecabe*.

E

ECHETLUS [Gr. Echetlos]. Greek hero. A peasant armed with a plow handle (echetle), he killed many Persians at the battle of Marathon.

ECHETUS [Gr. Echetos]. In Homer, a cruel king of Epirus (Hom. Od. xviii, 85).

ECHIDNA. A monster, half woman, half serpent. To Typhon* she bore a brood of monsters such as Cerberus*, the Nemean Lion (see HERACLES), the Chimaera*, etc.

ECHION. 1. One of the Sparti*. Married Agave*, the daughter of Cadmus*, and helped to build Thebes. 2. One of the Giants*. 3. Son of Hermes*, one of the Argonauts*.

ECHO. Greek nymph in Boeotia, enamored of Narcissus*. When her love was not returned she pined away until only her voice (echo) was left (Ov. iii, 349f.).

EËTION. King of Thebes in Cilicia, father of Andromache* (Hom. Il. i, 366; vi, 416).

EGERIA. Roman fountain nymph. Said to have been the wife and adviser of Rome's second king, Numa Pompilius (Liv. i, 19, 21). On her death she was changed into a spring near Aricia in Latium (Virg. vii, 763). Venerated at Rome as a goddess of birth.

EGESTAS [Lat. = indigence]. Roman personification of poverty, in Virg. situated in the underworld as a demon (Virg. vi, 276).

EGESTES. Another name for Acestes*.

ELECTRA [Gr. Elektra]. 1. Daughter of Agamemnon* and Clytaemnestra*, sister of Iphigenia* and Orestes*. Took young Orestes to safety upon the murder of their father. On Orestes' return as a grown man, she helped to punish their father's murderers. The three great Greek tragedians, Aeschylus, Sophocles, and Euripides, each depict her character in their plays: Choephori, Electra, and Electra, respectively. 2. Daughter of Oceanus* and Tethys* and mother of Iris* and the Harpies*. 3. A Pleiad*; she bore Iasius* and Dardanus* to Zeus*.

ELECTRYON [Gr. Elektruon]. Son of Perseus* and Andromeda*, king of Mycenae and father of Alcmene*.

ELEUSINIAN MYSTERIES. Religious ceremonies held in honor of Demeter* and Persephone* at Eleusis*. When Demeter was wandering about in search of her abducted daughter, she was hospitably received at Eleusis. She herself is said to have instituted the mysteries in memory of her wanderings. Just as the disappearance and resurrection of Persephone was associated with the death and rebirth of nature, the ritual of the mysteries bore the character of a fertility service. In the course of time the cult of Dionysus and Orpheus also came to be associated with the mysteries, which thus became deeper in character. The festival was celebrated twice a year: the greater mysteries in September in memory of Persephone's descent into the lower world, and the lesser in February to mark her return to earth, which meant the beginning of spring. The ceremonies started with a procession, followed by purification rites during which the mystae (initiates) bathed in the sea. The actual mysteries took place in the telesterion, a closed hall. Details of the ceremonies there are not known. A.t.s. the fate of Persephone was illustrated dramatically in a kind of Passion Play, but this theory is emphatically rejected by other scholars. The main theme of the mysteries was that death is not an evil but a boon. Originally, only inhabitants of Eleusis were mystae; Athenians were also admitted later, and in the fifth century the Eleusinia reached the peak of their popularity.

All Greeks, even slaves, were allowed to take part, and the influence of the mysteries spread far beyond Greece; Sulla, Marcus Antonius, Cicero, and Augustus were among those initiated. The sanctuary was destroyed by Alaric in A.D. 395, after which the mysteries were officially forbidden by Theodosius the Great.

ELEUSIS. Town of Attica, on the gulf of the same name. Famous for the Eleusinian* mysteries, which were held there in honor of Demeter* and Persephone*. The 14-mile road which connects Eleusis with Athens was called the Sacred Road because Athenians, beginning with the 7th century B.C., were admitted to the mystic rites at Eleusis.

ELISSA or **ELISSAR.** See DIDO.

ELPENOR. Companion of Odysseus*, who fell from the roof of Circe's* palace in a drunken stupor and broke his neck (Hom. Od. x, 552f.). *Iconography.* On an Attic pelike (c. 440 B.C.) at Boston can be seen the meeting of Odysseus and the ghost of Elpenor. Groping for support against the wall face, Elpenor is coming up from the underworld.

ELYMUS [Gr. Elumos]. A Trojan, mythical ancestor of the Elymi, a people of Sicily.

ELYSIAN FIELDS. See ELYSIUM.

ELYSIUM. A beautiful plain at the extremity of the earth, where those favored by the gods dwell in perfect happiness after death.

EMATHION. Arabian king, son of Tithonus* and Eos*. He was slain by Heracles*.

ENARETE. Wife of Aeolus*, ancestor of the Aeolians*.

ENCELADUS [Gr. Enkelados]. One of the Giants*, struck by Zeus' thunderbolts and buried under Aetna. Every time he turns over, the earth trembles (Virg. iii, 578).

ENDEIS. Wife of Aeacus* and mother of Peleus* and Telamon*.

ENDYMION. Greek prince from Elis, loved by the moon goddess Selene*, who kissed him every evening in his sleep. At her request Zeus granted him eternal youth, then put him into everlasting sleep on Mt. Latmos, where Selene visits him every night. *Iconography.* Endymion can be seen on wall paintings, e.g. in the Casa di Sirico at Pompeii, where not Selene but Artemis is shown as his beloved. His sleeping figure is also found on reliefs and sarcophagi. He is a favorite subject of Baroque painting.

ENIPEUS. River in Thessaly. The river god was loved by Tyro*, who when visited by Poseidon* in the likeness of Enipeus, conceived two sons, Neleus* and Pelias*.

ENYALIUS [Gr. Enualios]. Spartan god of war; also another name for Ares*.

ENYO. Greek goddess of war, companion of Ares*. Identified with Bellona* by the Romans.

EOS [Gr. = dawn]. Greek personification of the dawn; daughter of Hyperion*. She was mother, by Astraeus*, of the winds. She abducted Cephalus* and Tithonus*, becoming mother by the latter of Memnon*. The dew was said to be Eos' tears for the death of Memnon. The Romans called her Aurora. *Iconography.* On Greek vases Eos is usually represented with wings and in rich clothing, or riding in a quadriga drawn by winged horses. On an amphora by Execias (c. 530 B.C.) in the Vatic. Museum Eos stands mourning by the body of Memnon, and a bowl by Calliades and Duris (c. 490 B.C.) shows winged Eos carrying the hero in her arms. A favorite subject is the abduction of Cephalus: an archaic relief from Camirus (6th century B.C.) has Eos speeding away with the youthful Cephalus in her arms, while on the frieze of the altar at Pergamum (2nd century B.C.) she is riding ahead of Helius. In later times there is, among others, the Aurora of Guido Reni.

EPAPHUS [Gr. Epaphos]. Son of Zeus* and Io, later king of Egypt and legendary founder of Memphis (Ov. i, 748).

EPEUS [Gr. Epeios]. 1. Son of Endymion*; he beat his brothers in a contest and received the kingship of Elis as his reward. 2. In Virg., the builder of the Wooden Horse of Troy (Virg. ii, 264).

A.t.s. also the founder of Pisa and Metapontum.

EPHIALTES. One of the Aloadae*.

EPICASTE [Gr. Epikaste]. 1. Another name for Jocasta*. 2. Name of the wife and the daughter of Augias*.

EPIDAURUS. City in Argolis on the Peloponnesus, famous in antiquity for its sanctuary of Asclepius* and still well known for the numerous remains of ancient monuments—a magnificent theater, a tholos (round building), a stadium, a gymnasium, and the ruins of several porticoes where sick pilgrims came to be cured by the deity.

EPIGONI. The sons of the seven heroes who tried in vain to conquer Thebes (see SEVEN AGAINST THEBES). They undertook a punitive expedition against the city to avenge the deaths of their fathers —the expedition of the Epigoni.

EPIMETHEUS. Son of the Titan Iapetus* and Clymene* and husband of Pandora*. Invented by the Greeks as the counterpart (Epimetheus = afterthought) of his brother Prometheus* (= forethought).

EPONA. Gallic goddess, guardian of horses, also venerated in Italy and the Danubian countries. There was probably a temple of Epona at Assche-Kalkhoven in Belgium.
Iconography. There is a votive relief (2nd century A.D.) in the Landesmuseum at Trier, Germany, showing Epona in a long dress, sitting sidesaddle on a horse and holding a filled tray in her right hand.

ERATO. Muse* of lyric poetry and love songs.
Iconography. She is represented with a lyre in her hand.

EREBUS. [Gr. Erebos = darkness]. Son of Chaos. The name is to denote the nether regions.

ERECHTHEUS. 1. Ancient Attic hero, called Erichthonius, son of Hephaestus* and Gaea*; like Cecrops* an ancestor of Attica. His mother gave him to the goddess Athena to rear. That is why, on becoming ruler of Attica, he introduced the worship of Athena into the country. Like Cecrops*, he is said to have decided the dispute between Poseidon and Athena

for the possession of Attica, and he was worshiped with the two gods in the temple called the Erechtheum on the Acropolis, where his tomb also was. Some say he is identical with Erichthonius who, as a child, was put in a basket and entrusted to the daughters of Cecrops (see AGLAURUS). 2. Son of Pandion* and the nymph Zeuxippe*, brother of Butes, Procne*, and Philomela*. He was king of Athens and grandson of Erechtheus (1). During his reign Athens is said to have been threatened by an army of Thracians and inhabitants of Eleusis, led by Eumolpus*. Urged by the oracle, Erechtheus sacrificed one of his daughters to the underworld, after which victory over the enemy was assured. Eumolpus died, but in answer to his prayer Erechtheus was also slain, by Zeus' avenging thunderbolt. According to another tradition, however, there was originally only one Erechtheus.
Iconography. A bowl by the so-called Codrus painter (2nd half of the 5th century B.C.) at Berlin shows Gaea handing her child Erechtheus to Athena, watched by a serious-looking Cecrops, the lower half of whose body is that of a serpent.

ERICHTHONIUS [Gr. Erichthonios]. 1. Son of Dardanus*; one of the founders of Troy. 2. Another name for Erechtheus (1)*.

ERIDANUS [Gr. Eridanos]. In Virg. (vi, 659), a river in the underworld. In Herod. (iii, 115), an unspecified river, identified by some contemporaries of Herod as the Po because the latter flows near the end of the "Amber Way" and legend has it that amber was formed from the tears shed by the Heliades* for the death of their brother Phaëthon*, who had plunged into the Eridanus.

ERIGONE. Daughter of Aegisthus* and Clytaemnestra*.

ERINYES. Greek avenging goddesses who, when a breach of the right of asylum or hospitality, murder of a relative, or perjury was committed, rose from the underworld, relentlessly pursued the offender, and finally drove him or her mad. Even in death the criminal did not find relief unless he had purged himself of guilt. In that case the Erinyes were called the Eumenides (= the kindly ones) and were well disposed. They were usually thought of as three sisters: Alecto, Tisiphone, and Megaera. By the Romans they were called the Furiae (Furies) or —in poetic language—Dirae (= the dreadful ones).

Iconography. Ancient art represents the Erinyes as women with fiery eyes and serpents in their hair. Their attributes are torches and whips. They are sometimes shown as huntresses, with kilted dress and hunting boots. The head of a sleeping Erinys of Hellenistic sculpture (2nd century B.C.) is preserved at Rome.

ERIPHYLE. Wife of Amphiaraus*. When her husband wished to withdraw from the expedition of the Seven against Thebes*, she betrayed his hiding place and forced him to go. She thus obtained the bribe offered by Polynices*—Harmonia's* necklace. She later persuaded her son Alcmaeon* to take part in the expedition of the Epigoni* and was rewarded with Harmonia's dress.

ERIS [Gr. = strife]. Greek goddess of discord, companion of Ares*. Her omission from those invited to the nuptials of Peleus* and Thetis* proved disastrous. In her anger she threw a golden apple marked, "For the most beautiful," into the midst of the guests. Hera*, Aphrodite*, and Athena* all laid claim to it, but it was finally awarded by Paris*, prince of Troy, to Aphrodite. These events led indirectly to the Trojan war. Eris was called Discordia by the Romans.

Iconography. Eris appears, often with wings, on Etruscan mirrors. The judgment of Paris recurs regularly in Renaissance and Baroque art.

EROS. Greek god of sexual love, son of Aphrodite* and Ares*. Originally he represented the primeval power that created order and cohesion out of chaos. He is identical with the Romans' Amor* or Cupid. As a philosophical term in Plato, the "eros" is the god-given desire in man for what is exalted and eternal.

Iconography. See AMOR.

ERULUS. See HERULUS.

ERYMANTHOS. Mountain in Arcadia,

familiar from one of the exploits of Heracles*.

ERYSICHTHON. Thessalian prince, punished by Demeter* with an insatiable hunger because he felled trees in a wood that was sacred to her. He finally devoured himself.

ERYTHEA [Gr. Erytheia]. Mythical island which the Greeks situated somewhere in the west, near the setting sun. It glowed red in the evening sun (*erythros* = red). It was here that Geryon kept his cattle which were removed by Heracles*.

ERYTUS or EURYTUS [Gr. Erutos]. King of Oechalia in Thessaly. He promised the hand of his daughter Iole* to anyone who could beat his sons at archery. Heracles* won the contest but when the promised reward was refused he slew Erytus and his sons and took Iole away.

ERYX. Son of Aphrodite* and Butes (2)* and king of the Elymi on Sicily. He was a renowned boxer and even dared to challenge Heracles*, an act which he paid for with his life (Virg. v, 392, 412f.). Another legend says he was turned to stone with the Medusa's head by Perseus* (Ov. v, 195f.).

ETEOCLES [Gr. Eteokles]. Son of Oedipus* and Jocasta* and brother of Polynices*. When Oedipus went into exile, his sons cared so little about him that he cursed them. They ruled jointly over Thebes, but Eteocles soon expelled his brother, who recruited several heroes for a campaign known as the Seven against Thebes*. Both brothers died in a hand-to-hand fight.

ETEONEUS. Armor bearers of Menelaus* at the siege of Troy (Hom. Od. iv, 22, 31).

ETNA. See AETNA.

EUADNE. See EVADNE.

EUANDER. See EVANDER.

EUMAEUS [Gr. Eumaios]. Swineherd in Ithaca*, the country of Odysseus*. When Odysseus finally returned to Ithaca after his wanderings, he was given a kindly welcome by Eumaeus, although the latter did not recognize his master. Odysseus later revealed his identity, and Eumaeus helped him to gain access to Penelope* and also to take revenge on the suitors (Hom. Od. xv, 371f.; xvi, 1f.; xvii, 507f.; xxii, 162f.).

EUMELUS [Gr. Eumelos]. Son of Admetus* and Alcestis*. He took part in the siege of Troy* (Hom. Il. ii, 714f.).

EUMENIDES. See ERINYES.

EUMOLPUS [Gr. Eumolpos]. Thracian priest of Demeter*. He is said to have instituted the Eleusinian mysteries, and is regarded as the ancestor of the Athenian family called the Eumolpides (Ov. xi, 93). Legend also speaks of a Eumolpus, son of Poseidon*, who fought with the Eleusinians against the Athenian hero Erechtheus (2)*. He was killed in this undertaking, but by a previous arrangement with his father Poseidon, Zeus struck Erechtheus dead with his thunderbolt. This Eumolpus and the Thracian priest are sometimes regarded as one and the same person, but most traditions agree there were two.

EUNEUS [Gr. Euneos]. King of the island of Lemnos, son of Jason* and Hypsipyle* (Hom. Il. vii, 468).

EUNOMIA [Gr. = orderly, order]. One of the Horae*.

EUPEITHES. Father of Antinous*. When his son, the most aggressive of Penelope's suitors, had been slain by Odysseus*, he tried to incite the people of Ithaca* against the latter, but was killed by Laertes* (Hom. Od. xxiv, 469f.).

EUPHEMUS [Gr. Euphemos]. Son of Poseidon* and Europa*, steersman of the Argonauts*. Medea* foretold that his family would rule Libya, and her prophecy was fulfilled when Battus*, a descendant of Euphemus, came to Libya and founded Cyrene.

EUPHROSYNE. One of the Charites*.

EUROPA. 1. Daughter of Tityus*; mother of Euphemus*. 2. Daughter of the Phoenician king Agenor* and Telephassa*. While she was walking along the seashore one day, she was approached by Zeus in the form of a handsome bull. Europa sat on the bull, which thereupon jumped into the sea and carried her off to Crete. There Zeus revealed himself in his true form and took her to Mt.

Dikte*, where she bore him Minos*, Rhadamanthys*, and, some say, Sarpedon*. She later married Asterion (Ov. ii, 833f.).

Iconography. The abduction of Europa is seen on some Greek pottery, e.g. a bowl from Aegina (c. 500 B.C.), now at Munich; also in an archaic relief from the temple at Selinus and a metope of the Sicyonian treasury at Delphi (middle of 6th century B.C.); and in several wall paintings, the best known of which is a Pompeian fresco in the Nat. Museum, Naples. From later times there are the paintings of Veronese and Peter Lely.

EURUS [Gr. Euros]. The southeast wind or storm wind.

EURYALUS [Gr. Eurualos]. 1. One of the Epigoni*, participator in the voyage of the Argonauts*, and comrade in arms of Diomedes (1)* in the Trojan war. 2. In Virgil he and Nisus are an almost proverbially close pair of friends (Virg. v, 294, 334; ix, 179, 199, 326, 431).

EURYBATES. Herald in the Greek army before Troy (Hom. Il. i, 320; ii, 184).

EURYCLEA [Gr. Eurukleia]. Slave of Laertes* and nurse of Odysseus*; she was the first to recognize him—by a scar—when Odysseus returned to his palace (Hom. Od. i, 429f.; xix, 353f.).

EURYDICE [Gr. Eurudike]. Wife of Orpheus*. When she died of a snake bite, Orpheus descended to Hades* and so charmed Persephone with his singing that he was permitted to take Eurydice back to the upper world, provided he did not look back at her on the way. But Orpheus was unable to exercise sufficient self-control, and Hermes* took Eurydice back to Hades for good.

Iconography. The scene in which Hermes is separating Orpheus from his beloved for the second time is shown on a magnificent relief at Rome (5th century B.C.). In later times the incident of Eurydice and the snake is often illustrated, e.g. on a picture by Poussin.

EURYGANEA. See OEDIPUS.

EURYLOCHUS [Gr. Eurulochos]. Companion of Odysseus* (Hom. Od. x, 205f.).

EURYMACHUS [Gr. Eurumachos]. One

of Penelope's* suitors (Hom. Od. xviii, 349f.).

EURYMEDON. King of the Giants* (Hom. Od. vii, 58).

EURYNOME. 1. Daughter of Oceanus*; mother of the Charites*. 2. Servant of Penelope* (Hom. Od. xxiii, 289f.). 3. Mother of Adrastus*. 4. Mother of Agenor*.

EURYPYLUS [Gr. Eurupulos]. 1. Thessalian king, one of the Greek heroes at the siege of Troy* (Hom. Il. v, 76f.; xi, 809f.). 2. Son of Telephus* and Astyoche*, ally of the Trojans. Slain by Neoptolemus (Hom. Od. xi, 520). 3. Son of Thestius*; he was killed by Meleager on the Calydonian* hunt for having insulted Atalanta*.

EURYSACES [Gr. Eurusakes]. Son of Ajax (2)* and Tecmessa, venerated as a hero at Athens.

EURYSTHEUS. King of Mycenae, son of Sthelenus (2)*. As a result of Hera's cunning, Heracles* spent a long period in the service of Eurystheus. It was during this time that the hero performed his Twelve Labors.

EURYTION. 1. A Centaur* who tried to abduct Hippodamea*, the bride of the Lapithian king Pirithous*, during the actual nuptials. This led to a savage battle between the Centaurs and the Lapithae*. 2. Son of Ares* who guarded Geryon's cattle. 3. In Virgil, a skilled Trojan archer (Virg. v, 514).

EURYTUS [Gr. Eurytos]. 1. Father of Dryope* (Ov. ix, 356). 2. See ERYTUS.

EUTERPE. Muse* of lyric poetry. *Iconography.* She is represented with a double flute.

EVADNE [Gr. Euadne]. Wife of Capaneus*. On her husband's death she put an end to her own life (Virg. vi, 447).

EVANDER [Gr. Euander]. Greek king in Arcadia, son of Hermes*. He came to Italy and founded a colony called Pallanteum* on the Palatine Hill. He brought civilization to the area and was honored as a hero at Rome. He aided Aeneas* in his struggle against Turnus* (Virg. viii, 54, 102, 514, 496).

EVENTUS BONUS [Lat. = good result]. Roman god of good harvests and of success in undertakings. His statue stood on the Capitol at Rome, near the temple of Jupiter Optimus Maximus.

F

FAMA. Roman personification of rumor (Virg. iv, 173f.; Ov. xii, 39f.).

FAMES. Roman personification of hunger. Virgil situates her at the entrance to the nether regions (Virg. vi, 276), Ovid in the icy land of the Scythians (Ov. viii, 780f.).

FATES. See MOIRAE.

FATUM [Lat. = what is spoken]. In Roman religion, the expressed will of the gods, originally concerning the future; hence decree of the gods, oracle. Later rather the inevitable, irrevocable will of the gods concerning the lot in life and death of man: destiny (cf. Gr. *moira*).

FATUUS. Another name for the Roman god Faunus* as an oracular deity. His oracle at Tibur (now Tivoli) near the spring Albunea* was well known (Virg. vii, 81f.).

FAUNA. See FAUNUS.

FAUNS. In Roman legend, shaggy forest demons with short horns, goats' hooves, and a short tail, like the Greek satyrs*. *Iconography.* Very well known is the bronze dancing faun from the Casa del Fauno at Pompeii. The famous Barberini faun, lying back and sleeping off the effects of a debauch, is at Munich. (It is of 3rd century B.C. but partly restored.) See also SATYR.

FAUNUS. Old Italian deity, guardian of fields and woods, agriculture, and cattle breeding. Some say he was king of Latium and father of Latinus* (Virg. vii, 47). He was called Fatuus as an oracular god, Lupercus (= warder-off of wolves) as the protector of cattle. He sometimes terrified human beings with bad dreams; hence another name—Incubus (= nightmare). Faunus had a female counterpart known as Fauna, sometimes identified with Bona Dea*.

FAUSTULUS. Roman shepherd who found Romulus* and Remus* and had them brought up by his wife Acca Larentia* (Liv. i, 4, 7).

FAVONIUS. Roman personification of the soft west wind, identical with the Greek Zephyrus*. He was the messenger of spring who promoted the growth of the crops (*favere* = to favor).

FEBRIS [Lat. = fever]. Roman goddess who gave protection from fever. Three temples were dedicated to her in Rome, one standing between the Palatine and Velabrum.

FELICITAS. Roman personification of good success. Her Roman temple was on the Forum Romanum.

FERALIA. See DI MANES.

FERENTINA. Goddess of the small mountain town of Ferentinum (now Ferento) in Latium. She was considered the patroness of the Latin League.

FERONIA. Old Italian goddess, revered particularly near Capena at the foot of Mt. Soracte. Also renowned was her sanctuary at Tarracina (now Terracina), where she was venerated as the goddess of the manumission of slaves. It appears that slaves could obtain their freedom by sitting down on a stone in the temple of Feronia.

FIDES [Lat. = faith]. Roman goddess of good faith. She had at least one temple at Rome, namely on the Palatine Hill. In the Capitol*, where the treaties Rome had signed with allies and subject peoples were kept under her protection, she was worshiped as Fides Publica Populi Romani.

FLORA. Roman goddess of flowers and field crops. Her festival, the Floralia, was licentiously celebrated about May 1. *Iconography.* Roman art represents her as a buxom girl garlanded with flowers, and that is how she is shown on coins, etc. A statue of Flora was found in the

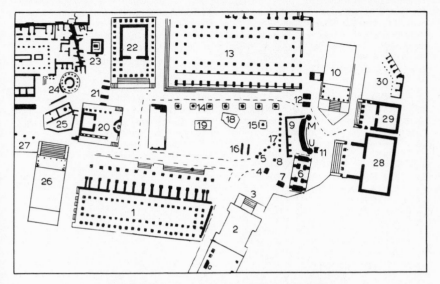

GROUND PLAN OF THE FORUM ROMANUM

1 - Basilica Aemilia, market hall with covered shopping arcade
2 - Curia or Senate chamber
3 - Comitium, square in front of the Curia where political and public meetings were held; later the much larger Campus Martius near the Tiber was used for this purpose
4 - The Black Stone, a very ancient monument, said by tradition to mark the tomb of Romulus
5 - Base of equestrian statue
6 - Triumphal arch of Septimius Severus
7 - Base of equestrian statue
8 - Commemorative column
9 - Rostra or platforms for public speakers
10 - Temple of Saturn
11 - Altar of Vulcan
12 - Triumphal arch of Tiberius
13 - Basilica Julia, market hall, clubhouse, and courthouse
14 - Seven commemorative columns
15 - Column of Phocas
16 - Two marble parapets adorned with reliefs
17 - Underground passages and wells
18 - Lacus Curtius—spring and altars where Curtius threw himself into the gaping cleft in the ground
19 - Equestrian statue of Domitian
20 - Temple of Divus Julius, the deified Julius Caesar
21 - Triumphal arch of Augustus
22 - Temple of Castor and Pollux
23 - Spring sacred to Juturna
24 - Temple of Vesta and, attached to it, the house of the Vestals
25 - Regia, originally the palace of the Roman kings, later the dwelling of the Pontifex Maximus
26 - Temple of the deified Emperor Antoninus and his wife Faustina
27 - Very ancient cemetery
28 - i. Temple of Concordia
29 - ii. Temple of the deified Vespasian
30 - iii. Colonnade of the Twelve Gods
   U = Umbilicus or navel, the center of Rome
   M = Millenarium or gilt milestone which indicated the distances from Rome to the chief cities in the Empire

---

Thermae of Caracalla at Rome. Flora also inspired many painters in later times, e.g. Gérard and Rembrandt.

FLORALIA. See FLORA.

FORDICIDIA. See TELLUS.

FORTUNA. Roman goddess of chance and happiness, originally probably a fertility deity, later identified with the Greek Tyche*. She was venerated—especially by women—under numerous epithets, e.g. Annonaria, Muliebris, Virilis, Respiciens, Primigenia, etc. There were several temples dedicated to her in Rome, but her greatest and most famous sanctuary was excavated after World War II in ancient Praeneste (now Palestrina); the oldest part (200 B.C.) had been extended by Sulla to form an impressive complex.

Iconography. She is usually shown standing and richly dressed. Her attributes are a cornucopia and a ship's rudder or a scepter.

FORUM ROMANUM. Originally a marshy plain between the Palatine and Capitoline, the first two of the hills of Rome to be inhabited, this site was drained by means of a canal in the earliest days of the city and made into a market place. It eventually became the political center of the Roman world, a square surrounded by temples and basilicas and adorned with monuments and triumphal arches.

FURIES. See ERINYES.

G

GAEA or GE [Gr. Gaia]. Mother Earth as a goddess, the oldest of the Greek deities. According to Greek cosmogony, she arose by her own power out of Chaos* and in turn produced the sky (Uranus*), sea, and mountains. By Uranus she became mother of the Titans*, Cyclopes*, and Centimani*. The Erinyes*, Giants*, and other monsters were also regarded as her children. She was the universal nurse and mother from whom all life sprang and to whom, when death came, all life returned. Her Roman equivalent was Tellus*, the "good earth."
Iconography. An archaic relief shows Gaea as a clothed female figure rising out of the earth. A seated goddess with a child on her lap, one of the figures on the W. façade of the Parthenon, is thought to be Gaea, and the child Thalassa (the sea). Gaea is also shown as a mother on Greek vases, e.g. pleading for the lives of her children the Giants on a bowl by Aristophanes (late 5th century B.C.); likewise on the altar at Pergamum (c. 200 B.C.). On sarcophagi she resembles Cybele, the Great Mother. Her attributes are a serpent, a cornucopia, and flowers or fruits.

GALANTHIS or GALINTHIAS. Maidservant of Alcmene*. When Hera* tried to prevent the birth of Heracles* to Alcmene, Galanthis deceived her by saying that Alcmene had already given birth. For punishment she was changed into a weasel (Ov. ix, 306f.).

GALATEA [Gr. Galateia]. (1) Greek sea nymph, daughter of Nereus*. She was the beloved of Polyphemus*, but a.t.s. she forsook him for Acis*. (2) Statue of a girl sculptured by Pygmalion*, who fell in love with the statue and prayed that the girl be brought to life. Aphrodite granted his wish.

GALINTHIAS. See GALANTHIS.

GALLI. Roman name for the Corybantes*.

GANYMEDE. Son of Tros*. Because of his extreme beauty he was taken to Olympus by the gods to become Zeus' cupbearer there. Some say he was kidnapped by Zeus or his eagle (Hom. Il. v, 266; Ov. x, 155).
Iconography. The abduction of Ganymede is a favorite subject for vase paintings and sculpture in later antiquity. Particularly famous is the bronze group by Leochares (4th century B.C.): a soaring eagle with outspread wings raising young Ganymede into the air. In other sculptures, gems, and sarcophagi, too, Ganymede is represented as a naked youth, sometimes with a mantle over his shoulder. He is usually accompanied by a dog.

GARGARENSES. Mythical nation consisting solely of men. The Amazons* were said to have intercourse with them for a time annually to ensure the continued existence of their race.

GE. See GAEA.

GELANOR. Son of Sthelenus (1)* and king of Argos. When Danaus* arrived in Argos with his daughters and laid claim to the throne, Gelanor, in obedience to a divine sign, handed power over to him.

GENII. In Roman mythology the Genius was originally a family ancestor who dwelt in the underworld and ensured the continuance of the family by its male members. In later times Genii were more generally beings who protected individuals and accompanied them throughout their lives. Each man had a Genius to whom he offered sacrifice on birthdays and other occasions. The protective spirit of women was called Juno.
Iconography. The Genius of departed ancestors was symbolized by the serpent, which is generally shown on house altars

and on shrines for the Lares in houses at Pompeii.

GERYON or GERYONES. A three-headed monster, son of Chrysaor*. He lived somewhere in the west and possessed a great herd of cattle which was stolen by Heracles*. The giant Eurytion (2)*, who was watching over the cattle, was killed on this occasion, and even Geryon, when he tried to stop Heracles, was slain by the hero.

GIANTS [Gr. Gigantes]. powerful beings of great stature, sons of Gaea*. Setting out from the Thessalian plain, they piled Mount Ossa* on Pelion* in order to storm Olympus* and dethrone the gods. With the help of Heracles* they were destroyed and buried under volcanoes (see AETNA) (Ov. i, 151f.).

Iconography. The battle between the gods and the Giants was a favorite theme in ancient art. The best known representation is the relief on the altar at Pergamum (c. 180 B.C.). The Giants shown there have many different forms: some are men to the waist, ending in the tail of a serpent, and others are winged. Of the late archaic period is the Battle of the Giants on the frieze of the Siphnian treasure house at Delphi (c. 552 B.C.), where the Giants are represented as helmeted hoplites. Among the surviving reliefs of the Hekatompedon on the Athenian Acropolis is a group consisting of Athena and the large, naked figure of a recumbent Giant.

GLAUCE [Gr. Glauke]. One of the Nereids*.

GLAUCUS [Gr. Glaukos]. 1. Greek fisherman of Anthedon (Boeotia). A magic herb that he had eaten compelled him to jump into the sea, and he was changed into an ocean divinity (Ov. xiii, 898f.). 2. King of Corinth, son of Sisyphus* and Merope*. He incurred Aphrodite's* anger, and she avenged herself when Glaucus was taking part in the funeral games of Pelias*, by causing his horses to go mad and tear him to pieces. His ghost, according to a later legend, used to scare the horses at The Isthmian* Games. 3. Leader of the Lycians in the Greek army at Troy (Hom. Il. ii, 876;

vi, 119f.). 4. Son of Minos* and Pasiphaë*; he was accidentally killed while a child but was restored to life with a magic herb.

GOLDEN AGE. In Roman mythology, the paradisiacal prehistoric age under the rule of Saturn*, a period of perfect peace and prosperity. War and fighting were unknown, and laws were superfluous. The earth produced its fruits spontaneously, and even among the animals peace prevailed (Ov. i, 89f.).

GOLDEN FLEECE. The golden fleece of the ram on whose back Phrixus* and Helle* departed for Colchis. Phrixus sacrificed the animal to Zeus and suspended the fleece from a tree in a wood sacred to Ares*, where it was guarded by a dragon (see ARGONAUTS).

GORDIAS or GORDIUS [Gr. Gordias or Gordios]. Phrygian farmer on whose plow an eagle landed—a sign that he would one day be king. Later an oracle designated him as king and he bacame the founder of Gordium, thenceforth the capital of Phrygian kings. The pole of his chariot, which was kept in the capital, was fastened with a skilfully devised "Gordian knot." This, the oracle said, could only be untied by a future conqueror of the world. Alexander the Great cut it with his sword.

GORGON. Female monster whose gaze turned the beholder into stone. Later three Gorgons were recognized: Medusa, Euryale, and Stheno, daughters of Phorcys* and Ceto*. They lived in the extreme west. Medusa was the best-known of them, partly owing to the legend of Perseus*, who succeeded in cutting off her head (Ov. iv, 772f.).

Iconography. The Gorgon's head was used as a terror-inspiring device on the Aegis*. The head, with serpents for hair, and sometimes also with the tongue sticking out, often figures on Greek vases as a decoration on warriors' shields. The Gorgon's head also appears on the older coins of the city of Athens, and on seals, temple antefixae, and mural paintings. An archaic relief is also known—one of the metopes of temple C at Selinus—on which Perseus is seen cutting off Medusa's head.

The Gorgon has a wide mouth containing fangs, and her tongue sticks out. Pegasus has been born from her blood and she is clasping him with her right hand (early 6th century B.C.). Later representations of the Gorgon or Medusa give the face a quieter and less horrible expression, e.g. the Medusa Rondanini at Munich—although here, too, the head is wreathed in snakes, while small wings sprout from the hair.

GORGONION. Head of the Gorgon* (see also AEGIS).

GRADIVUS. A name for Mars*.

GRACES. See CHARITES.

GRAEAE [Gr. Graiai]. Three daughters of Phorcys* and Ceto*, sisters of the Gorgons*. They were witches who had only one eye and one tooth among them, which they used by turns. They dwelt in the west and were the only ones who could show the way to the Gorgons.

GRATIAE. See CHARITES.

GRATION. One of the Giants*.

GYGES. One of the Centimani*.

H

HADES [Gr. Haides or Aides]. Greek god of the kingdom of the dead, son of Cronus* and Rhea*. When Cronus' three sons divided up the world among them, Zeus* was alotted the upper world, Poseidon* the oceans, and Hades the lower world or place of the departed spirits. He shared his throne with Persephone*, whom he had abducted from the upper world. The name Hades is also used for the god's kingdom. In Roman mythology the underworld is called not only Hades but also Orcus, Tartarus, or Avernus. There is a famous description of the lower world in Virgil's *Aeneid* (vi), when Aeneas visits it. The gloomy region is enclosed by several rivers: the Acheron*, the Styx*, and the Lethe*. In ancient literature two more are named: the Cocytus* and the Pyriphlegethon*. Cerberus*, the hound of hell, guarded the entrance; the god Hermes* accompanied the shades to the lower world, and Charon*, the gruff boatman, ferried them across the Styx. The fare was a coin placed in the dead man's mouth. Only the shades of those whose bodies had been buried or consumed by fire were admitted to Hades' kingdom. Hades was also master of the riches concealed in the depths of the earth. He was therefore also called Pluto (Gr. *ploutos* = rich) or, by the Romans, Dis (Lat. *dives* = rich). The narcissus and cypress (see CYPARISSUS) were sacred to him. *Iconography.* Hades is seldom represented in ancient art. Some Roman busts show him with long hair and beard and gloomy features. On vases, cameos, coins, and sarcophagi he is sometimes clothed in a short-sleeved chiton with an eagle-topped rod or cornucopia in his hand. On a wall painting in the Etruscan tomb at Colini near Orvieto Hades sits on a high throne with Persephone by his side. The god is covered with a lion's skin, wearing the animal's head like a helmet, and with a spear in his hand. In later times Hades is mainly shown abducting Proserpina (= Persephone), e.g. by Bernini and Rembrandt.

HAEMON [Gr. Haimon]. Son of Creon (1)*; betrothed to Antigone*. When the latter was condemned to death for disobeying Creon's orders, Haemon killed himself by her side.

HAEMUS [Gr. Haimos]. Son of Boreas* and king of Thrace. In his arrogance he compared himself and his wife Rhodope* to the divine couple, Zeus* and Hera*. For punishment Zeus changed them into the mountain ranges that bore their names (the Haemus Mountains are now known as the Balkans).

HALAESUS. In Virgil, Agamemnon's* charioteer who fled to Italy. He fought against Aeneas there and reputedly founded Falerii (now Civita Castellana) (Virg. x, 411).

HALCYONE. One of the Pleiades*.

HALIRRHOTIUS [Gr. Halirrhotios]. Son of Poseidon. He pursued Alcippe, a daughter of Ares* and Agraulus*, with his love, and for that was slain by Ares.

HALITHERSES. Soothsayer in Ithaca. He supported Telemachus* and Odysseus* in their fight against the suitors (Hom. Od. ii, 253; xvii, 68; xxiv, 451).

HALIUS [Gr. Halios]. Son of Alcinous* [Hom. Od. viii, 119].

HAMADRYADS. In ancient mythology, tree nymphs who were born and died with the tree in which they lived.

HAMMON. See AMMON.

HARMONIA. Daughter of Ares* and Aphrodite*. On her marriage to Cadmus* her presents from her mother included a dress and a necklace. These were later to bring great misfortune to Eriphyle* and Alcmaeon*.

HARPALYCE [Gr. Harpaluke]. Thracian princess, reared like an Amazon in the open air by her father, Harpalycus. She excelled particularly in running (Virg. i, 317). After her death she was venerated as a deity.

HARPOCRATES. Egyptian deity, identified with Horus*.

HARPIES. Monstrous creatures with the long claws of birds of prey and the faces of repulsive hags. They caused human beings to disappear without trace or tortured them in various ways. For instance, they stole Phineus' * food. But they were chased away by the sons of Boreas*, since when they have lived in the Strophades, where Aeneas* suffered their torments (Virg. iii, 225f.). Originally they were prob. personifications of the tempest and squall (Gr. *harpuiai* = snatchers). In Virgil they are demons of death who dwell at the entrance to the underworld (Virg. vi, 289).
Iconography. The best-known representations of the Harpies are the reliefs of the Harpy tomb (archaic, c. 500 B.C.), an Ionic monument from Xanthos (Asia Minor); this is a rectangular pillar, with reliefs on all four sides. A procession of figures brings offerings to the dead, and at the corners can be seen creatures with the head and torso of a woman and the tail and wings of a bird, carrying the souls of the dead away. Generally regarded as Harpies, they are thought by some to be Sirens*.

HEBE. Greek goddess of youth, daughter of Zeus and Hera. She preceded Ganymede* as the cupbearer of the gods on Olympus, and was given in marriage to Heracles* when he took his place among the gods. She was called Juventas by the Romans.
Iconography. Hebe was represented as a buxom young woman. On many Greek vases she is shown in a sleeveless chiton, as cupbearer of the gods or as the bride of Heracles (e.g. on an Apulian amphora). There was a famous statue—now lost—of Hebe, made of gold and ivory by Naucydes, a brother of Polycletus (5th century B.C.). Copies of this renowned work can be found on late Argive coins.

HECABE. See HECUBA.

HECAMEDE. [Gr. Hekamede]. Daughter of Arsinoös of Tenedos and slave of Nestor* (Hom. Il. xi, 624).

HECATE [Gr. Hekate = working afar]. Old Greek goddess belonging to the Titan* family, daughter of Zeus* and Demeter* or Perse*. When the Titans rebelled against Zeus, she was the only one who remained faithful to him. For this she was rewarded with power over sky, earth, and sea. She was also goddess of the underworld and identified with Persephone*. As goddess of the new moon she was identified with Artemis-Phoebe. Above all, she was goddess of sorcery and magic. She was the patroness of witches and helped them brew their potions. Accompanied by her barking black dog, she haunted cemeteries. She conjured up ghosts and phantoms from the underworld to terrify people. She was not much venerated in temples, but her statue with three bodies or three faces (one for each of the phases of the moon) was placed at crossroads, especially where three roads met. Hence her Latin name Trivia (= of the three ways). Black lambs, dogs, and honey were offered to her.
Iconography. In earliest Greek sculpture she is represented in single form, e.g. in works by Myron and Naucydes. The first statue of Hecate in triple form is the one —now lost—by Alcamenes (5th century B.C.) on the Acropolis. Numerous smaller Hecate groups have survived, in which three separate female figures clad in chitons are grouped around a cylindrical pillar, with their backs to it. Hecate usually has a burning torch in her hand and a dog with its head raised at her feet. On the altar of Pergamum she is shown with one body and three heads (c. 170 B.C.). She can be seen in single form on Greek vases and coins. In addition to the torch, her attributes are a serpent, a lash, a dagger, a key, and a sword, and on her head she sometimes wears the *kalathos,* a high wicker basket, or a crescent.

HECATONCHIRES [Gr. Hekatoncheires]. Monsters with a hundred arms, offspring of Uranus* and Gaea*. See CENTIMANI.

HECTOR [Gr. Hektor]. Eldest son of King Priam* and Hecuba*; husband of Andromache* and father of Astyanax.* Described in Homer's *Iliad* as the noblest of Troy's heroes. He was the bravest of the city's defenders. His solicitous love for his wife and child is depicted by Homer among others, in the *Iliad*, vi, 370f. By slaying Patroclus*, he incurred the wrath of Achilles* and finally fell a victim to it. His body was dragged three times around the walls of Troy by Achilles but was preserved from corruption by Aphrodite and Apollo. It was finally handed back to his father and burned with much ceremony on a funeral pyre (Hom. Il. xxiv, 23f., 725f., 762f.).

Iconography. Hector is often shown on Greek vase decorations that have the Trojan War for their subject. On an Attic amphora by Euthymides (c. 510 B.C.), now at Munich, the hero is seen arming for the fight: he is putting on his armor while Hecuba hands him his helmet. A Chalcidian amphora (c. 530 B.C.) at Würzburg depicts the farewell of Hector and Hecuba. The François vase (c. 570 B.C.) shows him standing at the gate of Troy with his brother Polites. His duel with Achilles, the mutilation of his corpse, and its return to Priam are subjects of Greek vase paintings. On cameos, coins, and frescoes, e.g. some in the Casa del Larario at Pompeii, Hector is represented in scenes from the Trojan War.

HECUBA or HECABE [Gr. Hekabe]. Daughter of Dymas; wife of King Priam* of Troy and mother of Hector*, Paris*, Cassandra*, Creusa*, and many other children. After the fall of Troy she was carried off into slavery (Hom. Il. vi, 251f.; xxii, 430f.; xxiv, 193f., 747f.).

Iconography. On Greek vases she is shown as a beautiful young woman in various scenes from the Trojan War. On a fresco in the Casa di Cecilio Iucundo at Pompeii she is seen gazing sadly from a window at a procession bringing Hector's body back to Troy.

HELEN. Daughter of Zeus or Tyndareus* and Leda*, reputed in antiquity to have been a woman of dazzling beauty. While still a child she was carried off by The-

seus* but was rescued by the Dioscuri*. She later married Menelaus* and bore him Hermione*. She was abducted by Paris* of Troy, an act which led to the Trojan War. On Paris' death she married his brother Deiphobus*. There are various versions of her fate after the capture of Troy; some say she returned to Sparta with Menelaus, others that she was banished to Rhodes and died there, or that she married Achilles* and bore him a son, Euphorion. In Homer she is regularly referred to as the cause of the Trojan War (Hom. Il. ii, 161; iii, 70, 282f., 458, etc.). Virgil, too, calls her the wicked spirit of Troy (Virg. ii, 573), especially since she voluntarily deserted her husband to follow Paris (Hom. Od. xxiii, 218, 221; Virg. i, 650; vii, 364).

Iconography. Helen is represented on many Greek vases in sumptuous clothes and without attributes. The scene in which Menelaus recovers his wife, for instance, is shown on an Attic oenochoe (c. 430 B.C.) in the Vatic. Museum, and on the scyphus of Hieron and Macron (c. 490 B.C.) at Boston. Menelaus is rushing toward Helen with his sword drawn or throwing it away, while Helen is fleeing. The same scene is painted on a fresco in the Casa del Menandro at Pompeii.

HELENUS [Gr. Helenos]. Son of Priam* and Hecuba*. He had the gift of prophecy, and when he fell into the hands of the Greeks he foretold their conquest of Troy. After the Trojan War he was taken off to Epirus as a slave by Neoptolemus*. After the latter's death he married Andromache*, who had also been taken from Troy as a slave. He inherited part of Neoptolemus' kingdom and founded a new Troy in Epirus, where he was visited by Aeneas on his way to Italy (Hom. Il. vi, 75f.; vii, 44f.; Virg. iii, 295, 334f., 374f.).

HELIADAE. The seven sons of the sun god Helius*, skilled in astronomy and navigation, and venerated as heroes, particularly on Rhodes.

HELIADES. Daughters of the sun god Helius* and sisters of Phaëthon*, for whose death they wept incessantly until their tears became amber and they themselves were changed into poplars (Ov. ii, 340f.).

HELICON. [Gr. Helikon]. Wooded mountain in Boeotia, sacred to the Muses*. The famous springs Aganippe* and Hippocrene* flowed here.

HELIUS [Gr. Helios]. Greek sun god, son of Hyperion*; brother of Selene* and Eos*. In the morning he rose up out of the Ocean* in the east with his quadriga, completed his journey around the firmament, and sank once more into the Ocean in the west at nightfall. He was all-seeing and all-knowing. He had by Clymene* a son Phaëthon*, to whom he lent his chariot, with disastrous consequences. By Perse* he was the father of Aeëtes* and Circe*. The worship of the sun as a deity reached Greece from the East. Helius was especially revered on Rhodes, e.g. in annual gymnastic games. Rhodes was also the site of the so-called Colossus, a 100-foot-high statue of Helius made c. 291 B.C. by Chares and destroyed in 225 B.C. by an earthquake. The Colossus of Rhodes was the sixth wonder of the world. At various places where Helius was venerated, there were herds dedicated to him, e.g. on the island of Thrinacia* (sometimes identified as Sicily). Cattle, rams, he-goats, and white horses were sacrificed to Helius. The cock and the eagle were sacred to him. The Romans revered the sun as Sol* Invictus (invincible sun).

Iconography. Helius was represented with his mantle flapping, an aureole around his head, and sometimes standing in the solar chariot. A metope of the Temple of Athena at Hellenistic Ilium shows him thus. He is also seen on many later reliefs relating to the Mithraic religion, e.g. in the Mithraeum under St. Prisca's at Rome. In early Christian art Christ is sometimes represented as Helius, e.g. in a mosaic in mausoleum M or "of the fisherman" in the necropolis under St. Peter's at Rome.

HELLAS. The usual name for ancient Greece; many mountains, regions, and cities of Hellas are associated with figures from Greek mythology or were centers for the worship of various deities. Thus Olympus was the throne of Zeus, Arcadia was the home of the god Pan, and sacred Delphi was the principal sanctuary of Apollo. For the most important mountains traditionally associated with Hellenic myths, for the main region of Hellas, for the chief islands in the Aegean Sea and some cities on the west coast of Asia Minor, and for a number of places in Hellas which were centers of veneration for gods and heroes, see maps.

HELLE. Daughter of Athamas* and Nephele*. She and her brother Phrixus* fled from her father's degenerate second wife, Ino*, who wanted to kill Nephele's children. Nephele aided her threatened offspring by sending them a winged ram with golden horns. Phrixus and Helle mounted the animal, which was to take them to Colchis. On the way, however, Helle fell into the sea to which she gave her name (the Hellespont). Phrixus reached Colchis safely, and there he sacrificed the ram to Zeus and suspended its fleece from a tree in Ares' forest (see GOLDEN FLEECE).

Iconography. The journey of Phrixus and Helle is rarely shown on vases but frequently on reliefs and wall paintings.

HELLEN. Son of Deucalion* and Pyrrha*, or of Zeus. Legendary ancestor of the Hellenes.

HELLESPONT. See HELLE.

HEPHAESTUS [Gr. Hephaistos]. Greek god of fire and the blacksmith's art, son of Zeus* and Hera*. As he was born a cripple, his mother threw him from Olympus* into the sea, where Thetis* and Eurynome*, daughters of Oceanus*, cared for him for many years. When Hephaestus later returned to Olympus, he was once more thrown from it, this time by Zeus in the course of a quarrel. After falling for a day he landed on Lemnos, where he was hospitably received and looked after by the inhabitants. Some say this fall was the cause of his limp. Aphrodite* was his wife. As the god of fire he was associated with all processes in which fire is needed. Hephaestus had his workshops under volcanoes, e.g. Aetna in Sicily and Mt. Mosychos on Lemnos, the island where he was particularly venerated and where the Cabeiri* were his helpers. He artistically forged arms and accouterments for countless gods and heroes, e.g. Zeus' scepter, Poseidon's* trident, Heracles' * shield, Achilles' * cuirass, etc. As an artist smith he is closely related to Athena*, the goddess of arts. A festival common to both deities was celebrated at Athens: the Chaldeia. The Roman god of fire, Vulcan*, was wholly identified with Hephaestus (Hom. Il. xviii, 394f.; i, 593; the "Homeric Laughter* of the gods" at the cripple Hephaestus: i, 599-600).

Iconography. The god is represented as a bearded man, wearing a round or conical workman's hat and holding blacksmiths' tools in his hand. He is seen on many vase paintings: his return to Olympus is shown on the François vase; as a crippled god he stands in relief on the frieze of the Siphnian treasury at Delphi (6th century B.C.). For the Hephaestus temple at Athens (the "Theseum") the sculptor Alcamenes made a bronze group of the crippled god with Athena (c. 420 B.C.), but nothing more is known about this work. A Roman sarcophagus shows Vulcan at work with his assistants, the Cyclopes. There are also two famous paintings of Vulcan's smithy, one by Tintoretto and the other by Velasquez.

HERA. The chief of the Greek goddesses, daughter of Cronus* and Rhea*. She was both the sister and the wife of Zeus*. She was so difficult and arrogant that Zeus was sometimes obliged to exercise his infinite power even on her, in order to make her stubborn character more pliable. The countless love affairs of her husband were so many sources of annoyance to Hera and led to domestic strife between the two deities. Nevertheless, she was held in great honor by gods and mortals. Her chief power was over nature, but she was also the guardian goddess of marriage and birth (see IL-ITHYIA). Ceremonies in her honor were held in spring all over Greece, but especially at Samos, which was wholly sacred to her, and in Boeotia. According to Homer, Argos, Mycenae, and Sparta were her favorite cities. The peacock, crow, and pomegranate were sacred to

her. The Roman goddess Juno* was identified with her.

Iconography. Hera is represented as a noble female figure, majestic and venerable. On her head she wears a diadem or, in earlier representations, a veil. She is also shown veiled on the frieze of the Parthenon (school of Phidias, c. 435 B.C.). For the Temple of Hera at Mycenae Polycletus made a famous gold and ivory statue of the goddess (c. 415 B.C.): Hera enthroned, with a scepter and a pomegranate in her hands. Also well known is the Ludovisi Hera, a Roman copy of a 4th-century Greek original, in which Goethe saw the ideal of feminine beauty and dignity. There is, further, the standing figure of the Barberini Juno at Rome, remarkable for the unusual pleating of her dress. Many representations of the goddess have been found on Samos, e.g. on coins of the island. A famous sanctuary of Hera has been excavated at Paestum in southern Italy, and many votive offerings have been found, including statuettes of the enthroned goddess, with a child in her left arm and a pomegranate in her right hand. A remarkable fact is that a 12th-century church near the Hera sanctuary was dedicated to the Madonna of the Pomegranate. The representations of this Madonna and Hera are quite identical.

HERACLES [Gr. Herakles]. Son of Zeus* and Alcmene*, one of the most popular and celebrated heroes of antiquity. The miraculous feats and heroic deeds ascribed to him are legion. He was said to have been born in Boeotia, having been begotten by Zeus when he visited Alcmene during the absence of her husband Amphitryon*. Zeus had predicted that Alcmene's child would rule the house of Perseus, but Hera* tried to prevent this by causing Eurystheus*, son of Sthelenus*, to be born before Heracles. She also sent two serpents into young Heracles' cradle to kill him and thus secure power for Eurystheus. Small as he was, Heracles strangled them and grew up without mishap. One of his tutors, Linus*, a musician, rebuked his pupil, but paid for it with his life, so hard did young

Heracles strike him with a lute. Sent by Amphitryon to the Cithaeron* mountains, he led a shepherd's life until he reached manhood. This is where Prodicus (a sophist, friend of Socrates and Plato) situates his well-known allegory of Heracles at the crossroads: the hero chose the difficult path to virtue and not the broad road to sensual pleasure. Arriving in Thebes, he liberated the Thebans in a short campaign from the crippling tribute imposed on them by Erginus, king of Orchomenus. Creon*, king of Thebes, gave him his daughter Megara in marriage. Eurystheus now demanded that Heracles should serve him. This so enraged the hero that he killed his own children. By way of punishment the oracle of Delphi commanded him to perform twelve labors in the service of Eurystheus. These, if well done, would ensure him immortality. The twelve labors were as follows: 1. To kill a lion that was ravaging the neighborhood of Nemea and was invulnerable. Heracles strangled it and afterwards wore its head and hide as a helmet and armor. 2. To slay a water snake (Hydra) at Lerna in Argolis. This monster had seven or more heads, and as soon as the hero cut one off, two more grew in its place. Using burning branches, he managed to sear the wounds and render the Hydra harmless; he dipped his arrows in the monster's gall. 3. To capture alive a large boar living in the woods on Mt. Erymanthos in Arcadia. He returned to Mycenae with the animal on his shoulders and so terrified his master Eurystheus that he hid in a barrel. 4. To capture a hind sacred to Artemis*. It had golden horns and brazen hooves. 5. To remove the Stymphalian Birds* from Lake Stymphalus in Arcadia. These were man-eating birds which had beaks and claws of steel and used their steel feathers as arrows. Heracles drove these monsters off with an iron rattle. 6. To clean the stables of King Augeas* of Elis, which 3,000 cattle had fouled for thirty years. Heracles diverted the rivers Peneus and Alpheus* through the stables and completed his task in one day. Augeas had promised him one-tenth of his herd as reward but refused

to pay Heracles afterwards. The hero thereupon laid waste the king's land and slew Augeas and all his sons except Phyleus*, who had recognized Heracles' rights. Heracles is said to have founded the Olympic Games* on this occasion. 7. To catch the Cretan bull. Poseidon* had presented the animal to Minos*, who was to offer it in sacrifice. When Minos neglected to do so, Poseidon drove the bull mad. 8. To capture the wild, man-eating mares of the Thracian king Diomedes*, who fed them on the flesh of visitors to the country. Heracles fed Diomedes to the mares and successfully brought the animals back to Mycenae. 9. To fetch the girdle of Hippolyta, queen of the Amazons. After a hard battle against the Amazons, Heracles slew Hippolyta and took the girdle. On his way back he saved Hesione*, daughter of the Trojan king Laomedon*, from the claws of a monster that Poseidon had sent to ravage Troy because Laomedon had refused to reward Poseidon for his help in building the walls of Troy. The king was on the point of sacrificing Hesione to the animal to allay Poseidon's wrath when Heracles rescued her. Heracles also destroyed the monster, for which act Laomedon had promised him his immortal horses. The king once more failed to keep his word, and Heracles therefore laid Troy waste and slew the king. 10. To steal Geryon's* cattle from the fabulous land of Erythea*. His long journey thither took him through Lybia and Europe, where he forced the sun god Helius* to ferry him to Erythea in his boat. On the way back the hero drove the herd straight across Europe, fighting against many hostile tribes and individuals (Cacus*, Eryx*, Alcyoneus*, etc.). 11. To fetch the Apples of the Hesperides. The apples were a present from Gaea* to Hera on her marriage to Zeus and were guarded somewhere in the west by a dragon. Heracles forced the sea-god Nereus* to show him the way, and after many dangerous encounters (Antaeus*, Busiris*, Emathion*, Prometheus*, etc.) he arrived in the land of the Hyperboreans*, where Atlas* supported the firmament on his shoulders.

Heracles asked Atlas to fetch the apples and took over his task in his absence. Others say that Atlas himself tried to take the apples to Eurystheus but that Heracles tricked him into carrying the heavens for a moment. When Atlas agreed, Heracles left him to his fate and hastened to Mycenae. 12. The last labor consisted in fetching Cerberus* from the underworld. At Mt. Taenarum in the S. of the Peloponnese the hero went down into Hades*, where he met Perseus*, Theseus*, Pirithous*, etc., managed to chain the hound of hell, and took him back to Eurystheus. Having completed his labors, Heracles went to Thebes, presented his wife Megara to his friend Iolus, and went to king Erytus*, who promised his daughter Iole to whoever excelled him in archery. Heracles won the contest, but when Erytus withheld the reward Heracles took a bloody revenge by, among other things, murdering the king's son Iphitus. When Apollo refused to cleanse Heracles of his guilt, the hero stole the tripod from Apollo's temple. Zeus prevented the threatened struggle between Apollo and Heracles by ordering the latter to sell himself as a slave to the Lydian queen Omphale*. During this period he took part in the Calydonian* hunt and the voyage of the Argonauts* and punished the Cercopes*. He also undertook a punitive expedition against Troy (see Ninth Labor above), slew Laomedon and gave Hesione in wedlock to his friend Telamon. He also performed warlike feats in Peloponnesus: his revenge on Augeas (see Sixth Labor above) and his expedition against King Neleus* of Pylos. Neleus and his sons, except Nestor*, who was absent, were slain. In Sparta Heracles fought against Hippocoön* and gave the throne to Tyndareus*. In Calydon he fell in love with Deianira*, who had another suitor, Achelous. There was a duel between the two rivals, in which Achelous assumed many different forms but lost. Then came the hero's encounter with the Centaur* Nessus*, who tried to abduct Deianira when Heracles asked for his help to cross a river. Nessus was killed but prepared a horrible revenge

(see below). Tradition, finally, records his aid to Aegimius* and his duel with Cycnus*. On a punitive expedition against Erytus he killed the latter and carried Iole off as booty. The jealous Deianira treated a garment with Nessus' blood, which the dying Centaur had told her would revive Heracles' love for her. The hero, who was about to offer sacrifice to Zeus, put the garment on; the poisonous salve then started to corrode his flesh. Seeing that his end was approaching, Heracles climbed Mt. Oeta* and made a funeral pyre which Philoctetes* lit, receiving Heracles' bow and arrow as reward. As the flames rose, Athena* bore the hero in a chariot with four horses to Olympus*, where Hebe* was given to him in marriage. Heracles was originally the hero of the Dorians but later of entire Greece. Egyptian and Eastern tales and nature myths refer to the figure of Heracles, who was finally revered as a paragon of the highest moral courage which overcomes all evil. He was venerated as a savior and benefactor of humanity, and also as an oracular deity. The Kynosarges gymnasium at Athens was dedicated to him as patron of such institutions. Many cities in Greece held a festival called the Herakleia in his honor. The Romans knew him as Hercules*.

Iconography. The oldest art sometimes shows Heracles as a child or youth, but usually as a powerfully built man with a broad chest, muscular neck, and short hair. In the oldest representations on black-figured Greek vases (c. 700 B.C.) he wears armor or a short chiton, and is armed with a sword or bow. After 650 B.C. he is usually shown as a powerful nude carrying a lion's skin and a club. The many sculptures of Heracles include statues by Myron and Lysippus. The latter work was the original on which the well-known Farnese Hercules at Rome was based; it shows a rather resigned-looking hero resting his left armpit on his club, which is draped in the lion's skin. The numerous scenes from his life are depicted countless times on vases, sarcophagi, reliefs, and frescoes, e.g. as a small child strangling the snakes (Casa dei

Vettii at Pompeii), in the service of Omphale (Casa di Sirico at Pompeii), or in the Garden of the Hesperides (Casa di Sacerdote Amando at Pompeii), etc. A bronze from Herculaneum shows him as a beardless youth struggling with the hind of Artemis. His twelve labors were the subject of the metopes of the temple of Hephaestus at Athens and that of Zeus as Olympia. Among the best-known of the very many representations of Heracles on vases are the scene with Busiris and that in which Heracles brings Cerberus to a terrified Eurystheus; both occur on the Caere hydria (middle of 6th century B.C.).

HERACLIDS. Descendants of Heracles*. Upon the latter's death his children were expelled from Peloponnesus and fled to Attica. The great-grandchildren of Heracles' eldest son Hyllus* succeeded in reconquering Peloponnesus and shared it among themselves. This event, known as the "return of the Heraclids," referred to what we call the Dorian migration and served to give a "historical" basis to Dorian power in Peloponnesus. Not only the Dorians but also the kings of Lydia and Macedonia considered themselves Heraclids.

HERCULES. The Latin name for Heracles*. The cult of Heracles spread to Rome via Sicily and southern Italy. The shrine known as Ara Maxima Herculis Victoris on the Forum Boarium was one of the oldest sanctuaries in the city. According to tradition it was founded by Hercules himself, or by Evander* (Virg. viii, 102, 172, 271; Liv. x, 23, 3). Rome also boasted a temple dedicated to Hercules Invictus and another to Hercules Pompeianus. Oil merchants venerated him as their patron under the title of Hercules Olivarius.

HERMAE. Fairly tall pillars, slightly tapered upward and topped by a head or bust of Hermes* in an archaic style. They were set up in streets and squares in Greek cities. The head of Heracles*, Athena,* Dionysus*, etc. was sometimes substituted for that of Hermes. Hermae were occasionally used by the Romans as boundary posts or as indoor ornaments.

In the latter case the Roman practice was to set up portraits of their ancestors as hermae in their homes, as can be seen in many patrician houses at Herculaneum and Pompeii.

HERMAPHRODITUS. Son of Hermes* and Aphrodite*. When, as a youth, he repulsed her love, the lake nymph Salmacis asked the gods to unite their bodies for all time. The youth was changed into a "hermaphrodite"—half man, half woman (Ov. iv, 288f.).

Iconography. On earlier reliefs associated with the cult of Dionysus, Hermaphroditus is sometimes shown as a Bacchante carrying a thyrsus. He is often seen as a recumbent nude in Hellenistic sculptures. The Romans sometimes represented him with a faun, engaged in love play. He also occurs on Pompeian frescoes, e.g. in the Casa di Olconio Rufo.

HERMES. Greek god of everything involving dexterity and cunning. He was the son of Zeus* and Maia*, born on Mt. Cyllene in Arcadia. While still a child he stole fifty head of cattle from Apollo*, who let him keep them in exchange for a lyre which Hermes had made from the shell of a tortoise. Hermes was the messenger of the gods, and as such he also led the shades of the dead to the underworld. He was the protector of men in dangerous undertakings, and god of commerce, in which skill and good judgment play a part. For the same reason he was also god of thieves and cheats. He was well disposed and brought blessings to humanity, and every stroke of good luck (= *hermaion*) was attributed to him. He gave wealth, eloquence, and persuasiveness. He was considered the inventor of many practical and pleasant things, such as the lyre, the flute, weights and measures, and sport. He attended to public safety on roads and squares, and protected the traveler. Statues of him were set up by the roadside everywhere (see HERMAE). The worship of Hermes spread from Arcadia all over Greece. Small domestic animals, incense, and honey were offered to him. The Romans identified him with Mercury*.

Iconography. In early art Hermes was

originally represented as a powerful man with a beard, and that is how he is shown on Greek vases, clad in a traveling cloak, a broad-brimmed, flat hat, and winged boots, and with a herald's rod (caduceus*) in his hand. Alternatively, he sometimes wears winged sandals and sometimes a winged hat. Later he became a beardless, lithe young man with an intelligent, friendly look. There is a famous statue by Praxiteles: Hermes carrying the infant Dionysus (4th century B.C.); equally well known is Hermes Resting, a bronze from Herculaneum, showing the god sitting on a rock nude, with only wings on his heels. As conductor of the souls of the dead, Hermes also frequently occurs on funerary monuments, e.g. the famous relief in the Villa Albani at Rome, representing the farewell of Orpheus and Eurydice in which Hermes is seen in traveling dress, with his hat hanging around his neck. Hermes is sometimes depicted as a shepherd, carrying a ram. When shown as the god of commerce, e.g. on the Hermes of the Capitol, he carries a moneybag.

HERMIONE. Daughter of Menelaus* and Helen*. Before the expedition against Troy she was betrothed to Orestes*, but her father later tried to marry her to Neoptolemus*. In the subsequent quarrel between the two suitors Neoptolemus is said to have been killed.

HERO. The beloved of Leander, a young man of Abydos. Each night Leander swam the Hellespont to visit Hero in Sestos on the other side. She used to light a lamp to guide him. One stormy night the lamp blew out and Leander was drowned. In despair Hero cast herself into the sea.
Iconography. The story of the two lovers is illustrated on the coins of the cities of Sestos and Abydos, on gems and in several frescoes at Pompeii (Casa dei Vettii). Leander is seen swimming toward a tower on which Hero stands with a lamp in her right hand.

HEROES. Greek name for persons of the past who by their great or brave deeds brought blessings to the people and the country and who therefore deserved divine honor. Although they were mortal, their extraordinary qualities raised them far above normal people. It was important to make sure of their good will, and they were therefore venerated with temples, altars, and sacrifices. Sometimes they were demigods and had divine fathers or mothers, as was the case with Heracles*. The Greeks generally revered as a hero the founder of their particular city.

HERSE. Daughter of Cecrops*; mother by Hermes* of Cephalus*.

HERSILIA. Wife of Romulus* and, like her husband, deified after his death (Ov. xiv, 829f.).

HERULUS or ERULUS. Son of the goddess Feronia*. He had three lives and was finally slain by Evander* (Virg. viii, 563).

HESIONE. Daughter of Laomedon*, king of Troy. To appease the anger of Poseidon*, Hesione was to be sacrificed to the monster the god had sent to Troy. Heracles* slew the monster and rescued Hesione (Ov. xi, 194f.).

HESPERIA [= land of the west]. 1. old name used by the Greeks for Italy and by the Romans for Hispania (Spain). 2. Nymph, daughter of the Trojan river god Cebren (see AESACUS).

HESPERIDES [= daughters of the west]. Daughters of Nyx* or Atlas*. In a garden somewhere in the west they and a dragon guarded the golden apples which Gaea* had given Hera* as a wedding present. Heracles* removed the apples, but they were brought back later by Athena*.

HESPERUS [Gr. Hesperos, Lat. *vesper* = evening]. Greek personification of evening or the evening star.

HESTIA. Greek goddess of the domestic hearth, daughter of Cronus* and Rhea*. Among ancient peoples the hearth fire had a sacred character; that was where sacrifices were offered and where suppliants and guests enjoyed protection and asylum. Hestia was offered a share of all the sacrifices made there. She was the protectress of the home. The Greek city-state had its hearth in the Prytaneum or city hall, where a fire was kept going in honor of Hestia. When colonies were founded, the emigrants took embers from this fire with them as a symbol of the link between the mother city and the new colony. Hestia was a virgin goddess, and her service was performed by virgins. The goddess appears to have had no temples of her own, but a special altar was reserved for her in many sanctuaries. At every solemn sacrifice the first libation was poured for her, and the first of the field crops and newborn livestock were offered to her. The Romans venerated her as Vesta*, whose worship was much more definite and important than that of the Greek Hestia.

Iconography. Hestia is represented in early art as a chaste, veiled matron in a long robe, with a scepter, torch, or lamp in her hand. Apart from many representations on Greek pottery (e.g. the François vase), statues of the goddess were sculptured by Phidias, Scopas, and others, but are not known to us.

HICETAON [Gr. Hiketaon]. Son of Laomedon* and brother of King Priam* of Troy* (Hom. Il. iii, 147).

HIPPOCOÖN [Gr. Hippokoön]. Son of Oebalus* and brother of Tyndareus*. He expelled his brother from Sparta and usurped the throne until he was slain by Heracles*.

HIPPOCRENE [Gr. Hippokrene = horse spring]. A spring on Helicon which gushed forth under the hoof of the horse Pegasus*. The water of the spring gave poetical inspiration.

HIPPODAMEA [Gr. Hippodameia]. 1. Wife of Pirithous*; the war between the Lapithae* and the Centaurs* started at her wedding. 2. Daughter of Oenomaus* and Asterope. She bore Atreus*, Thyestes*, and Alcathous* to Pelops*.

HIPPOLOCHUS [Gr. Hippolochos]. Son of Bellerophon* and father of Glaucus (3)*.

HIPPOLYTA. Queen of the Amazons*. She possessed a precious girdle, a gift from the god Ares*, and Heracles* was ordered by Eurystheus to fetch it. At first she was prepared to give it away, but Hera* incited her to war against Heracles. She was slain in the battle. Some say that

Heracles was assisted by Theseus*, and that Hippolyta, of her own free will, followed the latter to Athens and became mother of Hippolytus* by him.

HIPPOLYTUS [Gr. Hippolutos]. Son of Theseus* and Antiope*. His stepmother Phaedra* fell in love with him. When her love was not requited, she complained to Theseus that he had tried to seduce her. The enraged Theseus prayed to Poseidon* to punish him. While Hippolytus was driving along the seashore in his chariot, the god caused a monster to rise from the sea. The horses bolted, dragging their master after them till he died (Ov. xv, 497f.). He was restored to life by Asclepius* and thenceforth lived in a sacred wood near Aricia (Latium), where he was venerated under the name of Virbius (Virg. vii, 765f.).

HIPPOMEDON. One of the seven kings who marched against Thebes (see SEVEN AGAINST THEBES).

HIPPOMENES. Son of Megareus. He defeated the Arcadian princess Atalanta* in a race and married her. For offending Cybele* they were both later changed into lions (see ATALANTA).

HIPPOTES. Father or grandfather of Aeolus*.

HIPPOTHOÖN. Son of Poseidon* and Alope*. Upon Cercyon's* death he ruled over Eleusis.

HIPPOTHOUS [Gr. Hippothoös]. Son of Priam* (Hom. Il. xxiv, 251).

HOMERIC LAUGHTER. The hilarious laughter of the Olympian gods at the sight of the crippled god Hephaestus*. Described by Homer (Il. i, 599) as follows: "Then unrestrained laughter broke out among the glorious gods when they saw Hephaestus, officious and panting, hobble across the hall."

HORAE. Greek goddesses, daughters of Zeus* and Themis*. They represented the order of nature and the changing seasons and also protected the moral order. They are generally spoken of as three in number: Dike*, Eunomia* and Irene*. The Greeks knew only two Horae: Thallo (= blossoming) and Carpo (= ripeness). Their number later changed to four, to correspond to the four seasons. Homer (Il. v, 749f.) describes them as guardians of the gates of Olympus.

Iconography. They are represented as lightly clad young women, and, in older works, without attributes (e.g. François vase). Later they are often represented as the Seasons (e.g. on a familiar Roman relief in Paris), with the appropriate attributes—flowers, wreaths, fruits, basket, sickle, a shepherd's crooks, etc. There is also a famous fresco by Guido Reni in Rome.

HORATIUS COCLES. Legendary hero of Rome's earliest history. When the Etruscans were besieging Rome and had already occupied the Janiculum Hill, Cocles single-handedly defended the bridge leading to the city against overwhelming odds, while the Romans destroyed the bridge behind him. He then escaped by swimming the Tiber (Liv. ii, 10).

HORUS. Egyptian god, son of Isis* and Osiris*. As a sun god he was identified by the Greeks with Apollo*. He was also the god of queens. As the child of Isis and Osiris he was called Harpocrates.

Iconography. As a god of heaven Horus is represented in the form of a falcon. As Harpocrates he is shown as a child with his finger at his mouth.

HYACINTHUS [Gr. Huakinthos]. A beautiful youth, beloved of Apollo*. When the god accidentally killed him with a discus, he caused the flower of the same name to spring from Hyacinthus' blood (Ov. x, 162f.).

HYADES. A constellation that rises near the rainy season. Myths concerning many constellations were current, and the Hyades were regarded as women who had grieved for the death of their brother Hyas and been changed into stars.

HYAS. See HYADES.

HYDRA. Gigantic water serpent with seven or more heads, who ravaged the region of Lerna in Argolis and was killed by Heracles*. Virgil (vi, 576) situates the Hydra in the underworld as a guardian.

HYGEIA [Gr. Hugieia]. Greek goddess of health, daughter of Asclepius*. The goddess Athena was also venerated under the epithet of "Hygeia."

Iconography. Hygeia is shown as a young woman, standing clad in a chiton and holding in her right hand a bowl from which she feeds a snake. She is often seen on coins. In later times there is a painting of her by Rubens.

HYLAS. Friend of Heracles*. When he went ashore in Mysia to fetch water during the voyage of the Argonauts*, he was abducted by Naiads. Heracles spent so long searching for his missing friend that the Argonauts continued their voyage without him.

Iconography. Hylas is shown on several coins of Kios and on some frescoes at Pompeii, e.g. in the Casa del Efebo.

HYLLUS [Gr. Hullos]. Son of Heracles* and Deianira* and ancestor of the Heraclids*.

HYMEN or **HYMENAEUS** [Gr. Humen or Humenaios]. In Greece and Rome, the wedding song sung by the bride's attendants as the bride was led from her parents' home to her husband's. Also personified as the god of marriage, and in that capacity a member of Aphrodite's* company.

HYPERBOREANS. A mythical race supposed to live in the far north (*huperBoreas* = beyond the N. wind). They live in perpetual sunshine and perfect contentment. The race was dedicated to Apollo*, who enjoyed living in their midst.

HYPERION. One of the Titans*, father of Helius*, Selene*, and Eos*. In Homer also another name for Helius*.

HYPERMNESTRA or **HYPERMESTRA.** One of the fifty daughters of Danaus*, the only one who disobeyed her father by not murdering her husband, Lynceus*.

HYPNOS [Gr. = sleep]. Greek personification of sleep, considered to be a brother of Death (Thanatos*). Both deities lived in the underworld. The Romans called Hypnos Somnus*.

Iconography. Hypnos is represented as a nude young man with wings on his shoulders or temples; his attributes are a poppy stem and a horn. On funerary reliefs he is sometimes shown as a bearded old man, with wings on his shoulders and leaning on a staff or inverted torch. There is also a Hellenistic statue (3rd century B.C.) which represents Hypnos as a young man walking forward with his head and torso slightly bent. In his raised right hand he holds a horn from which he drops opium, and in his left hand a poppy stem.

HYPSIPYLE. Daughter of Thoas*, the king of Lemnos. During the stay of the Argonauts* on Lemnos she bore Jason* two sons, Thoas and Euneus. When the women of Lemnos slew all the men of the island in anger at their infidelity, Hypsipyle managed to save her father. When her act was discovered, she was compelled to flee, finally finding refuge at the court of King Lycurgus* in Nemea.

HYRIEUS. A Boeotian king who was robbed by Agamedes* and Trophonius* but took successful counter-measures (see AGAMEDES).

I

IACCHUS [Gr. Iakchos]. Title of Dionysus* and prob. also of Triptolemus*, used in the Eleusinian* mysteries. Possibly a personification of the Greek *iakchos*, a cry of joy or hymn in honor of Bacchus.

IAMBE. Daughter of Pan* and Echo*. Cheerful and full of high spirits, she succeeded in consoling Demeter* with her amusing remarks when the goddess was mourning the loss of her daughter. She became the first priestess of Demeter.

IAMUS [Gr. Iamos]. Mythological ancestor of the Iamides, a priestly family of Olympia.

IAPETUS [Gr. Iapetos]. One of the Titans* or Giants*, and father of Atlas*, Menoetius*, Prometheus*, and Epimetheus*.

IAPYX. 1. Son of Daedalus* or Lycaon* who settled in Iapygia (old name for Apulia). 2. In Virgil, the physician of Aeneas* (Virg. xii, 391, 402). *Iconography*. A fresco in the Casa del Sirico at Pompeii shows a warrior with a thigh wound being attended to by an older man; many believe this represents the wounded Aeneas and Iapyx.

IASIUS or IASION [Gr. Iasios]. Son of Zeus* and Electra (3)*. Was father by Demeter* of Plutus*. Enraged by his arrogance, Zeus slew him with a thunderbolt.

IASO. Greek goddess of healing, daughter of Asclepius*.

ICARIUS [Gr. Ikarios]. 1. Athenian who was taught the cultivation of the vine by Dionysus. When some shepherds, having drunk the wine, became intoxicated, they slew Icarius in the belief that he had poisoned them. The gods placed him among the stars as Boötes (= drover). 2. Son of Oebalus* and father of Penelope*. He promised the hand of his daughter to whoever beat him in a race. Odysseus* was the lucky man (Ov. vii, 183f.).

ICARUS [Gr. Ikaros]. Son of Daedalus*, with whom he was imprisoned in the Labyrinth on Crete. They escaped by means of wings attached to their shoulders with wax. Icarus flew too close to the sun, which melted the wax, and he fell into the sea, later named the Icarian Sea after him. According to legend he is buried on the small island of Icaria to the W. of Samos (Ov. viii, 183f.). *Iconography*. See DAEDALUS.

IDA. 1. Mountain range in Phrygia and Mysia near Troy (now Kaz Dagh, 5748 ft.). The Judgment of Paris is said to have been pronounced here (see PARIS). In Homer, the seat of Zeus during the siege of Troy (Hom. Il. viii, 47f., 438f.). 2. Highest mountain in Crete (8060 ft.), where, according to legend, Zeus* was born in a cave.

IDAEA [Gr. Idaia]. Greek nymph, mother by Scamander* of Troy's first king, Teucer (1)*.

IDAS. Son of Aphareus*. He abducted Marpessa, an Aetolian princess and granddaughter of Ares*. Apollo also sought her favor and Zeus allowed her to make her own choice. She chose Idas. After taking part in the Calydonian* hunt and the expedition of the Argonauts*, he died in a batle with the Dioscuri*.

IDMON. Soothsayer who accompanied the Argonauts* although he knew he would not survive the expedition. He died on the way in Bithynia, where the town of Heraclea (now Eregli) is said to have been founded around his grave.

IDOMENEUS. Grandson of Minos, king of Crete; leader of the Cretans in the Trojan War and famed for his heroic deeds in that struggle (Hom. Il. i, 145; ii, 405, 645f.). Returning home after the fall of Troy, he was caught in a storm. He then vowed to Poseidon that he would sacrifice the first living creature that he saw in his home country. Although this turned out to be his son, he kept his word. He thus incurred the wrath of the gods, who drove him from Crete and caused him to land in Calabria (Virg. iii, 400). He later went back to Crete and on his death was buried at Knossos*.

ILIA. See RHEA SILVIA.

ILIONE. Eldest daughter of Priam* and Hecuba* (Virg. i, 653).

ILITHYIA [Gr. Eileitia]. Old Greek goddess, patroness of midwives, later identified with Hera* or Artemis*.
Iconography. On an Attic amphora (c. 540 B.c.) Ilithyia, wearing a richly decorated peplos and with a wreath on her head, watches the birth of Athena and makes a gesture of amazement.

INACHUS [Gr. Inachos]. Son of Oceanus* and Tethys*, father of Io*. After the Flood (see DEUCALION) he made the Argolian plain inhabitable again and founded the city of Argos. He was also venerated as the god of the river of the same name.

INCUBUS. See FAUNUS.

INDIGETES. See DI INDIGETES.

INO. Daughter of Cadmus* and Harmonia*; second wife of Athamas*. She incurred the anger of Hera* (see ATHAMAS). Upon her death she was received by Poseidon* and venerated as a sea goddess under various names, e.g. Leucothea (Ov. i, 567f.) and Italia. According to Roman legend the Nereids* took her to the mouth of the Tiber to escape Hera's vengeance. At Rome she obtained Carmenta's protection and was worshiped under the name of Matuta*.

IO. Daughter of the Argive king Inachus*. Jealous of Zeus' passion for Io, Hera* changed her into a cow and set Argus* to watch her. When Argus was killed by Hermes* at Zeus' command, Hera tormented the cow with a gadfly until, after many wanderings, including a crossing of the Bosporus (= cow-ford), she arrived in Egypt, where she reassumed her original form and bore Epaphus* to Zeus (Ov. i, 567f.).
Iconography. She is usually represented as a woman with small horns at her temples. That is how she is shown on many Greek vases and on wall paintings,

the best-known of which is the fresco in the Casa di Livia on the Palatine at Rome: Io is seated before a rock and watched by an armed Argus while Hermes approaches stealthily from the other side. Correggio's painting, "Io and Jupiter," is renowned.

IOLAUS [Gr. Iolaos]. Son of Iphicles (1)* and friend of Heracles*, whom he helped to kill the Lernaean snake. He also built the funeral pyre for his dying friend (Ov. ix, 394f.).

IOLE. Daughter of Erytus*, king of Oechalia; she loved Heracles*.

ION. Legendary ancestor of the Ionians, son of Xuthus* and Creusa (3)* or of Apollo*. The Athenians chose him as their king.

IPHIANASSA. See IPHIGENIA.

IPHICLES [Gr. Iphikles]. 1. Son of Amphitryon* and Alcmene*, half-brother of Heracles*. He accompanied the hero on several expeditions. 2. Son of Thestius*, one of the Argonauts* and participant in the Calydonian* hunt, on which Meleager* killed him.

IPHIGENIA [Gr. Iphigeneia]. Daughter of the Mycenaean king Agamemnon* and Clytaemnestra*. When the Greek fleet lay at anchor off Aulis, ready to sail for Troy, Artemis* caused a calm and prevented the departure. Calchas* declared that the goddess would only be appeased if Agamemnon sacrificed his daughter. After much internal conflict Agamemnon summoned his daughter from Mycenae on the pretext of marrying her to Achilles*. When the sacrifice was about to take place, Artemis at the last moment put a hart in Iphigenia's place and took the girl to Tauris (now the Crimea), where she became a priestess in the temple of the goddess. One of her tasks was to sacrifice to Artemis any stranger who set foot in the land. One day Iphigenia's brother Orestes* and his friend Pylades* visited the temple at Tauris. A reunion between brother and sister followed, then Iphigenia fled with the two men to Greece. She is called Iphianassa in Homer (Hom. Il. ix, 145), who makes no mention of a sacrifice. The figure of Iphigenia inspired various writers in antiquity and later times: Euripides (*Iphigenia in Aulis, Iphigenia in Tauris*), Racine, Vondel, Goethe, Gluck.

Iconography. The sacrifice of Iphigenia is a favorite theme of wall paintings. She appears as a young woman with an expression of calm resignation, e.g. in the Casa del Poeta Tragico at Pompeii and on a sarcophagus relief at Rome. She is shown as a priesteess at Tauris together with Orestes and Pylades on various Pompeian frescoes, e.g. in the Casa del Citarista, the Casa di Marco Olconio, and the Casa di Pinario Ceriale. In later times there are paintings by Ricci, Pittoni, Bencovich, and Tiepolo.

IRENE [Gr. Eirene = peace]. Greek personification of peace; one of the Horae*.

Iconography. Irene is represented as a woman in flowing garments, with a scepter, horn of plenty, torch, or rhyton. The marble statue of Irene with Plutus (= wealth) in her arms, by Cephisodotus (c. 380 B.C.), is well known.

IRIS [= rainbow]. In Greek mythology, the rainbow that links heaven and earth, considered as the messenger of the gods. In particular she bore Hera's* messages to human beings (Virg. iv, 694).

Iconography. Artists show Iris as a young woman with wings on her shoulders and a rod or pitcher in her hand. She occurs chiefly on Greek vases.

ISIS. Egyptian goddess of fertility, wife of Osiris* and mother of Horus*. Her functions were many and varied: she gave fertility to the Nile valley, was the law giver, the goddess of birth and queen of the underworld, and in a general way safeguarded the welfare of the state and of man. Her importance greatly increased in Hellenistic times, and in imperial Roman times her cult was observed throughout the Empire, although the authorities had originally opposed it and forbidden its services. The religion of Isis was a mystery cult which, among other things, commemorated the grief of Isis as she sought her murdered husband Osiris, and her joy when he was restored to life. There is a striking resemblance between this and the myth of Cybele* and Attis*.

Iconography. Isis is represented as a woman with the head of a cow. In Greek and Roman art the goddess is shown as a woman with her hieroglyph, a throne, or a cow's horns with the sun's disk between them, on her head; she is also found with the child Horus on her lap. Her attributes are a serpent, an ear of corn, a lotus, a half-moon, and a sistrum (a metal rattle).

ISMENE. Daughter of Oedipus* and Jocasta*. In the tragedies of Sophocles she appears as Antigone's* weaker sister.

ISTHMIAN GAMES or ISTHMIA. Contests held by the Greeks every two years on the isthmus of Corinth. They were held in honor of Poseidon* and were organized by the Corinthians. After Corinth was destroyed, this task was taken over by the Sicyonians. There were contests in athletics, horse-racing, and later also poetry and music. The Isthmian games were considered less important than the Olympic* or Pythian* games. Legend ascribes their establishment to Poseidon and partly to Theseus*, the national hero of the Athenians. That was why Athenians in particular went in large numbers to the Isthmian games from early times on. Solon offered a reward of 100 drachmas for every Greek victory in the games. Apart from that the prize consisted of a palm branch and a wreath. Until imperial Roman times the Isthmia were held and well attended, so that announcements of general importance were often made during the games. On the site of the games there were a temple of Poseidon, a stadium for foot racing, a hippodrome for horse racing, a gymnasium for athletics, and a theater. Few traces of these are left.

ITALUS. Ancient Italian hero, son of Penelope* and Telegonus*. He was king of the Oenotrians or the Siculi, who were regarded as the oldest inhabitants of Italy.

ITHACA. One of the Ionian Isles off the east coast of Greece. According to tradition—supported by archaeological finds—the island described by Homer as the home of Odysseus*. The poet speaks of two mountains, four harbors, the nymphs' cave, and other details which tally closely

with actual features of Ithaca (Hom. Od.
i, 186; xiii, 96f., 103f., 351). Dörpfeld
(c. 1929) thought he could identify Leu-
kas with Homer's Ithaca, but the dis-
coveries have lessened the plausibility of
his theory.
ITYLUS [Gr. Itulos]. Son of Zethus*
and Aëdon*, killed by his mother by mistake.
ITYS. Son of Tereus* and Procne*. Wishing to revenge themselves on Tereus,
Procne and her sister Philomela* killed
Itys and served his flesh as food to Tereus
(Ov. vi, 636f.).

IULUS or **JULUS.** See Ascanius.
IXION. King of the Lapithae*, admitted
by Zeus* to the gods' table despite his
murder of his father-in-law. But when
Ixion tried to seduce Hera*, Zeus hurled
him into Tartarus*, where he was tied
to a fiery wheel in perpetual motion (Ov.
iv, 461). He was the father of Pirithous*,
and also of the Centaurs* by a cloud in
the form of Hera (Ov. xii, 504).
Iconography. The punishment of Ixion is
depicted on some Greek vases from southern Italy: naked and entwined by serpents,
he is shackled to a burning wheel.

J

JANUS. Old Italian god of doors and gates [*janua* = door] and of the course of the year. He was also the god of all beginnings: the first month (= *Januarius*) of the year and the first day of every month, the beginning of every hour and of man's life. He was said to have been king of Latium and to have founded the Janiculum citadel (Virg. viii, 357). His temple, or rather archway, was in the Forum at Rome. The army marched to battle through this arch, which was shut in time of peace. He was often honored together with Vesta*.
Iconography. Janus is shown with two faces, one bearded and the other originally not, to symbolize the sun and the moon; later both were bearded. He carries a key in his right hand. The double-headed Janus is first seen on coins; later coins (2nd century A.D.) show him with as many as four (Janus quadrifrons).

JASON. Son of Aeson*, the king of Iolcus. Aeson was driven from the throne by his brother Pelias*, and gave his son to the Centaur Chiron* to rear. When Jason was grown up he demanded that his father's and his own rights be recognized by Pelias. Pelias concurred on the condition that Jason fetch him the Golden Fleece* from Colchis (or Aea*). Jason undertook the expedition at the head of the Argonauts* and, after carrying out certain difficult conditions, obtained the Golden Fleece from King Aeëtes* (see ARGONAUTS). He was helped in this task by the king's sorceress daughter Medea*, who later followed Jason to Iolcus. Here they learned that Pelias had killed Aeson, whereupon Medea craftily contrived Pelias' death. Jason abdicated in favor of Acastus* and went with Medea to Corinth, where he fell in love with and married Creusa (1)*. Medea took a terrible revenge on Creusa; she revenged herself on Jason by killing the children she her-

self had borne him. Jason, in despair, committed suicide (Ov. vii, 1f.).
Iconography. A red-figured Attic vase painted in the style of Duris (c. 480 B.C.) shows Jason, under Athena's protection, emerging from the dragon's mouth; from a tree in the background hangs the Golden Fleece. A fresco at Pompeii (Casa degli Amorini Dorati) shows Jason with Pelias.

JOCASTA [Gr. Iokaste]. Wife of Laius* and mother of Oedipus*. She later married Oedipus, not knowing he was her son. When she learned the truth she hanged herself. Jocasta was thus a victim of the curse that hung over the Labdacides*.

JOVE. See JUPITER.

JUNO. Old Italian deity, protectress of women, marriage, and birth, and as such honored under many titles: Virginalis (= of the virgin), Matronalis (= of the married woman), Jugalis (= of marriage), Pronuba (= bridesmaid), Lucina (= of childbirth). As every man had a Genius*, so every woman had her Juno as protective spirit. Juno was later identified with the Greek Hera*, and wife of Jupiter*. Together with Jupiter and Minerva* she was venerated on the Capitol* (Juno Capitolina). The month of June was sacred to her, and as Juno Moneta (= warner?) she watched over the state finances and had a temple on the Arx, one of the two peaks of the Capitoline Hill. Her main festival occurred on March 1. Lambs and other livestock were sacrificed to her. In Virg. she is represented as a bitter enemy of the Trojans, being still resentful of the judgment of Paris*, a Trojan prince who failed to award her the beauty prize (Virg. i, 4, 51; ii, 612).
Iconography. See HERA.

JUPITER or JUPPITER, or JOVE. Chief god in the Roman pantheon, son of Saturn* and Rhea*, brother of Neptune* and Pluto*. Juno* was both his sister and his wife. He was the god of the bright sky (Ju-ppiter, from *dies* = radiant, *pater* = father), identical to the Greek Zeus*. The Romans venerated him chiefly as Optimus Maximus (= most good, most powerful) and as controlling the universe and the elements, whence his titles such as Tonitrualis (= god of thunder), Fulminator (= god of lightning), etc. He protected the laws and the state and revealed his will in miracles and oracles. He led the Roman armies to victory (title Victor) and stayed their flight (title Stator). His chief sanctuary was on the Capitol, and there he was venerated with Juno and Minerva* and the authorities made their official sacrifices to him. On their return from wars victorious generals also offered him thanks there. He was also the patron of the old Latin League (Latiaris = god of the Latins). As the Roman Empire expanded, various foreign gods were identified with him, e.g. Ammon* in Egypt. The many festivals held in his honor included the Ludi Romani and the Feriae Latinae. The eagle was his messenger and symbol, the thunderbolt his attribute.

Iconography. See ZEUS.

JUTURNA. Sister of Turnus* the king of the Rutulians. Jupiter* loved her and made her nymph of a spring in Latium. In Virgil she supports her brother in his fight against Aeneas* (Virg. xii, 141, 229, 469).

JUVENTAS [Lat. = youth]. Roman personification of youth (see HEBE).

K

KER [Gr. = death demon]. The ancient Greeks believed that every human being had his own *ker* or death demon (e.g. Hom. Il. xxii, 210); *ker* later took on the more general meaning of avenging goddess.

KESTOS [Gr. = girdle]. The embroidered girdle of Aphrodite*. It was the girdle that gave Aphrodite her irresistible fascination.

KLOTHES [Gr. = spinners]. Homeric name for the Fates or Moirai* (Hom. Od. vii, 197).

KOAS [Gr. = fleece]. Greak name for the Golden Fleece* (Herod. vii, 193).

KNOSSOS [Lat. Cnossus]. Important ancient city on the north coast of Crete, several miles south of the port of Heraklion; now famous for the excavations on the site of the "palace of Minos."

KORE [Gr. = maiden]. Another name for Persephone* in the mysteries of Demeter*.

KRONIA. The festival held annually by the Athenians in honor of Cronus* and the Golden Age*. The Roman counterpart of this celebration was the Saturnalia*.

KUBERNESIA [Gr. *kubernetes* = steersman]. Greek feast held at Athens in honor of Nausithous* and Phaeax, the steersman of the Athenian national hero Theseus*; according to legend it was instituted by Theseus personally after his successful expedition to Crete.

L

LABDACIDES. Descendants of Labdacus. They included Laius*, Oedipus*, Eteocles*, and Polynices*.

LABDACUS [Gr. Labdakos]. King of Thebes, grandfather of Oedipus*. His descendants, the Labdacides*, derive their name from him.

LABYRINTH. Legendary maze in Crete, laid out by Daedalus*. It was the abode of the Minotaur*. The complicated ground plan of the palace of Knossos excavated by Evans (from 1900 onward) suggests that it was this that gave rise to the legend of the Labyrinth. The origin of the word confirms this theory: *labrys* = double ax, the sacred symbol venerated in the palace of Knossos.

LACHESIS [= the allotter]. One of the Moirai*.

LACUS CURTIUS. A spot in the Forum Romanum, still recognizable by the paving (travertine, late Republican period), where there was a kind of well, reputed to be the hole into which the heroic Marcus Curtius* jumped, offering his life to save the city. Others say the hole was caused by lightning and consecrated and enclosed by consul Caius Curtius in 445 B.C.

LADON. The dragon who guarded the apples of the Hesperides*.

LAERTES. Aged father of Odysseus*. During his son's absence he led a retired and wretched life in the country. On Odysseus' return Laertes helped to take revenge on the suitors (Hom. Od. i, 189f.; xxiv, 498f.).

LAESTRYGONES. In Homer, man-eating giants. When Odysseus* landed among them, some of his companions fell victims to their cruelty (Hom. Od. x, 106, 119, 199).

LAIUS [Gr. Laios]. Son of Labdacus* and king of Thebes. Husband of Jocasta*, he was the father of Oedipus*. As an oracle foretold that his own son would slay him and later marry Jocasta, he gave Oedipus to a shepherd to kill. The prophecy was nevertheless fulfilled (see OEDIPUS).

LAMIA. In Greek mythology, a kind of vampire or werewolf who seized small children and sucked their blood.

LAMPETIA. Daughter of Helius*. Together with Phaëthusa* he guarded the cattle of Helius on the island of Thrinacia*. When Odysseus' companions slaughtered some of the cattle, she informed her father (Hom. Od. xii, 375).

LAMPUS [Gr. Lampos]. Son of Laomedon* (Hom. Il. iii, 147).

LAMUS [Gr. Lamos]. King of the Laestrygones*, legendary founder of Formiae (now Formia) in Latium (Ov. xiv, 233).

LAOCOÖN [Gr. Laokoön]. Trojan priest of Apollo* who tried in vain to prevent his fellow citizens from bringing the Wooden Horse* inside the walls of Troy. Athena, the patroness of the Greeks, then sent two gigantic serpents which coiled around Laocoön and his two sons and killed them (Virg. ii, 201f.).
Iconography. One of the most famous sculptures of antiquity is the Laocoön group in the Vatican Museum. In this work three sculptors of Rhodes—Agesander, Polydorus, and Athenodorus— represented Laocoön and his two sons being crushed by two serpents. It dates from the second half of the 1st century B.C. and displays the same baroque style as the great altar of Pergamum. It was found in a damaged condition in Rome in 1506, and the arms were wrongly restored. In September 1957 fragments of a Laocoön group were found in a cave near Sperlonga (Italy); these are thought to be the "original."

LAODAMUS. 1. Son of Eteocles* and king of Thebes. In the war of the Epi-

79

goni* he slew Aegialeus* but died later at the hands of Alcmaeon*. 2. Son of Antenor*. 3. Son of Alcinous*.

LAODAMIA [Gr. Laodameia]. 1. Daughter of Bellerophon*, mother of Sarpedon* by Zeus*. 2. Daughter of Acastus* and wife of Protesilaus*. When the latter was slain by Hector she had no further desire to live.

LAODICE [Gr. Laodike]. 1. Water nymph, mother of Niobe*. 2. Daughter of Priam* and Hecuba*.

LAOMEDON. Son of Ilus* and one of the founders of Troy. He built his city walls with the aid of Poseidon* and Apollo*, but when the work was completed he refused the gods their agreed hire. Poseidon then sent a sea monster which laid the country waste. When Laomedon was about to sacrifice his daughter Hesione to the monster in order to appease the god, Heracles* rescued the girl and slew the monster. Laomedon once more refused to pay the reward, and the hero destroyed Troy. Laomedon and all his sons except Podarces* lost their lives (Hom. Il. v, 640, 649; xx, 236f.; xxi, 442.; Ov. xi, 194f.).

LAOTHOË. Daughter of Altes*, mother by Priam* of Lycaon (2)* (Hom. Il. xxi, 85).

LAPITHAE. A warlike people of Thessaly, famous for their battle against the Centaurs* at the wedding of their king Pirithous*, when the Centaurs tried to abduct the bride. The battle ended in the complete annihilation of the Centaurs (Ov. xii, 210f.; Hom. Od. xxi, 297). *Iconography.* The battle between the Lapithae and Centaurs is a theme much treated in ancient art. A fresco from Pompeii (now in Naples Museum) shows the Centaurs being received by Pirithous, the king of the Lapithae. The battle is depicted on, *inter alia,* the well-known François vase, where the Lapithae fight with lances while the Centaurs defend themselves with branches and stones. Of the sculptures that represent the fight the best-known are that on the W. façade of the temple of Zeus at Olympia and the metopes of the Parthenon.

LARA or LARUNDA. Italic fountain nymph who betrayed the love affair between Jupiter* and Juturna*. By way of punishment Jupiter made her dumb. Legend says she was the mother of the Lares* compitales.

LARARIUM. Shrine for the Lares* in the Roman home. This was originally a kind of small cupboard near the domestic hearth, later a shallow rectangular or arched niche in the wall of the atrium or peristyle. This niche was often flanked by half-columns topped by a tympanum. The Genius* of the emperor is sometimes represented between two Lares on the back wall. This was a result of the reorganization of the Lares cult by the emperor Augustus, who decreed that the Genius of the emperor, in the form of a sacrificing figure clad in a toga, should be venerated between the two Lares. This regulation, which referred mainly to the public cult of the Lares compitales, was often also followed for private worship.

LARENTALIA. See ACCA LARENTIA.

LARES [sing. Lar]. Roman tutelary spirits of the home and fields. The cult of the Lares is probably derived from the worship of the departed head of the family, for he was supposed to bring blessings to the home and fertility to the fields. Together with the Penates (see DI PENATES), the Lares were venerated as guardians of the home (Lares familiares) in a small chapel or shrine, called the Lararium*, which was placed in the atrium or peristyle of the house. Sacrifice was offered to them at meals and on feast days. Where fields or roads met, honor was paid to the "Lares compitales" or "Lares viales" as protectors. Other titles under which the Lares were worshiped were "permarini" (guardians of the sea) and "rurales" (guardians of the land). But above all they were venerated as the Lares domestici, privati, patrii or familiares, i.e. protectors of the home. That cities, too, had their Lares is seen from the temple built to the city's Lares in Pompeii after the earthquake of A.D. 63 had caused great destruction there. The chapel of the Lares of the city of Rome was on the slopes of the Velia hill, between the Forum and the Palatine.

Iconography. The Lar was represented as a young man dancing, wearing shoes and a kilted tunic. In one upraised hand he carried a horn-shaped cup and in the other a dish. Lares mainly occur as bronze statuettes and on wall paintings. When Augustus reorganized the cult of the Lares, he decreed that the emperor's Genius, represented as a figure wearing a toga and offering sacrifice, should be venerated between two Lares. Similarly, the Genius of the dead head of the family can be seen between two Lares in many private Lararia, e.g. the magnificent one in the Casa dei Vettii at Pompeii.

LARUNDA. See LARA.

LARVAE. In Roman mythology, the mischievous spirits of dead family members who went round spreading terror and destruction. They were thus the opposite of the benevolent Lares*.

LATINUS. Son of Faunus* and the nymph Marica*. He was king of Laurentum* in Latium and the ancestor of the Latins. According to Roman legend, when Aeneas* landed in Latium with his fellow Trojan exiles, Latinus received him hospitably and gave him his daughter Lavinia* in marriage (Virg. vii, 45, 52, 69, 96, etc.).

LATIUM. Division of ancient Italy, S.E. of Rome, situated between the Tiber, the Apennines, and the Tyrrhenian Sea. Originally limited to the area around Mons Albanus (now Monte Cavo), it later expanded in a direction as far, approximately, as Caieta (now Gaeta). In Roman tradition Latium was the region where Aeneas settled, and in Virgil's *Aeneid* the area south of Rome is the scene of the battle between the invading Trojans and the resisting native population. See map, AENEAS IN LATIUM.

LATONA. See LETO.

LAURENTUM. Ancient Latin city on the coast to the S. of Rome, said by tradition to have been the capital of King Latinus*, father-in-law of Aeneas*. At present an excavation site about 6 miles S. of the Lido di Roma.

LAUSUS. In Virgil, son of the Etruscan king Mezentius*. He was slain by Aeneas* (Virg. vii, 649; x, 816).

LAVERNA. Roman goddess of lawful or unlawful gain, and hence also of thieves. Her altar in Rome was near the Porta Lavernalis.

LAVINIA. Daughter of Latinus* and Amata*. Although she was betrothed to Turnus*, the king of the Rutulians, she was given in marriage to Aeneas* by her father. She thus became one of the stakes in the grim battle between Turnus and Aeneas, which is described by Virgil in the last books of the *Aeneid* and ends in the death of Turnus. Aeneas married Lavinia and became father by her of Silvius* (Virg. vi, 763; xii, 937). The city of Lavinium founded by Aeneas in Latium was named after her (Virg. xii, 194).

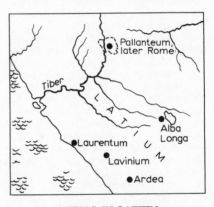

AENEAS IN LATIUM

Virgil describes how Aeneas and his Trojans, after long wanderings, encamped near the mouth of the Tiber (Virg. vii, 157). Rome did not yet exist, but on one of the famous seven hills, the Arcadian Evander had founded a settlement which he called Pallanteum (Virg. viii, 54). Laurentum was the capital of Latium and the residence of King Latinus, the future father-in-law of Aeneas (Virg. viii, 1). Ardea was the seat of Turnus, king of the Rutulians and leader of the resistance to the Trojans who invaded Latium (Virg. vii, 411). Lavinium was founded by Aeneas after he had established himself firmly in Latium; he named the city after his wife Lavinia (Virg. xii, 194). Alba Longa was founded by Aeneas' son Ascanius.

LEANDER [Gr. Leandros]. See HERO.

LEARCHUS [Gr. Learchos]. Son of Athamas* and Ino*. His father, stricken with madness, slew him (Ov. iv, 515).

LEDA. Daughter of Thestius*; wife of the Spartan king Tyndareus*. Zeus loved her for her extraordinary beauty and visited her in the form of a swan. She then laid two eggs; the Dioscuri* were hatched from one, Clytaemnestra* and Helen* from the second. According to others Polydeuces and Helen were hatched from one and Castor and Clytemnaestra from the second.

Iconography. Leda and the swan were a favorite subject for artists in antiquity and also in later times. The various Leda groups known to antiquity included one by Timotheus, one of the sculptors of the Mausoleum (4th century B.C.). In Hellenistic times there are also several representations of Leda clasping the swan to her bosom. The same scene occurs on gems, reliefs, and Pompeian wall paintings (e.g. in the Casa della Regina Margherita and the Casa dei Vettii). In later times there are works by Da Vinci, Michelangelo, Falconet and Vieira. Later paintings often show a secondary motif, the children resulting from this union.

LEMURES. Name applied by the Romans to the spirits of the dead. The good spirits were worshiped as household gods (see LARES); the evil spirits (see LARVAE) were appeased and warded off by strange ceremonies, called the Lemuria, held on May 9, 11, and 13. On those days the head of the household made an offering of black beans.

LEMURIA. See LEMURES.

LENAEA. Feast in honor of Dionysus, held in January at Athens at one of the temples of the god, the Lenaeum. A festive procession and a convivial public meal were among the main celebrations. The city of Athens bore the cost of the meat, and young wine was drunk and offered in sacrifice.

LERNA. A marsh to the S. of Argos in which a gigantic serpent dwelt. It was killed by Heracles*.

LETHE [Gr. = forgetfulness]. A river in the underworld of the Greeks and Ro-

mans. The shades of the dead drank from it and then forgot their earthly existence (Virg. vi, 714).

LETO or LATONA. Daughter of the Titan Coeus* and Phobe*, and mother by Zeus of the twins Apollo* and Artemis*. A Delian legend says that the jealous Hera pursued her all over the world, preventing her from finding a place where she could give birth to her children, until Zeus fastened the floating island of Delos* to the bottom. There she found peace at the foot of Mt. Cynthus, where she bore her children. Delos was sacred from then on. Leto took a terrible revenge on Niobe*, who mocked her for having so few children. There is also an account in Ovid of the punishment meted out to the Lycian peasants who so insolently drove Leto away (Ov. vi, 331f.).

Iconography. Leto was represented clothed in a chiton and wearing her hair long, often with her two children in her arms. Among ancient works of art is a famous Leto group by Praxiteles (4th century B.C.). She is also depicted on vases, coins, and reliefs, including the well-known altar from Pergamum (2nd century B.C.). The episode of the Lycian peasants is the subject of works in later times, e.g. by Bloemaert and Elsheimer.

LEUCIPPE [Gr. Leukippe]. 1. Greek nymph who was with Persephone* when the latter was abducted by Hades*.

LEUCIPPUS [Gr. Leukippos]. King of Messenia, father of Phobe and Hilaera. His daughters were abducted by the Dioscuri* (Ov. viii, 306).

LEUCOTHEA. See INO.

LEUCOTHOË [Gr. Leukothoë]. Daughter of the Persian king Orchamus. Apollo*, who was enamored of her, gained access to her by assuming her mother's form. Her irate father had her buried alive, but Apollo changed her into a fragrant plant (Ov. iv, 199f.).

LEVANA [Lat. *levare* = to lift]. Roman goddess who protected newborn children and promoted acknowledgment of such children by their fathers. It was the custom to place a newborn baby on the ground in front of the father, who acknowledged paternity by lifting the child.

LIBER. Old Italian deity of the procreation and productivity of nature. He was identified with Dionysus* at an early date and honored as the god of viniculture. His feast, Liberalia, was held on March 17.

LIBERA. Roman goddess who was identified with Proserpina*; daughter of Ceres* and sister of Liber*. She was also revered as Ariadne*, the wife of Dionysus*.

LIBERTAS [Lat. = freedom]. Roman personification of freedom, venerated as a goddess, e.g. in temples of the Aventine hill and the Forum at Rome (Liv. xxiv, 16, 19). She was originally the goddess of personal freedom and later of the freedom of the Roman Empire.
Iconography. She is represented on many Roman coins as a woman with a Phrygian cap, laurel wreath, and a lance.

LIBITINA. Old Italian goddess of corpses and burials. All the requisites for funerals were stored in her temple, where they could be hired, together with gravediggers and any other personnel needed for the funeral.

LIBYA. Daughter of Epaphus* and Memphis*. She was loved by Poseidon*. The known part of Africa was called Libya after her.

LICHAS. Heracles' attendant who brought him the robe that Deianira* had poisoned with the blood of Nessus*. He was slain by Heracles (Ov. ix, 211f.).

LICYMNIUS [Gr. Likumnios]. Son of Electryon*; he accompanied Heracles on many of his expeditions.

LINUS [Gr. Linos]. A handsome Greek youth who died an early death. According to one legend he was the son of Apollo* and the Muse Urania*, and was killed by his father in a contest. Legends of Argos make him the son of Apollo and Psamathe*, the daughter of a king of Argos; fearing her father's anger, Psamathe gave her son to shepherds to rear. When he grew up he was devoured by dogs. Psamathe was killed by her father, and Apollo, in his wrath, sent a plague to Argos which mainly affected children. In Theban legends Linus was a son of Apollo and the Muse Terpsichore*. He

was an excellent musician and taught Orpheus* and Heracles*; when he reprimanded the latter for his mistakes, Heracles killed him. The Greek word *linos* (= dirge) is associated with Linus.

LITYERSES. Son of the Phrygian king Midas*. He challenged each of his guests to a reaping contest and, when the visitor lost, cut off his head. He was slain by Heracles*.

LOCRUS [Gr. Lokros]. Son of Zeus and Maera (1)*.

LOTOPHAGI [= lotus eaters], legendary kindly people who lived on the fruit of the lotus. When Odysseus landed in their country on his wanderings, his crew ate the lotus fruit and forgot their homeland (Hom. Od. ix, 84f.).

LOXIAS. Name of Apollo* as the god of unfathomable oracular pronouncements.

LUA. Roman goddess to whom captured arms were dedicated by burning (Liv. viii, 1, 6.)

LUCIFER [Lat. = light bearer]. The morning star, mentioned in Ovid as the son of Aurora* and father of Ceyx* (Ov. xi, 271, 295, 346).

LUCRETIA. Wife of Tarquinius Collatinus, a cousin of the last king of Rome; Tarquinius Superbus. The latter's son Sextus seduced Lucretia, who later committed suicide. Collatinus and his friends then expelled the Tarquinian dynasty from Rome. For the city this meant the end of the monarchy and the beginning of the Republic.

LUNA [Lat. = moon]. Roman moon goddess, identified with the Greek Selene*. Daughter of Leto* and sister of Sol * (Helius*), later identified with Artemis*. Her temple at Rome stood on the Aventine hill (Liv. xl, 2, 2) and was destroyed in the great fire in Nero's reign.

LUPERCAL. See LUPERCUS.

LUPERCALIA. Very old Roman festival of purification, held on February 15 in honor of Lupercus*. His priests, the Luperci, sacrificed goats in the Lupercal cave at the foot of the Palatine. Then, clad only in the skins of the slaughtered animals, they walked through the streets of Rome, lashing everyone they met with thongs cut from goat skins. Childless wives in particular tried to get in their way, as it was thought that blows from the Luperci could cure barrenness, which was felt to be a great disgrace. Because of the licentiousness associated with the festival Augustus forbade all young men to take part in it.

LUPERCUS [Lat. = warding off wolves?]. Roman title for the Greek god Pan*, also identified with the old Italian deity Faunus*. A cave at the foot of the Palatine hill was called Lupercal and dedicated to him. The festival of the Lupercalia* in honor of Faunus-Pan was celebrated on February 15.

LYAEUS [Gr. Luaios = he who frees]. Epithet for Dionysus*-Bacchus as the god who freed people from cares.

LYCAON [Gr. Lukaon]. 1. A king of Arcadia who arrogantly tested the divinity of Zeus by serving him a dish made of his son's flesh. The irate god turned him into a wolf. (Gr. *lukos* = wolf) (Ov. i, 163f.); 2. Son of Priam* and Laothoë, taken prisoner by Achilles* and sold as a slave. He was later killed while escaping (Hom. Il. xxi, 35f.).

LYCOMEDES [Gr. Lukomedes]. King of the Dolopians on the island of Skyros. Achilles* spent some time at his court and became father of Neoptolemus* by his daughter Deidamea.

LYCON [Gr. Lukon]. Son of Hippocoön*, slain by Heracles.*

LYCORIAS [Gr. Lukorias]. A sea nymph, daughter of Nereus and Doris*.

LYCURGUS [Gr. Lukourgos]. 1. Son of Dryas*; king of the Edonians in Thrace.

He opposed the introduction of the Dionysiac cult into his country and ordered all grapevines to be cut down. Zeus punished him with blindness and an early death (Ov. iv, 22). 2. Son of Pheres* and king of Nemea.

LYCUS [Gr. Lukos]. 1. Son of Poseidon* and Celaeno*. 2. Son of Hyrieus*. Was hospitably received in Thebes, where he acted as guardian to Labdacus* and later Laius*. His brother Nycteus* on his deathbed instructed him to take vengeance on Epopeus*, who had abducted Nycteus' beautiful da..ghter Antiope*. Lycus did so and handed Antiope over to the caprices of his wife Dirce*. 3. Son of Pandion and legendary founder of Lycia in Asia Minor, which is named after him. 4. Son of Dascylus; king of Mysia. He entertained the Argonauts*, including Heracles*. In return, Heracles conquered for him the country of the Bebryces, which was afterwards called Heraclea.

LYNCEUS [Gr. Lugkeios]. 1. Son of Aegyptus*; husband of one of the daughters of Danaus*. He was the only husband to survive the treacherous attack of the Danaids. 2. One of the Argonauts, famed for his keen sight; he could see right through the earth (Ov. viii, 304).

LYNCUS [Gr. Lugkos = lynx]. King of the Scythians, who learned agriculture from Triptolemus*. He wished, however, to keep the glory of this accomplishment for himself and made an attempt on Triptolemus' life. Demeter* prevented further harm and changed Lyncus into a lynx (Ov. v, 650f.)

M

MACAR or MACAREUS [Gr. Makareus]. Son of Aeolus*. He cherished an incestuous love for his sister Canace*. 2. A companion of Odysseus* (Ov. xiv, 159). 3. One of the Heliadae*.

MACHAON. Son of Asclepius*. Together with his brother Podalirius* he led a detachment of Thessalians in the battle for Troy. Both brothers were famous as physicians (Hom. Il. ii, 732; iv, 193f.; xi, 506f.). Machaon was buried and venerated at Gerenia, an ancient city of Messenia.

MAENADS [Gr. Mainades = raving]. See BACCHANTES.

MAERA [Gr. Maira]. 1. Daughter of Proteus* and companion of the goddess Artemis*. Zeus* pursued her with his attentions until Artemis killed her out of jealousy. 2. Daughter of Atlas*.

MAGNA MATER [= Great Mother]. The title under which the goddess Cybele* (identified with Rhea*) was venerated in Lydia and Phrygia. The full title was Magna Mater deorum Idaea (= Great Mother of the Gods who is adored on Ida*). Her cult spread over Greece from the 6th to the 4th century B.C. and was introduced into Rome in 205 B.C. (see CYBELE).

MAIA. Arcadian nymph, daughter of Atlas* and Pleione*. She was loved by Zeus* and gave birth to the god Ares* in a cave on Mt. Cyllene*.

MAJESTA or MAIA. Italian goddess, wife of Vulcan*. Sometimes confused with the Greek Maia*. The month of May (Lat. Maius) was named after her.

MANES. See DI MANES.

MANTO. Daughter of Tiresias* of Thebes. On the capture of Thebes by the Epigoni* she was taken prisoner to Apollo* at Delphi, who ordered her to found an oracle of Apollo at Colophon (Asia Minor). There she became mother of the seer Mopsus*. According to another tradition she came to Italy and became mother by Tiberius of Ocnus*, the founder of Mantua (Virg. x, 199). Others say the city was named after another Manto who was the daughter of Heracles*. Mantus* is also associated with Mantua.

MANTUS. An Etruscan god of the underworld. His name is related to the Etruscan city of Mantua (see MANTO).

MARICA. Italian nymph, married to Faunus* and mother of Latinus* (Virg. vii, 47). A.t.o. she was the mother of Faunus. She had a sacred wood near Minturnae (now Minturno) on the border of Latium and Campania (Liv. xxvii, 37, 2) and there was also near Minturnae a lake named after her.

MARO or MARON. Companion and tutor of young Dionysus*, priest of Apollo* at Ismarus (Thrace).

MARS. Italian god of war, venerated along with Jupiter* and Quirinus* on the Capitoline (see CAPITOL) at Rome in very early times. C. 510 B.C. this Capitoline triad was replaced by Jupiter, Juno*, and Minerva*, but Mars still remained one of the gods most revered at Rome. The month of March was dedicated to him. He was invoked as a god of spring and reawakening nature, and the feast of Ambarvalia* (= procession round the fields), which was later dedicated to the fertility goddess Dea Dia*, was originally in honor of Mars. As time went on he increasingly took on the character of a war god. His priests were the Salii (= leapers), a very old college of priests who owed their name to the leaping procession which they led through Rome and at which the Carmen Saliare was sung, a song whose words had ceased to be understood even in antiquity. The drilling ground at the bend in the Tiber was called the Campus Martius (= field of Mars). There the censors offered the purificatory sacrifice (lustrum) in his honor.

As a god of war he was wholly identified with the Greek Ares*, and Venus* was therefore considered to be his wife. The "hastae Martiae" (spears of Mars) were kept in the Regia on the Forum at Rome. If these spears shook, it was an important omen of approaching war. A general about to go into battle had to set these spears in motion with the words, "Mars vigila" ("Mars, awake"). As Mars Gradivus (= marching into battle) he led Rome's armies to victory. He was said to be the father of Romulus* and Remus* (Virg. i, 274), and he was therefore considered the father of the entire Roman people. The wolf and the woodpecker were sacred to him, and his retinue included Fuga and Timor, the personifications of flight and fear. Of the temples dedicated to him at Rome the best-known is the temple of Mars Ultor (= avenger) on the Forum of Augustus.
Iconography. See ARES.

MARSYAS [Gr. Marsuas]. Greek satyr*, an extremely skilled player of the double flute which Athena had thrown away because playing it made her cheeks bulge and deformed her face. He was rash enough to challenge Apollo himself to a contest but lost. In punishment for his arrogance he was flayed alive. This was reputed to have happened in a cave near Celaenae in Phrygia, in which the river Marsyas rises (Ov. vi, 382f.).
Iconography. The scene in which Athena has thrown her flute away and Marsyas is about to recover it is depicted in a celebrated work by Myron (late 6th century B.C.). A bronze statuette of Marsyas in the British Museum is prob. a copy of Myron's sculpture. It shows Marsyas as a naked, bearded satyr, holding his right hand above his head and making a defensive gesture with his left. His torture is represented on, *inter alia*, a well-known Hellenistic statue: Marsyas is tied by his hands and feet to a tree, awaiting his punishment. Marsyas is also shown on reliefs, vases, and many coins.

MATRALIA. See MATUTA.

MATRONALIA. See JUNO.

MATUTA or MATER MATUTA. Ancient Roman deity, originally the goddess of dawn. She was later invoked by women in labor and was also venerated as the protectress of the sea and of harbors. The Romans sometimes identified her with Ino*-Leucothea. Her feast was the Matralia on June 11.

MAVORS. Old and poetic name for Mars* (Virg. viii, 630f.).

MEDEA [Gr. Medeia]. Daughter of King Aeëtes* of Colchis. She was a sorceress and helped Jason to gain possession of the Golden Fleece*. She then fled with him to Greece, where she married him. When Jason was besieging Iolcus, intending to punish Pelias*, she craftily contrived Pelias' death. Then she and Jason settled in Corinth, where Jason later repudiated her in favor of the Corinthian princess Creusa (1)*. In her rage Medea sent the bride a poisoned dress, which consumed her flesh, and then she killed her own children. She fled to Athens on a cart drawn by dragons (Ov. vii, 1f.). The cruel revenge that Medea took on Jason is the subject of the famous tragedy of Euripides, *Medea*. Some say Medea landed later in Persia, whose inhabitants were thenceforth called Medes.
Iconography. On Greek vases Medea is usually represented as an Eastern woman in a Phrygian cap, e.g. on an Attic amphora from Ruvo (late 5th century B.C.) and on an Apulian vase now at Munich. On wall paintings and Roman sarcophagi she wears Roman dress, e.g. on a fresco from Herculaneum. There is a well-known sarcophagus at Berlin on which the whole Medean tragedy is recorded: the handing of the poisoned wedding gift to Creusa, Creusa's death, Medea's murder of her children and her flight in the cart drawn by dragons. In more modern times there is Feuerbach's famous painting of Medea.

MEDON. 1. Son of Oileus* and stepbrother of Ajax*. When Philoctetes* was left behind on Lemnos, Medon led his troops at Troy. He died at the hands of Aeneas* (Hom. Il. ii, 727; xv, 332f.).
2. A herald in Ithaca who was kindly disposed toward Penelope* and was therefore spared when the suitors were slain (Hom. Od. iv, 677; xxii, 357f.).

MEDUSA. See GORGON.

MEGAERA [Gr. Megaira = the wrathful one]. One of the Erinyes* (Virg. xii, 846).

MEGALENSES, LUDI. See CYBELE.

MEGAPENTHES. Son of Meneclaus*. He is said to have driven his stepmother Helen* from Sparta after the death of his father (Hom. Od. xv, 100f.).

MEGAREUS. Boeotian king, father of Hippomenes*. He sacrificed himself in the campaign of the Seven* against Thebes, since Tiresias* had foretold that Thebes would conquer if one of the Sparti* voluntarily gave his life (Ov. x, 605).

MEGES. Son of Phyleus* and leader of the Epeans or Dulichians at the siege of Troy (Hom. Il. ii, 627; v, 69).

MELAMPUS [Gr. Melampous]. A Greek soothsayer who received the gift of prophecy as a child, when serpents licked his ears while he was asleep. From then on he likewise understood the language of animals. Also famous as a physician, he cured the women of Argos of a mental illness.

MELANIPPE. 1. Sister of Hippolyta*, the queen of the Amazons*. Heracles took her prisoner and did not let her go until she had procured the queen's girdle. 2. Mother or, a.t.o., mistress of Aeolus*. 3. One of the sisters of Meleager (see MELEAGRIDES).

MELANIPPUS. 1. Son of Astacus; he was one of the bravest defenders of Thebes when the city was attacked by the Seven* kings. He slew Tydeus* but died by the hand of Amphiaraus*. 2. One of the sons of Agrius*. 3. Son of Theseus* and Perigune*.

MELANTHIUS [Gr. Melanthios]. Son of Dolius, the goatherd of Odysseus*.

MELEAGER [Gr. Meleagros]. Son of Oeneus* and Althaea*, of Calydon in Aetolia. He took part in the expedition of the Argonauts* and was the chivalrous and brave leader of the hunt for the wild boar that was ravaging Calydon (see CALYDONIAN HUNT). It was Meleager who killed the boar with his spear and received its head and skin as his prize. As Atalanta* had been the first to wound the

beast, Meleager gave his prize to her. But the sons of King Thestius* of Pleuron, two brothers of his mother, were jealous and rebelled against this award, taking Atalanta's prize from her. Meleager slew the malcontents, an act which led to war between the Aetolians and the men of Pleuron. Meleager's mother, full of grief for the death of her two brothers, cursed Meleager, who then withdrew from the fight. The Aetolians consequently fared very badly and begged Meleager to come back into action at their side. His wife finally persuaded him to do so, and the fight was soon decided in favor of the Aetolians. Althaea's curse, however, caused one of Apollo's* arrows to wound Meleager mortally. Another version of this legend was known to antiquity, viz. that when Meleager was born the Moirai* foretold that the boy would not live longer than the brand which lay in the hearth would burn. Althaea hid the brand away and carefully preserved it. Later, when Meleager had slain his uncles, she threw the brand on the fire, thus bringing about her son's death (Ov. viii, 260f.). *Iconography.* Meleager is represented as a young, curly-haired hunter, naked or with a mantle loosely over his left arm. He is usually accompanied by a dog. Scopas' statue of him (4th cent. B.C.) was famous. Meleager appears not only individually on statues (Berlin, Vatican) but also on Greek vases and sarcophagi in the Calydonian hunt scene. Vases and mirrors sometimes depict the scene in which he presents the boar's pelt to Atalanta. In more modern times Meleager was a favorite subject for Rubens, Jordaens, and many others.

MELEAGRIDES. The sisters of Meleager*, who bewailed the death of their brother so unceasingly that Artemis* changed them into guinea fowl (Ov. viii, 534f.).

MELIA. Greek nymph, daughter of Oceanus*. She bore Phoroneus* and Aegialeus or Phegeus to Inachus*. A.t.o. she was the mother of Amycus* by Poseidon*.

MELIBOEA [Gr. Meliboia]. 1. Daughter of Oceanus* and mother of Lycaon*.

2. The only daughter of Niobe* to be spared by Artemis*. She was so terrified by the death of her brothers and sisters that she was afterwards called Chloris (= the pale one).

MELICERTES [Gr. Melikertes]. Son of Athama* and Ino*. When Ino in her madness jumped into the sea with her young son, they were both made sea deities. Melicertes was then called Palaemon by the Greeks and Portunus by the Romans. The Isthmian* Games were said to have been instituted in his honor. (Ov. iv, 522).
Iconography. His portrait occurs on Corinthian coins.

MELISSA or MELITTA. A nymph, daughter of the Cretan king Melisseus. She fed the infant Zeus* with goat's milk and taught man the use of honey (Gr. *melitta* = bee); Melissa was also a title applied to the priestesses of Demeter* and Artemis*.

MELISSEUS. Legendary king of Crete, father of Melissa*.

MELITE. In Roman legend, a sea nymph (Virg. v, 825).

MELITTA. See MELISSA.

MELPOMENE. Muse* of music and song and especially of tragedy.
Iconography. She is represented in a long garment, often veiled or with vine tendrils in her hair. In her hand she holds a tragic mask, and on her feet she wears cothurni (boots worn on the stage).

MEMNON. Son of Tithonus* and Eos*. With his Ethiopians he came to the aid of Troy, besieged by the Greeks, and performed many heroic deeds. He slew, among others, Antilochus*, son of Nestor*. When he finally died, slain by Achilles*, Zeus was so touched by Eos' tears that he granted him immortality. In Egypt, near Thebes, stand the "pillars of Memnon"; they are statues of Pharaoh Amenhotep III (c. 1400 B.C.), erected in his funerary temple. In 27 B.C. one of the huge statues was partly destroyed by an earthquake and, according to the testimony of many visitors to the monuments in antiquity, gave forth at sunrise a musical sound as of a breaking string. This statue was called the pillar of Memnon and the sound was construed as the greeting of the famous hero to his mother the Dawn. Ovid speaks of the birds of Memnon that rose from the ashes of his funeral pyre and fly each year to Troy (Ov. iii, 576f.).
Iconography. On Greek vases Eos is occasionally shown grieving by Memnon's body, e.g. on a black-figured Attic amphora (c. 530 B.C.) in the Vatican Museum.

MEN. In Phrygian mythology, a male personification of the moon.

MENDES. Egyptian god of productive nature, identified with Pan* by the Greeks.

MENELAUS [Gr. Menelaos]. Son of Atreus* and brother of Agamemnon*. He was married to Helen*, daughter of Zeus* or of Tyndareus*, from whom he inherited the throne of Sparta. When Helen was abducted by Paris*, he called upon the Greek kings to join him in an expedition to Troy. At the siege of Troy he performed many heroic feats, vanquishing Paris in a duel, fighting Aeneas* and Hector*, and defending the corpse of Patroclus*, etc. He was one of the men who entered Troy in the Wooden Horse*. After the fall of Troy, he returned with Helen to Sparta, which they reached only after many years' wandering. Their only child was Hermione* (Hom. Il. ii, 408f.; iii, 205f., 449f.; vii, 94f.; xvii, 237f.; Od. iv, 44f.; Virg. ii, 264; vi, 525).
Iconography. Menelaus occurs on many Greek vase paintings depicting the Trojan War. On an Attic kylix by Duris (c. 490 B.C.), now at Paris, he is seen dueling with Paris: he is putting the latter to flight and Aphrodite is staying Menelaus' hand. An oinochoë (c. 430 B.C.) in the Vatican Museum depicts the scene in which Menelaus recovers Helen at Troy: he has thrown his sword away and is running toward her. Also famous is the Hellenistic statue (second half of 3rd century B.C.) of Menelaus holding the body of Patroclus. Various copies of this sculpture exist, including the one at Rome, which has been known as the Pasquino group since the 16th century.

MENIPPE. Daughter of Orion*, sister of

Metioche. Both girls had received the gift of great beauty from Aphrodite* and equaled Athena* in their skill at women's crafts. When their native district, Aonia, at the foot of Helicon*, was struck by the plague, they voluntarily offered themselves in expiatory sacrifice to the gods of the underworld. They were placed among the stars.

MENOECUS or MENOECEUS [Gr. Menoikos or Menoikeus]. Father of Creon* and Jocasta*.

MENOETIUS [Gr. Menoitios]. 1. One of the four sons of Iapetus* and Clymene*. He was cast into Tartarus by Zeus*. 2. Son of Actor* and father of Patroclus* (Hom. Il. xi, 765f.). 3. Herdsman of Hades* on the island of Erythea*. He informed Geryon* of the theft of the latter's cattle by Heracles*.

MENTES. 1. Leader of the Cicones in the Trojan War (Hom. Il. xvii, 73). 2. Leader of the Taphians in the Trojan War. When the goddess Athena* visited Telemachus*, she assumed the form of Mentes (Hom. Od. i, 105f., 417f.).

MENTOR. Son of Alcimus of Ithaca* and friend of Odysseus*. On his departure for Troy, Odysseus entrusted him with the education of Telemachus* (hence the modern meaning of "mentor": someone who counsels others, especially in matters of study) and put him in charge of his home. Athena* sometimes assumed the form of Mentor when she visited Telemachus (Hom. Od. ii, 225f., 267f.).

MEPHITIS. Italian goddess, venerated especially in areas where there were volcanoes or solfataras. People prayed to her for protection against poisonous or otherwise harmful natural gases.

MERCURY [Lat. merx = merchandise]. Roman god of commerce and profit, and originally of the grain trade in particular. Later wholly identified with the Greek Hermes*. By 495 B.C. he had a temple in Rome, associated with a kind of exchange. Mercury's chief festival was celebrated on May 15.

Iconography. Mercury is represented in exactly the same way as Hermes, e.g. on a painting in a shop in the Via dell'

Abbondanza at Pompeii: Mercury is shown, clad in a loose cloak, with wings on his sandals and hat, coming out of a temple holding a purse filled with money in his right hand. He obviously awards profit to the industrious merchant.

MERCURY'S WAND. See CADUCEUS.

MERIONES. A Cretan, comrade in arms. and charioteer of Idomeneus* (Ov. xiii, 358f.).

MEROPE. 1. Daughter of Oceanus. 2. Daughter of Atlas* and wife of Sisyphus*. She was one of the Pleiades*, but her star gave the least light because she was ashamed of her marriage with a mortal. 3. Wife of Polybus* and foster mother of Oedipus*.

MEROPS. 1. King of Ethiopia, husband of Clymene*, who was the mother of Phaëthon* by Helius*. 2. King of Cos. After the death of his wife he was inconsolable, and Hera* placed him among the stars. 3. King of Percote on the Hellespont. His two sons fell at Troy, slain by Diomedes* (Hom. Il. ii, 831).

MESTRA. Daughter of the Thessalian king Erysichthon*. Her father, possessed by an insatiable hunger, sold her as a slave. But Poseidon* had given her the gift of being able to assume any form, so that she kept returning to her father, who each time sold her again.

METANIRA [Gr. Metaneira]. Wife of Celeus*, the king of Eleusis, and mother of Demophon*.

METIOCHE. One of the two daughters of Orion* (see MENIPPE).

METIS [Gr. = counsel]. Daughter of Oceanus* and Tethys*. She provided the emetic which caused Cronus* to vomit up the children he had swallowed. Zeus* married her, but fearing her child would surpass him in power and usurp his throne, he later swallowed her. Instead of a child being born to Metis, Pallas Athena* sprang from Zeus' head.

METOPES. Thin slabs, originally probably of clay, later of marble, which fill the spaces between the triglyphs in the Doric entablature. Metopes and triglyphs are parts of the Doric frieze; the metopes are usually decorated with scenes from mythology in relief. See diagram.

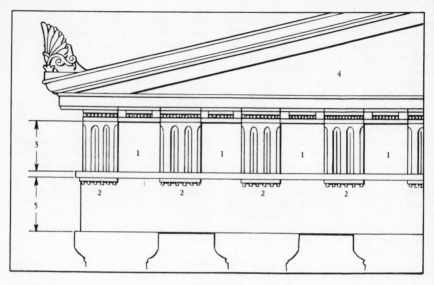

METOPES

Metopes (1) are typically located between the triglyphs (2) in the frieze (3), which is situated between tympanum (4) and architrave (5).

MEZENTIUS. King of the Etruscan city Caere (now Cerveteri) and father of Lausus*. He was deposed for his cruelty and fled to Turnus*, whom he helped in his resistance to the invading Trojans. He was slain by Aeneas in a battle (Virg. vii, 648; viii, 482; x, 786, 907).

MIDAS, son of Gordius and king of Phrygia. Dionysus* once passed through his country and his companion Silenus*, befuddled with wine, lost his way or was kidnapped. Midas received Silenus hospitably and took him back to Dionysus. The god allowed Midas to ask whatever he wished as a reward. Midas expressed the foolish wish that everything he touched should be changed into gold. The wish was granted, but as even the food and drink he tried to consume turned to gold, he would have died of hunger had Dionysus not taken back his favor. For this purpose Midas had to bathe in the river Pactolus, which has ever since carried gold in its sand (Ov. xi, 90f.). In a music contest between Apollo* and Pan*, Tmolus, who had been chosen as judge,

awarded the prize to Apollo. Only Midas disapproved of the decision, and Apollo punished him by changing his ears into those of an ass. Midas hid his deformity under his Phrygian cap, but it was observed by his barber. Unable to keep silent, the latter dug a hole in the ground and whispered his discovery into it: "Midas has ass's ears." Later, a reed grew in the hole and when the wind blew, the reed uttered the same words (Ov. xi, 146f.).

Iconography. The myth of King Midas is rarely illustrated in antiquity, although the music contest was a favorite subject of Renaissance and Baroque painters.

MINERVA. Roman goddess of arts and sciences and patroness of handicrafts. She was identified with the Greek goddess Athena*, and hence was also goddess of war. She was further venerated as goddess of healing (Minerva Medica). The Etruscans adopted the cult of Athena and worshiped her as Menerva or Minerva. It was they who introduced the goddess to Rome, where her main sanctuary was on the Capitol*. She, Juno*, and Jupiter* formed the Capitoline triad. There was also an important temple of Minerva on the Aventine hill and another in the Forum of Nerva. Her chief festival fell on March 19.

Iconography. In Roman art Minerva is entirely identified with Pallas Athena: she wears a helmet and carries the shield with the Gorgon's head and sometimes a lance in her hand. Her attributes are the owl and the serpent (see ATHENA).

MINOS. 1. Legendary king and lawgiver of Crete; son of Zeus* and Europa* and brother of Rhadamanthys*. Upon his death he was appointed judge in the underworld (Virg. vi, 432). 2. Grandson of the preceding and king of Crete. Pasiphaë* was his wife, Ariadne* and Androgeus* two of his children. With his fleet he dominated the surrounding seas and put Athens under tribute (see AEGEUS). He had the Labyrinth* laid out for the Minotaur* and compelled the Athenians to send seven youths and seven maidens as sacrifice for the monster every nine years. Theseus* put an end to this evil. Daedalus*, who had been held a prisoner on Crete by Minos, escaped and found asylum at Cocalus' * court in Sicily. When Minos came there in search of him, he was given a kindly reception by Cocalus but was later basely murdered by him. "Minos" is probably a title for the rulers of Crete in the golden age of the island (c. 1600-1400 B.C.). Cretan culture of that time is called Mycenaean, and excavations have confirmed the power and wealth of Crete in those days.

Iconography. Coins of Knossos* and Phaestus show Minos as a bearded man wearing a diadem. On Greek vases he is sometimes seen as a judge on a throne or together with Theseus and the Minotaur.

MINOTAUR [Gr. Minotauros = Minos' bull]. In Greek mythology, a monster with a man's body and a bull's head, born to Pasiphaë*, the wife of Minos*. Minos once asked Poseidon to make a bull rise from the sea and promised to sacrifice it to the god. When he failed to keep his word, Poseidon caused Pasiphaë to conceive an unnatural passion for the ani-

mal. The Minotaur was the fruit of this love, and it ravaged the island until Heracles* captured it. Minos then enclosed it in the Labyrinth* that Daedalus* had built for him. For a time the city of Athens was obliged to hand over youths and maidens for sacrifice to the Minotaur (see AEGEUS), until Theseus*, aided by Ariadne*, finally slew the monster (Ov. vii, 404f.).

Iconography. The Minotaur is shown as half man and half animal on gems from Crete and silver coins of Knossos. The conflict with Theseus is depicted on many vases, e.g. a bowl by Aeson (4th century B.C.), now in Madrid, on which the hero is pulling the Minotaur out of the labyrinth by the ear; the bull's head and human arms of the monster are visible.

MINTHE or MENTHE [Gr. = mint]. A nymph who was loved by Hades* but was changed into the plant of the same name by the jealous Persephone*.

MINYADES. The three daughters of Minyas*: Leucippe, Arsippe, and Alcathoë, who opposed the cult of Dionysus*. The god punished them with madness, and they roamed the world restlessly until Hermes* changed them into bats.

MINYAS [Gr. Minuas]. King of Orchomenos in Boeotia; mythical ancestor of the Minyans and hence also of the Argonauts*.

MISENUS. 1. Companion of Odysseus*. 2. Comrade in arms of Hector*, and later in the service of Aeneas*. He was trumpeter to Aeneas' fleet, challenged Triton*, and was drowned by him. Cape Misenum (now Miseno) on the Gulf of Naples is named after him (Virg. iii, 239; vi, 173, 212, 234).

MITHRA or MITHRAS. Ancient Aryan god of light, referred to in both the Veda of the Indians and the Persian Avesta, where he is the "helper" in the fight for what is good and just. As a light god he was early identified with the sun in India. Mithraism probably came to Europe in the first century B.C. and attained very great importance in the imperial era of Rome. The Roman legions spread the cult over the entire Empire and Mithraea (temples of Mithra) have been found in all its provinces. So far thirteen have been discovered in Rome. The Mithraic religion was a mystery cult that was modified in the course of time by syncretism. Mithraism was a dangerous opponent of Christianity as the latter spread. Its influence was at its peak about A.D. 300, when the victory of Constantine the Great at the Pons Milvius near Rome (A.D. 312) turned the tide. Christianity then became the state religion, and apart from small revivals, e.g. under Julian the Apostate, Mithraism ceased to have any further influence. The content of this mystic religion is still the object of study by scholars and is being made progressively clearer by excavations. The Dutch "digs" under the Church of S. Prisca at Rome, for instance, have clarified ideas about Mithraism in the last few years.

Iconography. On the numerous reliefs and paintings that have been found, particularly in Mithraic temples, Mithra is represented as a youthful, beardless figure, usually clad in a short tunic, with a fluttering mantle around his shoulders and a Phrygian cap on his head. He sometimes wears close-fitting trousers. The best known representations show him killing a bull: his left hand holds the bull by the neck, his right encloses a dagger and is raised ready for the mortal plunge. Mithra is occasionally shown as the sun god, with an aureole round his head.

MNEMOSYNE. Greek goddess of memory, daughter of Uranus* and mother of the Muses* by Zeus*.

MNESTHEUS. A Trojan, companion of Aeneas* on his wanderings (Virg. iv, 288; ix, 171, 781).

MOIRAE [Gr. moira = fate]. In Greek mythology, the goddesses of fate. Considered since the time of Hesiod (c. 700 B.C.) as three in number: Clotho, who spun the thread of life; Lachesis, who measured it; and Atropus, who cut it off. They were called Parcae by the Romans. Homer speaks of a single Moira, a mysterious power to which even the gods are subject and whose decisions are irrevocable. The Moirae were considered to be daughters of Zeus* and Themis* and were represented as ugly old women.

Iconography. In older art they appear without attributes (e.g. on the François vase); on later monuments Clotho (= spinner) is seen with a spinning wheel, Lachesis (= measurer) with a rod or a globe on which she writes, and Atropos (= who cannot be turned) with a scroll, a wax tablet, or a sundial.

MOLOSSUS [Gr. Molossos]. Son of Neoptolemus* and Andromache*.

MOMUS [Gr. Momos]. Greek god, son of Nyx, and personification of scorn and stinging criticism.

MOPSUS [Gr. Mopsos]. 1. Son of Ampyx and the nymph Chloris. He took part in the Calydonian hunt* and was the soothsayer of the Argonauts* (Ov. viii, 316). As a seer he was also regarded as a son of Apollo*. 2. Son of Rhacius or Apollo and Manto*, and a famous soothsayer. Together with Amphilochus* he founded the oracle of Apollo at Colophon (Asia Minor).

MORPHEUS. Greek god of dreams, son of Hypnos*. He appeared in human form to people in their dreams. His brothers appeared as animals, and Phantasus* as an inanimate object (Ov. xi, 635).

MUCIUS SCAEVOLA. Legendary hero of Rome's earliest history. When Porsinna and his Etruscans were besieging the city, Mucius forced his way into the enemy camp and tried to assassinate Porsinna. His attempt failed and he was arrested, but he spoke to Porsinna in such a courageous fashion that he made a great impression on the king. To reinforce his words and to show his contempt for pain and torture he put his right hand into a brazier and allowed it to burn off without displaying any sign of weakness. Struck by this bravery, Porsinna set him at liberty. By this action Mucius acquired the nickname of Scaevola (= left hand) (Liv. II, 12).

MURCIA. Roman goddess of uncertain origin. She was also called Murtia or Myrtea, the myrtle goddess, and was identified with Venus*. At Rome she had a temple in the valley between the Aventine and the Palatine (Liv. I, 33, 5).

MUSES. Greek goddesses of song, music, poetry, art, and the sciences; daughters of Zeus* and Mnemosyne* or of Uranus* and Gaea*. Their cult is said to have been brought to Helicon* by the Aloadae*. Their number varies in the course of time: at first only one was known, and later three were named: Melete, Mneme, and Aeode, probably fountain nymphs in Pieria (W. Thrace). They are, however, generally considered nine in number: Clio (history), Euterpe (music or lyric poetry), Thalia (comedy), Melpomene (tragedy), Terpsichore (dancing), Erato (lyric and love poetry), Polyhymnia (hymns), Urania (astronomy), and Calliope (epic poetry). The district of Boeotia around Helicon was ever the favorite abode of the Muses; it was there that they were most venerated, and the springs Aganippe* and Hippocrene* were sacred to them. Other places frequented by the Muses were Delphi* and Parnassus*, where Apollo* became their leader (Musagetes = leader of the Muses). But the Muses were also venerated elsewhere in Greece, especially in places that were rich in springs. The Romans identified the Camenae with the Muses.

Iconography. On the François vase the Muses are still shown without their attributes, except Calliope, who is playing the flute. Later on they are depicted with the objects that are typical for each of them: Calliope with a stylus; Clio likewise with a stylus and a scroll, often also with a case of books; Euterpe with a flute, Melpomene with a mask, a sword, and a crown of vine leaves; Terpsichore with a lyre and plectrum; Erato with a stringed instrument; Thalia with a comic mask and a wreath of ivy; Urania with a globe and a stylus. Polyhymnia is distinguishable only by her serious expression and her closely fitting clothes. Many ancient statuary groups of the Muses have been preserved, e.g. in the Vatican museum. Also well known are the relief from Mantinea showing the Muses standing (style of Praxiteles, 4th century B.C.) and the votive relief by Archelaus of Priene (c. 125 B.C.), which illustrates the apotheosis of Homer, and Mt. Helicon with the Muses.

MYGDON. 1. King of the Bebryces*, slain by Heracles*. 2. King of the Phrygians who fought alongside Priam* against the Amazons*.

MYLITTA. Assyrian goddess of fertility and procreation, identified with Aphrodite* by the Greeks.

MYRMIDONS [Gr. *murmex* = ant]. A race inhabiting the district of Phthia in Thessaly and ruled by Achilles*. They are said to have originated in Aegina. When a terrible plague depopulated the island, Zeus changed the ants into human beings at the request of Aeacus*. The legend says that this "ant race" migrated to Thessaly under the leadership of Peleus*, Aeacus' son (Ov. vii, 618f.).

MYRRHA [Gr. Murrha]. Daughter of Cinyras* and mother by him of Adonis*. She was changed into a myrtle (Ov. x, 298f.).

MYRTEA. See MURCIA.

MYRTILUS [Gr. Murtilos]. Son of Hermes*; charioteer of Oenomaus*. He betrayed his master to Pelops*, who had promised him half of Oenomaus' kingdom. Pelops did not keep his word but threw Myrtilus into the sea. Hermes placed him among the stars.

N

NAIADS [Lat. Naiades, Gr. Naides = swimmers]. In antiquity, river and fountain nymphs. They possessed the gift of prophecy and were regarded as patronesses of poetry and music. They also promoted fertility and the power of growth.

NAPAEAE [Gr. Napaiai]. In classical mythology, dell nymphs.

NARCISSUS [Gr. Narkissos]. Son of Cephissus* and Liriope; a youth of extraordinary beauty who spurned the love of the nymph Echo*. Aphrodite* punished him by causing him to fall in love with his own reflection in the water. Consumed by this insatiable love, he pined away and was changed into the flower of the same name (Ov. iii, 339f.).
Iconography. Narcissus is represented as a beautiful, naked youth with long hair. Sometimes he is a hunter wearing sandals and with a spear, club, or sword. There are several bronze statuettes; the best-known—at Naples—is, however, erroneously identified as Narcissus. The scene showing Narcissus at the spring is a favorite theme of Pompeian wall painting (e.g. in the Casa del Poeta Tragico, the Casa della Reina Margherita, the Casa di Olconio Rufo, the Casa di Loreio Tiburtino, etc.). In later times we have paintings by Poussin and Lemoyne. The nude figures on the famous Fountain of the Kneeling Boys by G. Minne at Ghent (Belgium) are also representations of Narcissus.

NAUPLIUS [Gr. Nauplios]. 1. Son of Poseidon* and Amymone*; legendary founder of Nauplia (now Navplion), a port on the Gulf of Argolis. 2. King of Euboea, father of Palamedes*. His son was put to death by the Greeks at Troy, and Nauplius took revenge by lighting fires on the cliffs of his island to misguide the Greeks returning from Troy; many ships were wrecked and sank. According to a tradition still surviving in Navplion, it was this Nauplius, not the son of Poseidon, who founded the city.

NAUSICAÄ [Gr. Nausikaa]. Daughter of Alcinous*, king of the Phaeacians*. When Odysseus* suffered shipwreck and was cast ashore on Scheria*, the island of the Phaeacians, he was noticed by Nausicaä, who received him courteously and hospitably and took him to her father's palace. She is one of the most fascinating characters in Homer's *Odyssey* (Hom. Od. vi, 17f.; vii, 2f., 290f.; viii, 457f.).
Iconography. The meeting of Odysseus and Nausicaä is depicted on various Greek vases, e.g. an Attic pyxis by Aeson (c. 425 B.C.), now at Boston. A bust of Nausicaä occurs on a coin of Mytilene.

NAUSINOUS [Gr. Nausinoos]. Son of Odysseus* and Calypso* or, a.t.o., of Odysseus and Circe*.

NAUSITHOUS [Gr. Nausithoos]. Son of Poseidon* and Periboea*. He was king of the Phaeacians* and settled his people on Scheria*, where they were later ruled by his son Alcinous* (Hom. Od. vii, 56f.).

NEAERA [Gr. Neaira]. Greek nymph, mother by Helius* of Lampetia* and Phaëthusa*.

NECTAR. The beverage of the Greek gods, which was prepared from honey and gave them immortality.

NEITH. Egyptian goddess of war and strife. She was particularly venerated at Sais in the Nile Delta and identified with Athena by the Greeks.
Iconography. The goddess is represented as a woman wearing the red crown of Lower Egypt. Her attribute is a shield bearing two crossed arrows.

NELEUS. Son of Poseidon* and Tyro*. He was the twin brother of Pelias*, and the two quarreled about the succession to the throne. Neleus then went to Messenia and became king of Pylos. When Heracles* visited him with a request to cleanse him from blood guilt, Neleus refused. Heracles then destroyed Pylos and killed Neleus with all his sons, except Nestor* (Ov. ii, 689).

NEMEA. A valley in Argolis, where the present town of Nemea stands. It was in this valley that Heracles* slew the Nemean lion. The valley was also the scene of the Nemean Games*.

NEMEAN GAMES or NEMEA. Games held every two years in the valley of Nemea* by the ancient Greeks in honor of Zeus*. The inhabitants of Argos organized the games, which were later held at Argos itself. The Nemea consisted of the usual athletic contests, horse racing, and poetry and music competitions, and were held near the sanctuary of Zeus. They became an important national festival c. 537 B.C.

NEMESIS [Gr. = distribution, indignation]. Greek goddess, personification of avenging justice, which gives to each according to his merits. Presumption, or conduct going beyond the bounds set to human nature, was particularly punished by Nemesis. The temple and statue of the goddess at Rhamnus, a village in the N. of Attica, were renowned in antiquity. She was therefore also called Rhamnusia.
Iconography. She is represented as a fully clothed female figure with a serious expression. In her left hand she holds an ell-wand, rein, lash, sword, or balance. Her attributes are like those of Fortuna: a wheel and a ship's rudder. Of the statue of Nemesis at Rhamnus, so famous in antiquity, nothing is known to us except that it was of colossal dimensions and was sculptured by Agoracritus of Paros, a pupil of Phidias.

NEOPTOLEMUS [Gr. Neoptolemos]. Son of Achilles* and Deidamea*. He was summoned to Troy on the death of his father because it had been foretold that the city could not be taken without his assistance. Upon his arrival at Troy the war started up again (*neos ptolemos* = new war), giving him his new name, for he was originally called Pyrrhus.

He was one of those who entered Troy in the Wooden Horse*. He killed Priam* and threw Astyanax* from the city walls. After the fall of Troy he was given Andromache* as his share of the spoils. Later he married Hermione* and gave Andromache in marriage to Helenus*. As Acastus* had seized Neoptolemus' country, Phthia, during his absence, Neoptolemus went to Epirus. When he finally returned to Phthia, he gave his territory in Epirus to Helenus. The revenging hand of Hermione's betrothed Orestes*, struck him down at Delphi. He was buried there and venerated as a hero by the population (Virg. ii, 469; iii, 328f.).
Iconography. On a bowl by the painter Duris (c. 480 B.C.) at Vienna, Odysseus is seen handing Achilles' armor to the young Neoptolemus, who receives his dead father's helmet and cuirass with a solemn expression.

NEPHELE. Greek nymph, Athamas'* first wife and mother of Phrixus* and Helle*. When she was repudiated by Athamas, she protected her children from the threats of their stepmother Ino*.

NEPTUNE. Roman god of water and the sea. Nothing is known with certainty of the origin and real function of Neptune. On his first appearance in the history of Rome he already possesses all the features of the Greek god Poseidon*. On the occasion of a religious festival in 399 B.C. he is mentioned along with Apollo, Latona, Diana, Hercules, and Mercury (Liv. v, 13, 6). Although his worship became better defined after he was identified with Poseidon, Neptune occupied a less elevated position in Roman eyes than Poseidon in the eyes of the seafaring Greek nation. Neptune's main function was as patron of racecourses and horses. His title as such was Neptunus Equester (*equus* = horse) and the only temple of Neptune at Rome was near the Circus Flaminius on the Campus Martius. His festival, the Neptunalia, was held on July 23; practically nothing is known of what it comprised.
Iconography. See POSEIDON.

NEREIDS. The fifty beautiful daughters of Nereus* and Doris*, friendly sea nymphs who rendered assistance to sailors.

Iconography. In ancient art the Nereids appear in the retinue of Poseidon, Amphitrite, Thetis, and other sea deities. On the older black-figured Greek vases they are fully clothed, e.g. a Corinthian hydria (6th century B.C.), now at Paris, which shows them in mourning garments standing around Achilles' deathbed. On later vase paintings they are seen nude or only partly clothed, riding on dolphins, sea horses, or other sea animals, and likewise on Roman frescoes and sarcophagi. A peculiar representation of flying Nereids is found on an Etruscan bronze cista from Palestrina. Finally, there is the celebrated Nereid monument from Xanthos (Lycia, Asia Minor), a marble funerary monument, part of which is now housed in the British Museum. It consists of a high podium topped by a small temple surrounded by pillars. Between the pillars stood statues of the Nereids. The podium and the façades of the temple are decorated with reliefs; two friezes adorn the podium and two the architrave and cella of the temple. The figures of the Nereids between the pillars are shown in rapid movement, with fluttering, transparent garments. The style is Attic-Ionic and dates the work to c. 400 B.C. In the Renaissance and Baroque periods the Nereid was a figure much used in the decoration of fountains and garden monuments.

NEREUS. Greek sea god, son of Pontus* and Gaea* and father of the Nereids*. He was a wise, genial old man who possessed the gift of prophecy and could assume any form. He made use of the latter faculty when Heracles* came and asked the way to the garden of the Hesperides*. The special domain of Nereus and his fifty daughters was the Aegean Sea, and many a sailor in distress there received from him.

NESSUS [Gr. Nessos]. A Centaur* who tried to assault Deianira*, the wife of Heracles*, when Heracles asked him to carry Deianira across the Euenus, a mountain stream in Aetolia. Heracles slew the Centaur, who, before he died, presented his spilled blood to Deianira, saying it was magical and could assure her of Heracles' love for all time. When Deianira later administered it to her husband, it caused him to die a terrible death (Ov. ix, 98f.).

Iconography. Greek vases show Nessus as a Centaur with a sword and club; later he is armed with a bow and arrow, e.g. on a Roman mosaic at Madrid. The well-known "Nessus amphora", an early Attic vase (c. 630 B.C.) bears paintings of the meeting between Heracles and Nessus in late geometrical style (New York Metropolitan Museum). A similar amphora of this period is at Athens. Nessus is frequently represented by Renaissance and Baroque painters, e.g. Pollaiuolo, Veronese, and da Bologna.

NESTOR. Son of Neleus* and Chloris* and king of Pylos. He was the only one spared when Heracles* slew his father and brothers. He fought the Centaurs*, took part in the Calydonian hunt* and was one of the Argonauts*. Though advanced in years, he took part in the Greek expedition against Troy, where, as the oldest of the Greek heroes, he excelled in wise advice, eloquence, and bravery (Hom. Il. i, 248f.; ii, 370f.; iv, 293f.; Od. iii, 157f., 343f., etc.).

NIKE [Gr. = victory]. Greek personification of victory. She was a divine being, but unlike the Roman Victoria*, she had no special temples or festivals. Nike appears mainly in the company of other deities, notably Zeus and Pallas Athena.

Iconography. Nike was represented as a winged female figure with garments flowing in the wind. In Hellenistic art particularly, she wears a laurel wreath or a palm branch, while in Greek vase painting she often carries a rod in her hand. The representations of Nike on Greek coins were numerous, but ancient sculpture also produced many Nikai. The archaic Nike of Delos (1st half of 6th century B.C.) is presented frontally, while the legs are placed sidewise to suggest movement. From the peak period of Greek art comes the famous Nike by

Paesonius (420 B.C.), a figure gliding downward with her dress billowing out behind her. The statue crowned a 36-ft. pillar erected at Olympia in 425 B.C. to commemorate the victory of the Messenians, and it is still at Olympia. A famous Hellenistic Nike is the Victory of Samothrace (Louvre, Paris). With outstretched wings she alights on the forecastle of a ship, her dress pressed tight against her body by the wind. The statue was sort of a fountain monument, erected at Samothrace c. 185 B.C. as a votive offering from the people of Rhodes. A magnificent Roman Nike or Victory is the bronze statue at Brescia: a winged figuré writing on a shield held in her left hand. Nike is also sculptured in terra cotta, both in statuettes and in reliefs; the temple of Athena Nike on the Acropolis at Athens was enclosed by a marble balustrade (late 5th century B.C.), the outside of which was decorated with reliefs showing Nikai offering sacrifices, leading a bull to the sacrifice, etc. Damaged parts of these magnificent reliefs are housed in Athens (Acropolis Museum). The best known part is a Nike fastening her sandal. For representations, see Victoria.

NIOBE. Daughter of Tantalus* and wife of King Amphion* of Thebes. Proud of her offspring—seven handsome sons and seven winsome daughters—she considered herself superior to Leto*, who had only two children: Apollo* and Artemis*. As a punishment for her arrogance, Apollo and Artemis killed all Niobe's children in one day. Overcome by grief the wretched mother was changed into a rock (Ov. vi, 146f.). Mt. Sipylus near Magnesia (Asia Minor) is still pointed out as the Rock of Niobe. This is because of the 26-ft.-high rock sculpture, representing a seated woman, hewn out of the mountain face there. According to Pausanias this is a likeness of Cybele*; others regard it as the weeping, petrified figure of Niobe of which Homer speaks (Il. xxiv, 614.).

Iconography. Niobe and her children falling to the arrows of Apollo and Artemis

NESTOR'S RESIDENCE AT PYLOS

In Homer, Pylos is the residence of the oldest of the Greek heroes, the wise Nestor (Hom. Od. iii, 4). Modern Pylos, also called Neocastro or Navarino, lies on the south side of Navarino Bay in historic surroundings (naval battle of Navarino). Near the town and on a hill stands the Venetian fort that guards the entrance to the magnificent bay, which is protected on the seaward side by the island of Sphacteria, familiar from the Peloponnesian War. Fourteen miles to the northwest of modern Pylos lies ancient Pylos with the hill of Eglianos. It was on this hill that a palace complex was discovered, with a surface area of about 6,000 sq. yds. The ruins date back to 1200 B.C., *i.e.*, the Mycenaean era. The palace contains a throne room with a circular fireplace in the middle, and there are clear indications that it was more than one story high. The objects found include a large quantity of pottery and a terra cotta bath. This is thought to be the palace where Telemachus came to inquire about his father, who had been away for so long (Hom. Od. iii), and where a bath was prepared for him by Nestor's daughter Polycasta (Hom. Od. iii, 464f.). A beehive tomb containing sarcophagi was discovered 90 yds. to the north of the palace; naturally enough, it is popularly known as Nestor's tomb.

are frequently depicted on Greek vases, e.g. the Niobid or Argonaut krater (Louvre, Paris), a red-figured vase of c. 435 B.C. On this vase curved lines are used for the first time to suggest undulating ground. Also familiar is the Niobe group of Florence (4th century B.C.), showing Niobe as an arrogant woman, holding her youngest daughter close to her, with grief in her eyes, yet awaiting fate with a regal bearing. Niobe's punishment is illustrated also on wall paintings and various sarcophagi.

NIOBIDS. The fourteen (in Homer twelve) children of Niobe* who paid with their lives for their mother's presumptuousness.

Iconography. See NIOBE.

NIREUS. Son of Charopus and Aglaea. After Achilles* he was the most handsome of the Greek heroes at Troy.

NISUS [Gr. Nisos]. 1. King of Megara and founder of Nisaea, the port of Megara. Once when Minos* marched against Megara and besieged Nisaea, Nisus' daughter Scylla* became enamored of him. She cut her father's purple hair, knowing full well that Nisus' life and the country's independence were linked to his possession of this miraculous hair. Megara fell and Nisus died but was changed into a sparrow hawk, while Scylla too became a bird of prey (Ov. viii, 35f.). 2. Son of Hyrtacus and companion of Aeneas*. He and Euryalus formed a classic friendship. Both were killed in a daring night attack on the camp of the Rutulians, Aeneas' enemies in Latium (Virg. v, 294; ix, 199, 234, 314, 326, 373, 431).

NIXI [Lat. *nitor* = to bear]. Roman deities who assisted women in labor (Ov. ix, 294).

NOTUS [Gr. Notos]. The south wind.

NOX [Lat. = night]. Roman personification of night (Virg. v, 721).

NUMITOR. King of Alba Longa*, father of Rhea Silvia*. He was deposed by his brother Amulius* but later restored by his grandsons Romulus* and Remus (Liv. i, 3; Virg. vi, 768).

NYCTEUS [Gr. Nukteus]. Son of Hyrieus* and king of Thebes. He was the brother of Lycus* and father of Antiope*.

NYMPHAEUM. See NYMPHS.

NYMPHS [Gr. *numphai,* Lat. *nymphae*]. Natural deities of a lower order in antiquity. Regarded as daughters of Zeus*, they animated nature in all its forms. Each spring, mountain, river, and tree had its own nymphs, who were called Oreads*, Dryads*, Hamadryads*, Nereids*, Naiads*, etc., depending on their abode. They were venerated in woods and caves and especially at springs, where nymphaea —buildings dedicated to nymphs—were erected, which developed into luxurious residences, especially in Roman times. There were several nymphaea in Imperial Rome, e.g. the ostentatious Septizonium on the Palatine Hill, which was built by Septimius Severus. There was a gigantic, pompous façade, 265 ft. long and three to seven stories high, profusely ornamented with columns, cornices, and fountains. Countless nymphaea are found even in Roman houses, e.g. at Pompeii, Herculaneum and Ostia. The sacred character of the originally rustic nymphaea gradually disappeared in Roman times.

NYX [Gr. Nux = night]. Greek personification of night.

Iconography. The goddess of night is represented as a young woman dressed in a star-spangled garment. On some Greek vases she is seen riding in a quadriga. Her attribute is an inverted torch.

O

OCALEA [Gr. Okaleia]. Wife of Abas (1)* and mother of Acrisius*.

OCEANIDS. Greek sea nymphs, daughters of Oceanus* and Tethys*.

OCEANUS [Gr. Okeanos]. Son of Uranus* and Gaea*; Greek personification of the vast ocean that was believed to surround the earth and from which the sun, moon, and stars rose daily. His wife was Tethys*, who bore him a countless number of sea gods and Oceanids*.

OCNUS [Gr. Oknos]. Son of Tiberis* and Manto*. Regarded as the founder of Mantua (Virg. x, 198). According to another tradition he was the son or brother of Auletes and founder of Felsina, later called Bononia (now Bologna).

OCYPETE [Gr. Okupete]. One of the Harpies*. ..

OCYRHOE [Gr. Okurhoë]. Daughter of Chiron* and the nymph Chariclo. For posing as a prophetess she was changed into a mare by Apollo* (Ov. 633f.).

ODYSSEUS [Lat. Ulysses or Ulixes]. Son of Laertes* and Anticlea* and king of Ithaca*. Penelope* was his wife and Telemachus* their son. When the Greek army was being assembled for the expedition to Troy and Odysseus was being compelled to take part, he tried to get out of it by feigning madness; he was found plowing his fields with an ox and an ass and sowing salt in the furrows. To test him Palamedes*, who had come to recruit him for the expedition, placed the infant Telemachus on the ground before the plow, and Odysseus betrayed himself when he avoided plowing over the boy. In the Trojan War he revealed himself a courageous warrior, but he particularly excelled in sagacity and eloquence. He was therefore much in demand as a negotiator or spy. Before the start of the Trojan War he was sent to Troy to demand Helen's return. He managed to trace Achilles* when the latter

had hidden himself on Skyros to avoid being sent to Troy, and the Wooden Horse was his astute idea. In Homer's *Iliad* he is an important figure: he led the Cephallenians in the struggle (iv, 329f.), and together with Diomedes* he undertook a reconnaissance visit to the Trojan camp (x). His main significance, however, is as the chief character in Homer's epic, the *Odyssey*, in which the poet describes Odysseus' adventures and wanderings after setting sail for home when Troy had been destroyed by the Greek army, and the difficulties that awaited him at home in Ithaca. He roamed about for ten years before reaching his homeland. In the course of his wanderings he came to the country of the Lotophagi*, and then to that of the Cyclopes*, where by a ruse he put the giant Polyphemus* out of action. From then on he was pursued by the wrath of Poseidon*. On a visit to Aeolus*, the god of the winds, he was given a sack in which the winds were shut up, so that he could be sure of a safe voyage, but his inquisitive crew opened the sack and the ensuing storm drove them off their course and back to the island of Aeolus. After an adventure among the Laestrygones* he came to the isle of the sorceress Circe*, who showed him the way to the underworld, where the spirit of Tiresias* revealed his future fortunes to him. After surviving the allurement of the Sirens* and the dangers of Scylla* and Charybdis*, he reached the island of Thrinacia*, where his companions stole some of the cattle of Helius*, the sun god. Zeus punished them for this by shattering all the ships with his thunderbolts. Only Odysseus himself survived this disaster, being washed ashore on Ogygia*, where the beautiful Calypso* kept him with her for several years in the hope of having him for her husband. Odysseus, however, was consumed with homesickness and longing for his wife and children, and finally, on the express order of the gods, Calypso let him go. Once again he was shipwrecked in a storm caused by Poseidon. Naked and destitute, he managed to swim to the coast of Scheria*, where he was found by the king's daughter, Nausicaä*. He was given a hospitable welcome and cared for at the court of her father, King Alcinous*, and the Phaeacians finally landed him safe and sound on Ithaca. There the hero learned how Penelope had for years been besieged by young noblemen suing for her hand and impoverishing her. The goddess Athena, ever his faithful protectress, gave him the form of an old beggar. In this disguise, which only his son Telemachus* and the faithful swineherd Eumaeus* penetrated, he managed to gain admission to his palace, where Penelope, in the depths of despair and under pressure from her insolent suitors, had meanwhile promised her hand to the one who could bend the bow of her husband, now presumed dead. When none of the suitors proved capable of doing so, Odysseus at the critical moment—still disguised as a beggar—asked to be allowed to try. To everyone's horror he easily bent the bow and proceeded to fire arrows at all the suitors in turn, assisted by Telemachus and some faithful friends. In short, Homer describes Odysseus as a resourceful hero who suffered many vicissitudes but by faithfully facing up to all dangers secured his life's ideal.

Iconography. On Greek pottery Odysseus is often represented in scenes from the *Odyssey,* e.g. gouging out Polyphemus' eye, clinging to the belly of the ram that brought him safely out of the Cyclops' cave, tied to the mast of his ship in order to resist the Sirens' song, slaying the suitors, etc. On later red-figured vases and also on reliefs and wall paintings Odysseus is shown in a short chiton and a pointed cap, both typical of travelers and seamen. The most famous of the wall paintings are the so-called Odyssey landscapes (c. 40 B.C.), now in the Vatican Museum at Rome.

ODYSSEY. Epic by Homer which describes Odysseus' adventures in 24 cantos. *Iconography.* The votive relief by Archelaus of Priene (2nd century B.C.), representing the apotheosis of Homer, includes a figure personifying the *Odyssey.*

OEAGER or **OEAGRUS** [Gr. Oiagros]. Thracian king, father of Orpheus*.

OEBALUS [Gr. Oibalos]. 1. King of Sparta, father of Tyndareus* and Hippocoön* and grandfather of Helen*. 2. Father of Icarius (2)* and grandfather of Penelope*.

OECLES or **OECLEUS** [Gr. Oikleus]. Father of Amphiaraus*. He helped Heracles* in his war against Laomedon*, but was killed while doing so.

OEDIPUS [Gr. Oidipous = swollen foot]. Son of Laius* and Jocasta*, the Theban king and queen. Shortly after Oedipus' birth his father gave him to a shepherd with orders to kill the child on Mt. Cithaeron*, because an oracle had warned Laius that he would die by the hand of his own son. Taking pity on the child, the shepherd gave him to another, who took him to Polybus*, the king of Corinth. There Oedipus grew up in ignorance of his origin until, during a drinking bout, someone called him an illegitimate son of Polybus. Perturbed, he set out for Delphi to consult the oracle on the matter. The Pythia gave him the dreadful answer that he would kill his father and marry his mother, and that his descendants would be a scourge of humanity. Oedipus set off sadly for Corinth but, nearing Thebes, he found the narrow road blocked by a man in a chariot. A dispute ensued, which led to blows, and Oedipus killed the stranger. When he arrived in Thebes, he found the city in mourning and consternation: King Laius had recently been attacked and killed and a cruel Sphinx* was ravaging the city and country around. The monster gave each passer-by a riddle and killed him if he could not solve it. Creon (1)*, regent of Thebes, promised the throne and the hand of Jocasta to the man who could slay the Sphinx. Oedipus answered the riddle correctly, and the Sphinx threw herself from the rock. Oedipus was duly given the throne of Thebes and married Jocasta, thus fulfilling the terrible prophecy. He had two sons, Eteocles* and Polynices*, and two daughters, Antigone (1)* and Ismene*. Years later, when the land was visited by a plague, the oracle stated that it was because Laius' murderer was still unpunished. Oedipus caused all possible investigations to be made and gradually came to a realization of the truth. In despair he gouged out his own eyes and Jocasta took her life. He abdicated, but when his now full-grown sons mocked him, he left Thebes to live as a blind wanderer, accompanied by the noble Antigone. He was received affectionately by Theseus* of Athens and passed his last years in Colonus, near that city. The oldest tradition calls the queen not Jocasta but Epicaste and says Oedipus continued to rule Thebes after her death and married Euryganea and later again Astymedusa. The tragic figure of Oedipus is the chief character in the famous tragedies of Sophocles: *Oedipus Rex* and *Oedipus at Colonus*.

Iconography. Oedipus is a theme not much encountered in the fine arts. Only the interrogation by the Sphinx is occasionally seen on Greek pottery. On a bowl (1st half of 5th century B.C.) in the Vatican Museum Oedipus in traveling dress is seen sitting on a rock; in a reflective attitude, with his knees crossed, he gazes up at the Sphinx perched aloft on a pillar.

OENEUS [Gr. Oineus]. King of Calydon* in Aetolia, husband of Althea* and father of Meleager*, etc. He was reputed to have introduced wine growing (*oinos =* wine) into Aetolia and to have received the first vine from Dioynsus* himself. The Calydonian hunt* took place in his time. The sons of his brother Agrius* deposed him for a while, but he was restored to power by Diomedes (1)*. He was later slain by his nephews while traveling in Peloponnesus. Diomedes buried him in Argos at the spot afterwards known as Oenoë.

OENOMAUS [Gr. Oinomaos]. Son of Ares*, king of Pisa in Elis and father of Hippodamea (2)*. Warned by an oracle that he would die if his beautiful daughter

married, he promised her hand to the man who could beat him at horse racing. He did so because Poseidon had given him horses that were invincibly fast, and he was thus certain he would never need to let his daughter marry. Pelops*, however, bribed Myrtilus*, Oenomaus' charioteer, who replaced the lynch-pins of the chariot with wax, so that Oenomaus was killed in the race. Pelops thus won Hippodamea by a criminal deed.

Iconography. Scenes from the race between Oenomaus and Pelops are depicted chiefly on Greek vases. The preparations for the race are also represented on the sculpture on the E. façade of the temple of Zeus at Olympia (1st half of 5th century B.C.), which shows Oenomaus as a proud, self-assured man with a beard and wearing a helmet.

OENONE [Gr. Oinone]. Phrygian nymph, daughter of the river god Cebren. Paris* carried her off to Mt. Ida, and she became his first wife. Their son was Corythus*. Deserted later by her husband, she died of grief. Some say that when Paris was mortally wounded in the battle for Troy, he appealed to her because she had the power to heal him. Angry at his infidelity, she refused, but after his death she threw herself upon his funeral pyre in despair.

OENOPION [Gr. Oinopion]. King of Chios; said to have introduced wine growing to the island.

OENOTRIA [= wine land]. Old name for the southeastern part of Italy: Bruttium and Lucania. Also used poetically for the whole of Italy (Virg. i, 532).

OENOTROPAE [Gr. Oinotropai = wine changers]. Epithet for the three daughters of King Anius* of Delos; they possessed the power to change anything into wine and, a.t.o., also into oil or corn.

OENOTRUS [Gr. Oinotros]. Son of Lycaon (1)*, who emigrated to Italy, the southern part of which was named Oenotria* after him.

OETA [Gr. Oite]. A barren mountain range in the S. of Thessaly, about 650 ft. high. It extends from the Pindus Mountains to Thermopylae.

OGYGIA. The fabled island of the

nymph Calypso* (Hom. Od. i, 50f.; v, 55f.).

OICLES. See OECLES.

OILEUS. King of Locris and one of the Argonauts*. He was the father of Ajax (1)* and Medon*.

OLENUS [Gr. Olenos]. An inhabitant of Mt. Ida whose wife boasted she was more beautiful than the goddesses. For punishment they were both changed into stone.

OLYMPIA. A place in Elis dedicated to Zeus and scene of the Olympic Games; it was a collection of temples, altars, sacred groves, and sports buildings. It was entirely situated in beautiful surroundings in the valley where the Alpheus and Cladeus meet, amidst leafy plane trees and olives. The temple precinct of Olympia belonged originally to the nearby town of Pisa, which was later destroyed by the Elians and never rebuilt.

OLYMPIAD. The period of four years between successive Olympic Games. The Greek system of reckoning time by Olympiads was introduced c. 300 B.C. The start of the first Olympiad was taken as 776 B.C., the year in which lists of Olympic conquerors were drawn up for the first time.

OLYMPIANS or OLYMPIC DEITIES. The chief deities of the Greeks; they were popularly supposed to dwell on Mt. Olympus*. They are Zeus, Hera, Apollo, Artemis, Athena, Hermes, Ares, Hephaestus, Demeter, Aphrodite, and Hesia.

OLYMPIC GAMES or OLYMPIA. The well-known games held every four years at Olympia* by the Greeks. They constituted by far the most important festival in ancient Greece and exceeded in esteem and significance the other great contests-cum-festivals such as the Pythian*, Isthmian*, and Nemean* games. The Olympic Games became so important for the Greeks that they dated their era from the year 776, when the list of Olympic victors was compiled for the first time (see OLYMPIAD). The character of the Olympic Games was that of a religious event in honor of Zeus*, later associated with the commemoration of Pelops*. Among the religious ceremonies the athletic contests occupied the chief place.

The origin of the games is unknown, and traditions are at variance about it. The poet Pindar says that Heracles held the first games around the tomb of Pelops, but Pelops himself was also considered to have been the founder of the games. It is certain that other deities were honored with games at Olympia before Zeus, namely Ilithyia*, Gaea*, and Hera*. Lycurgus, the "legislator of Sparta," and the Elean king Iphitus are credited with having given the games their final form. The games were held in August or September, and the immediate organization was in the hands of nine or more *Hellanodikai* from Elis, who were nominated anew for every Olympic festival. It was their task to see to it that no slave or unworthy person took part in the contests. Competitors had also to be properly trained. The *Hellanodikai* finally acted as judges at the contests and awarded the prizes. An oath they took beforehand obliged them to perform their duties conscientiously. Some time before the Olympic Games heralds were sent all over Greece exhorting men to compete and announcing a religious peace for the duration of the games. Competitors came from all the cities and small states of Hellas— even the Greeks in Asia Minor, southern Italy, and Sicily made their way to Olympia; it was a large-scale national occasion for Greece, for which all wars and quarrels between the numerous city-states were set aside. Interest in the games was especially great, and official delegations from the various cities attended. The games originally lasted one day, later five or six. How the opening ceremony went is not known with any accuracy; it was certainly religious in character and sacrifices were definitely offered, while participants also took an "Olympic oath." The actual contest consisted at first of only a race in the stadium. Gradually the program was extended by the inclusion of a race in full armor, the pentathlon or five-fold contest—consisting of the long jump, running, throwing the discus and javelin, and wrestling—and the *pankration,* a form of free wrestling in which everything was permitted except biting and injuring eyes, and finally chariot racing with two and four horses. Competitors had to defray their own expenses, so that chariot racing, for instance, was reserved for the wealthy. Competitors had to observe certain regulations, the breach of which was to some extent a sin in view of the religious character of the contests. If necessary, the judges could impose fines and debar athletes from competing. The prizes, a palm branch and a wreath from the sacred olive tree, were awarded on the last day of the games. The victor also had the right to erect his statue in the sacred domain of the Altis. The games were finally closed with a banquet for all the competitors in the Prytaneum. The honor accorded to the victor was great not only at the games themselves but also afterwards in his home town. He was given the place of honor at official events, poets sang his praises, and often a statue was erected for him. Famous lyric poets such as Pindar and Bacchylides composed magnificent odes to the glory of Olympic victors. The Olympic Games were abolished by Emperor Theodosius in A.D. 393. By that time the wholesome, sporting ideal and the religious background of the games had lost much of their meaning. 1500 years later, in 1896, the games were revived in the form we now know by the Frenchman, the Baron Pierre de Coubertin.

Iconography. The various forms of sport practised at the Olympic Games are represented in many Greek vase paintings.

OLYMPUS [Gr. Olumpos]. The highest mountain in Greece (9573 ft.), on the border between Macedonia and Thessaly. The summit is snow-covered for a large part of the year and the mountain is very barren and inaccessible. For the Greeks Olympus was the abode of Zeus* and the main gods (see OLYMPIANS). It was never climbed in antiquity, and seldom even later.

OMPHALE. Queen of Lydia, whom Heracles* served as a slave for some time as punishment for having killed Iphitus. Omphale made the tough hero so effeminate that he wore women's clothes and did women's work.

Iconography. In antique art representations of Omphale, usually accompanied by Heracles, occur on reliefs and frescoes. She is often seen decked in the lion's skin of Heracles and with his club in her hand, while the hero has feminine attributes, e.g. in wall paintings at Pompeii (Casa di Sirico, Casa di Marco Lucrezio).

OMPHALOS [= navel].. The oval stone monument in the temple of Apollo at Delphi*. It was venerated as the center of the earth.

OPALIA. See OPS.

OPECONSIVA. See OPS.

OPHION. One of the eldest Titans*, married to Eurynome*. He reigned before Cronus* but was dethroned by him and cast into Tartarus*.

OPIS. A nymph in Diana's* retinue (Virg. xi, 532).

OPS or OPALIA. Roman goddess of the earth as the source of fertility, and also of abundance and wealth in general. As a goddess of rich harvests she is closely associated with Consus*. She was regarded as the sister and wife of Saturn* and was also identified with Rhea-Cybele*. Her festival, the Opalia, was celebrated on December 9. In A.D. 7 a shrine was erected at Rome in honor of Ceres* and Ops as protectresses of the harvest. The temple stood on the Forum near that of Saturn, and a feast was held there on August 10. Another ceremony was performed on December 18 near the altar of Ops Consiva in the Regia on the Forum. Only the official priest and the Vestal virgins had access to this altar, and even these only on that date. Rome had other temples to the goddess, including one to Ops Opifera (= bringing help) and a very important temple on the Capitol* (Liv. xxxix, 22, 4). Caesar transferred the state treasury to this temple and placed it under the protection of Ops Capitolina.

ORACLE [Lat. *orare* = to pray]. Place where a deity or supernatural power makes his will or intention known to those who consult him. In antiquity several oracles were known, including those at Dodona* (Zeus), Delphi* (Apollo) and Epidaurus* (Asclepius). The place

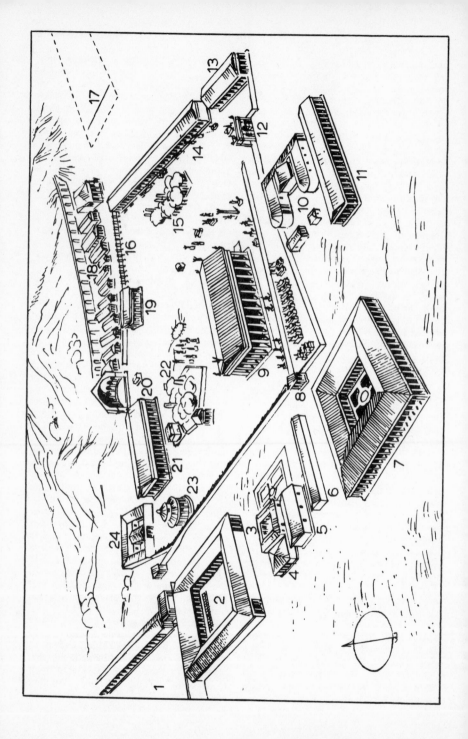

OLYMPIA AND THE SACRED TEMPLE DOMAIN OF ZEUS

Of the collection of temples and other buildings which is Olympia, the Altis—the partly walled-in temple domain at the foot of the Hill of Cronus—is the sacred center. Beyond the Altis lay secular buildings and grounds associated with the holding of the Olympic Games. After a French expedition had made important finds at Olympia in 1831, large-scale excavations were conducted in 1875-81 which were financed by the German government and which brought to light the most important remains of ancient Olympia. The work was resumed in the 1930s and later. In addition to the foundation and the remains of some buildings, important sculptures such as the Nike of Paeonius and the Hermes of Praxiteles, which now repose in the local museum, were also found. Ground plan:

1 - Gymnasium, space for athletic practice and the classic pentathlon. The ground is surrounded by colonnades and accommodations for the athletes.

2 - Palaestra for wrestlers and boxers.

3 - Theocoleon, a house for the priests.

4 - Heroum, a sanctuary of Pelops or his wife Hippodamea. Heracles, the legendary founder of the games, was probably also worshiped here.

5 - Megaron, a small square building once used as his assembly shop by the sculptor Phidias, whose works include the colossal statue of Zeus for the main temple. The Megaron has the same dimensions and lighting as the cella in the temple of Zeus. A Christian basilica was later built on its foundations.

6 - Long, narrow building, originally the workshop of Phidias.

7 - Leonidaeum, for the reception of guests. In Roman imperial times the main figures of Rome were accommodated here.

8 - Gateway to the Altis from Roman times; the most southerly of the two Altis walls adjoining this gateway is Roman; the more northerly one is the old Greek wall.

9 - Temple of Zeus in Doric style, dating from c. 465-450 B.C. It contained the celebrated gold-and-ivory statue of Zeus made by Phidias. The pediment sculptures, still partly preserved, represent (west façade) the battle between the Centaurs and Lapithae, with Apollo as umpire; (east

façade) preparations for the race between Pelops and Oenomaus. The statue of Zeus stood between the two heroes.

10 - Bouleuterium or council hall.

11 - Stoa or colonnade.

12 - Roman triumphal arch, giving access to the Altis. On the way to the Temple of Zeus stood the sacred olive tree whose branches were plucked to provide prizes for the winners in the Olympic Games.

13 - Stoa or colonnade.

14 - Porch of Echo.

15 - The great altar of Zeus.

16 - Pedestals for votive offerings.

17 - The stadium where the Olympic Games were held.

18 - Twelve treasuries founded by cities or states, including Sicyon, Epidamnus, Byzantium, Sybaris, Cyrene, Selinus, Metapontum, Megara, and Gela.

19 - Metroum or temple of the mother-goddess Rhea.

20 - Exedra of Herodes Atticus.

21 - Temple of Hera, dating from the late 7th century B.C.

22 - Pelopium, walled court, sanctuary, and tomb of Pelops, where a cult of the dead was practised.

23 - Philippeum, temple of Philip of Macedon.

24 - Prytaneum, building from which Olympia and the Games were administered.

where the deity manifested himself was sometimes a temple, sometimes a tree, spring, or sacred wood. In the latter three cases the applicant could try to obtain the divine pronouncement direct; at a temple oracle he had to apply to the priests. In the case of dream oracles such as that of Asclepius at Epidaurus, he obtained the god's revelations by "incubation," i.e. ritual sleep in the sanctuary, a practice that the Greeks borrowed from the Egyptians.

ORBONA [Lat. *orbus* = bereaved, childless]. Roman goddess, invoked by parents who had lost their children and wished to have more.

ORCUS. See HADES.

OREADS [Gr. Oreiades]. Mountain nymphs, the favorite companions of Artemis* (Virg. i, 500).

ORESTES. Son of Agamemnon* and Clytaemnestra*. When his father was murdered by Clytaemnestra and her lover, young Orestes was taken to the safety of his uncle Strophius' * home in Phocis by his sister Electra (1)*. Strophius' son Pylades* became his faithful friend. Eight years later Orestes returned to his native city, Mycenae, with Pylades and together they wreaked a bloody revenge on Clytaemnestra and Aegisthus*. For having murdered his mother Orestes was now pursued by the Erinyes* until the goddess Athena brought him before the Areopagus, the supreme court of her city, where the Erinyes accused him and Apollo* was his defender. The judges being equally divided about their verdict, Athena pronounced her deciding vote, which acquitted Orestes. Another legend says that Orestes, to be released from persecution, accepted the task of fetching the statue of Artemis from Tauris to Athens. He and Pylades, who went with him, met Orestes' sister Iphigenia* in Tauris and the three of them returned with the statue. Yet another tradition states that Orestes found peace of mind at Megalopolis in Arcadia, where there was a sanctuary of the Erinyes, who after Orestes' acquittal were called the Eumenides (= well-disposed). Returning to Mycenae, he slew the usurper Aletes* and married Hermione*. He died at an advanced age in Tegea. His bones were later transferred to Sparta. The subject of Orestes is treated by Aeschylus in his trilogy, the *Oresteia;* this consists of the tragedies *Agamemnon, Choëphori,* and *Eumenides,* which respectively deal with Agamemnon's return and death, Orestes' revenge, and his reconciliation with the Eumenides. Orestes also plays important roles in Sophocles' *Electra* and in Euripides' *Electra, Orestes,* and *Iphigenia in Tauris.*

Iconography. Orestes, usually accompanied by Pylades, is seen on numerous vases, reliefs, and sarcophagi. In particular, scenes from his life are reproduced on Roman frescoes, especially in houses at Pompeii: the Casa del Centenario, the Casa di M. Lucrezio, the Casa di Olconio Rufo, and the Casa del Pinario Ceriale.

ORION. A gigantic hunter from Boeotia who pursued the Pleiades until Zeus* in pity gave them a place among the stars. He was slain by Artemis* for an affront and placed as a constellation in the sky.

ORITHYIA [Gr. Oreithuia]. Daughter of King Erechtheus* of Athens. She was abducted by Boreas* and bore him Calais* and Zetes* (Ov. vi, 683).

Iconography. The abduction of Orithyia is shown on many Greek vases; on a red-figured Attic amphora, now at Munich, a winged Boreas can be seen in an upright attitude, lifting the astonished, gesticulating Orithyia from the ground.

ORMENUS [Gr. Ormenos]. Grandson of Aeolus* and legendary founder of Ormenium in Thessaly.

ORPHEUS. The famous Greek singer, son of the Muse Calliope* and Apollo* or Oeager*. Eurydice* was his wife. He sang so beautifully that he not only enchanted human beings but made wild animals gentle and even stirred inanimate nature. After Eurydice died he descended into the underworld and so moved Persephone*, the queen of Hades*, that Eurydice was permitted to follow him to the upper world provided he did not look around at her on the way there. Nevertheless he did look around, and when Eurydice was taken from him again he was inconsolable and roamed aimlessly and alone, without any interest in other women. Angered by his behavior, a band of Maenads* attacked him on the banks of the Hebrus (now the Maritsa) in Thrace and tore him to pieces. His limbs were tossed into the Hebrus and floated across the sea to Lesbos (Ov. xi, 1f.). Orpheus is said to have introduced mystery rites into Greece, and he inspired the followers of a secret doctrine: Orphism or the Orphic mysteries, which spread in Greece in the 6th century B.C.

Iconography. On the earlier monuments of antiquity Orpheus wears eastern dress and a Phrygian cap; later his clothing is more Greek, e.g. on the famous relief from the time of Phidias (c. 420 B.C.), the Roman copy of which is in Naples: Orpheus, with lyre in hand, takes a melancholy farewell of Eurydice as she is led back to the underworld by Hermes. An Attic red-figured krater (c. 440 B.C.) at Berlin shows Orpheus in Greek dress sitting on a rock, ecstatically playing his lyre. His head is wreathed in vine leaves. Thracian warriors in long cloaks listen, some with their eyes closed. Orpheus in the midst of wild beasts listening fascinated to him is one of the few pagan themes employed in early Christian art, e.g. in the Catacombs (symbol of Christ the Teacher and the Good Shepherd).

ORPHICA or ORPHIC HYMNS. A collection of eighty-seven poems of dogmatic-mystic content relating to the Orphic mystery cult. The later Greeks ascribed them to Orpheus*, but they only date back to the 2nd century A.D.

ORPHISM or ORPHIC MYSTERIES. Religious and philosophical movement that spread through Greece at the beginning of the 6th century B.C. It awoke particular interest among the followers of Pythagoras in southern Italy. The origins of Orphism lay in Thrace, the home of Orpheus*, who, according to tradition, spread knowledge of the mysteries of the Egyptians in Greece. Its doctrine contained a large admixture of elements of the Dionysiac cult, which was also native to Thrace. In the Orphic mysteries Dionysus* was the chief god, and he revealed himself in various forms. He was torn to pieces and devoured by the Titans*. Zeus* crushed the giants to death with his thunderbolts, and from their ashes there arose the new man, who had thus a divine spark in him but was also tainted with the evil of the Titans. The mysteries had the power to preserve man from the cruel punishment of sin after death. The adherents of Orphism were greatly interested in the hereafter, the idea of guilt and atonement, and the belief that man by his conduct in life could influence his fate after death. Another dogma of Orphism was reincarnation: the body was the prison of the soul, and purification was effected by a series of rebirths. The actual mysteries were not held in temples. There is complete ignorance about many aspects of the rites, although it is known that the *mystae* had to abstain from meat and beans before initiation. Sexual intercourse was also forbidden then. In antiquity there was a considerable literature on Orphism, but only a small proportion of it is now known to us. The so-called Orphica* are of later date.

ORPHNE. Nymph in the Greek underworld, married to Acheron*, god of the river of the same name (Ov. v, 539).

ORTHIA or ORTHOSIA. Title under which Artemis* was venerated, especially in Sparta.

ORTYGIA [= quail island]. Old name for the island of Delos*, and hence an epithet for the goddess Artemis*, who was born on Delos. Also the name of part of the city of Syracuse.

OSIRIS. Egyptian god of vegetation and of the water of the Nile. Various religious elements are perhaps fused together in the figure of Osiris. The Osiris myth is known to us only through the Greek writer Plutarch. Osiris was the son of the earth god Keb and the sky goddess Nuth. His brother Seth slew him, cut his body into fourteen pieces, and scattered them all over Egypt. His wife Isis reconstituted his body and restored him to new life. The resurrected Osiris was king of the land of the dead and had by Isis a son, Horus, who acted as his father's avenger.

Iconography. Osiris is represented as a mummy, with a whip and a crook in his hands.

OSSA. Mountain in the N.E. of Thessaly, in the coastal area called Magnesia. It is 6,405 ft. high and separated from Mt. Olympus* by the valley of the Tempe.

OTHUS. See OTUS.

OTRERA. Queen of the Amazons* and mother by Ares of Penthesilea* and Hippolyta*.

OTUS or OTHUS [Gr. Otos or Othos]. One of the Giants*, son of Aloëus* and brother of Ephialtes (see ALOADAE).

OXYLUS [Gr. Oxylos]. Son of Haemon*. When the Heraclids* conquered Peloponnesus, Oxylus was their guide and received Elis as his reward.

P

PAEAN [Gr. Paian, Paion or Paieon]. The physician of the gods (Hom. Il. v, 401, 899). Later also a title applied to various gods when besought to heal sickness, e.g. Apollo*, Asclepius*, etc. A paean is also a choral song in honor of Apollo, in which he is invoked or glorified as the Healer, and it finally took on the meaning of a song in praise of other gods besides Apollo.

PALAEMON [Gr. Palaimon]. The name under which Melicertes* was venerated by the Greeks after he became a sea god.

PALAMEDES. Son of Nauplius (2)* and Clymene (4)*, a wise and noble man. He was regarded as the inventor of the lighthouse, measures, the balance, dice, and some letters of the Greek alphabet. He took part in the expedition against Troy and was given the task of forcing the unwilling Odysseus* to take part. When Odysseus feigned madness, Palamedes was able to expose his deceit. From then on Odysseus plotted revenge, until he falsely accused Palamedes of treason during the siege of Troy. He caused a compromising letter, allegedly from Priam*, to be intercepted and secretly hid a sum of money in Palamedes' tent to make it look as if Palamedes had accepted a bribe from the enemy. The ruse succeeded, and Palamedes was unjustly executed (Virg. ii, 82; Ov. xiii, 56f.).

PALATINE HILL or MONS PALATINUS. The first of the seven hills of Rome to be settled. In antiquity the hill had three peaks: Palatium, Germalus, and Velia. In the course of time, by tilling, etc., the ground was leveled, so that its present surface area is greater than originally. The hill is about 170 ft. high and is the most characteristic of Rome by reason of its isolated position in the center of the city and close to the Tiber. The original settlement here was called Roma Quadrata. The hill is rich in history and is an ideal excavation site. There are traces of habitation from the 8th to the 6th century B.C. and remains of temples from various periods. Starting with Augustus, whose dwelling was on the hill (the "Casa di Livia"), the emperors built their palaces on the hill, much of which thus came to be covered by these edifices. They included the palaces of Tiberius, Caligula, Nero, and the Flavians, the last of which was extended by Septimus Severus. The word "palace" is derived from Palatium, the name of the hilltop.

PALES. Roman goddess of shepherds. She protected the flock and made it fertile (see PALILIA).

PALICI. Twin sons of Zeus* and the sea nymph Thalia or, a.t.o., of Vulcan*. They were chthonic demons who were venerated as heroes on the island of Sicily. They had a sanctuary in Palica, to the N.W. of Syracuse, near Aetna*, where a kind of trial by ordeal was practiced to test the trustworthiness of oaths (Virg. ix, 585; Ov. v, 406).

PALILIA or PARILIA. A national purification festival of Roman shepherds, held on April 21, the legendary foundation date of Rome. Straw fires were made through which the cattle were driven. The Palilia are usually associated with Pales*, goddess of shepherds, but a.t.o. the name Parilia = fertility festival (pario = to bear).

PALINURUS. The steersman of Aeneas*, who while sleeping fell into the sea off Lucania. He swam ashore but was killed by the Lucanians. A promontory near the scene of his death was named after him (now Palinuro) (Virg. iii, 202; v, 858; vi, 381).

PALLADIUM. Wooden statue of Pallas* Athena* which was worshiped on the citadel of Troy. As long as the statue stayed in the city Troy could not be taken. Diomedes* and Odysseus* stole it and took it to Greece (Virg. ii, 166). The Romans maintained that it was brought to Rome, and they kept a Palladium in the temple of Vesta* on the Forum Romanum.

PALLANTEUM. A city in Arcadia from which Evander's* ancestors came (Liv. i, 5). After his arrival in Italy Evander is said to have founded a city of the same name on the Palatine* (Virg. viii, 54), the site where Rome was to arise later.

PALLAS. 1. Epithet of the Greek goddess Athena* and the Roman Minerva*. 2. Son of Pandion* and brother of Aegeus*. 3. Son of Lycaon* and grandfather of Evander* (Virg. viii, 54). 4. Son of Evander; he was killed in the war against Turnus* (Virg. viii, 121, 466, 587; x, 487). 5. One of the Giants*.

PALLAS ATHENA. See ATHENA and PALLAS.

PAN. Greek god of woods, fields, and shepherds, whose chief abode was in Arcadia. He was the son of Hermes* and a nymph and had the horns, feet, and tail of a goat. Flocks, and also hunters, enjoyed his protection. He had invented the shepherd's flute and roamed among the mountains with it, delighting nymphs with his playing. He would sometimes suddenly appear to unsuspecting travelers and cause them to "panic." The Athenians were grateful to him for his aid in the battle of Marathon, where he had spread "panic" among the enemy. Pan was also a prophetic deity, and oracles were associated with some of his temples, e.g. at Akakesion in Arcadia. In the mountains there were numerous "caves of Pan" into which the cattle were herded in bad weather. Both the Athenian Acropolis* and Mt. Parnassus* near Delphi had a grotto of this kind. Some poets personify the Syrinx* or Pan-pipes as a nymph who was changed into a reed by Gaea to save her from Pan's attentions; Pan then made the reed into his shepherd's flute. The sacrifices offered to him consisted of small livestock and the products of the land: milk, unfermented wine,

and honey. The Romans identified him with the wood god Faunus (Ov. xi, 153; xiv, 515).

Iconography. Pan is represented as a satyr, with a crooked nose, a goat's horns and feet, a beard, tail, and hairy body, although earlier representations give him a more human appearance than later ones. A fresco from Pompeii, now in the Nat. Mus. at Naples, shows him as a beautiful naked youth with small horns, an olive wreath on his head, the syrinx in his right hand, and a staff in his left. He is seated on a rock and is about to play for three nymphs who are listening raptly. A goat with long, curled horns stands beside him. Another fresco from Herculaneum, also at Naples, shows him as a hirsute wood demon romping with a he-goat. Pan can also be seen on reliefs with Bacchic themes; his attribute there is the thyrsus*. Of the representations of Pan on Greek pottery the best-known is a painting showing Pan with a youth on an Attic red-figured krater (5th century B.C.), now at Boston. The artist is known by his work: the Pan painter.

PANACEA [Gr. Panakeia]. An herb capable of healing all diseases, sometimes personified in antiquity as a sister of Asclepius*.

PANATHENAEA [Gr. Panathenaia]. The principal festival in ancient Athens, held in honor of the patroness of the city, Athena*. The lesser Athenaea, which lasted two days, were celebrated every year. The greater, which lasted four days, were held every four years, always in the month we call August. The festival is said to have been instituted by Erichthonius*, was given its name by Theseus*, and had new festivities added to it by Pisistratus and Pericles. Apart from the usual athletic contests, recitations of Homer's poems were also held. The culminating point of the festival, however, was the solemn procession to the Acropolis, in which was carried a woolen peplos (= woman's robe) woven by the maidens of the city. The robe was then placed round the statue of Athena Polias (= of the city) in the Erechtheum. The procession was formed by the young men of Athens on horseback, girls carrying the implements of sacrifice, old men, warriors, the victors in the games, the envoys from other cities, and all the citizens. After the offering of the peplos there was a sacrificial ceremony. Also worthy of mention are the Panathenaeic amphorae of a special slender design which were filled with oil and presented as prizes to the winners of the games at the great Panathenaea; the vases date to c. 550-300 B.C. and are of the black-figured type. One side always shows Athena in armor between two columns, one crowned with a Nike* and the other with a cock. Scenes from the games are painted on the other side.

Iconography. The Panathenaean procession is represented in the frieze around the cella of the Parthenon. It is the work of Phidias and his school and is one of the greatest achievements of Greek sculpture. A part of the frieze is now in London, some slabs in the Acropolis Museum, and one in the Louvre; a part of the W. frieze, representing the magnificent procession of young Athenian horsemen, is still in position on the Parthenon. Among the figures still preserved in the frieze are a group of old men, jug carriers, men with animals for sacrifice, riders, and three gods of the two groups of six Olympians surveying the procession.

PANDAREUS [Gr. Pandareos]. Son of Merops (1)*. He was a friend of Tantalus*, at whose request he stole a bronze dog from a temple of Zeus in Crete. Some say he was turned to stone in punishment, others that he fled to Sicily. He was the father of Aedon*.

PANDARUS [Gr. Pandaros]. 1. Son of Lycaon and ally of the Trojans, famous as an archer. By wounding Menelaus* he broke the truce between the Greeks and the Trojans (Hom. Il. ii, 827; iv, 88; Virg. v, 496). 2. In Virgil, a brave Trojan, gatekeeper of Aeneas' * camp (Virg. ix, 722).

PANDION. 1. King of Athens, father of Erechtheus (2)*, Butes*, Procne*, and Philomela*. 2. Son of Cecrops*, who was expelled from Athens, fled to Megara, and ruled there. He was the father of Aegeus*.

PANDORA. A woman of rare beauty, made of earth and water by Hephaestus* at Zeus' * command and endowed by all the gods in turn with loveliness, cleverness, etc. (*pandora* = all gifts). Zeus, being angry with Prometheus* for having stolen fire, took revenge by presenting Pandora to Prometheus' brother Epimetheus*. Pandora brought with her a box full of plagues and disasters which she had been told to keep shut. Curiosity nevertheless made her open the box, and all evils spread over the earth. Thus the first woman was responsible for all mankind's suffering. Though Pandora tried to shut the box quickly, all that was left inside was Hope.

Iconography. The birth of Pandora is represented on a red-figured krater from Altamura, now in London.

PANDORUS [Gr. Pandoros]. Son of Erechtheus*.

PANDROSUS [Gr. Pandrosos]. One of the daughters of Cecrops*.

PANOPEA or PANOPE. One of the Nereids* (Virg. v, 240).

PANOPEUS. Son of Phocus*, companion of Amphitryon* and father of Epeus* (Hom. Il. xxiii, 665).

PARCAE. Roman goddesses of birth and fate. Originally two in number, they were later increased to three by analogy with the Moirae*, and were entirely identified with the Greek fate goddesses. The confusion is probably due to a mistaken etymology: *pario* (stem: *par-*) = to bring forth; *parior* (stem: *par-*) = to allot.

PARENTALIA. See DI MANES.

PARILIA. See PALILIA.

PARIS. Son of the Trojan royal couple Priam* and Hecuba*. Before his birth Hecuba dreamed she would bring a piece of burning wood into the world, and Aesacus* warned her that the child would be a danger to Troy. Paris was therefore exposed on Mt. Ida (1)*. Fed by a she-bear and found by a shepherd, he grew up among the shepherd people, who gave him the name of Alexander. When the goddesses Hera*, Aphrodite*, and Athena* quarreled for possession of the golden apple that Eris* had craftily thrown among the wedding guests of Peleus* and Thetis*, Paris was appointed judge by order of Zeus. Hera held out prospects of power and wealth to Paris, Athena promised him wisdom, and Aphrodite said she would give him the most beautiful woman in the world. Paris awarded the apple to Aphrodite, thus assuring the Trojans of the enmity of the other two goddesses, especially Hera. Although already married to Oenone*, he abducted the beautiful Helen*, wife of Menelaus*, whose guest he was. He took her to Troy and thus became the cause of the Trojan War. Homer and Virgil describe Paris as a weak character who did not play a heroic part during the siege of Troy. He sometimes acted bravely, but in general he was vacillating and spineless. Shortly before the fall of Troy he managed to wound Achilles* mortally but was himself slain soon afterwards by Philoctetes* (Hom. Il. iii, 16f., 424f.; xxii, 359; Virg. i, 27; iv, 215).

Iconography. Paris is represented as a handsome youth, usually wearing a Phrygian cap. Many monuments depict the Judgment of Paris, his abduction of Helen, and his slaying of Achilles. On an Ionic amphora (late 6th century B.C.) at Munich he is painted in a somewhat humoristic style, accompanied by his flock and sheep dog and being approached by Zeus, Zeus' messenger Hermes, and the three goddesses with a request for his judgment. An Attic vase by Hieron and Macron (490 B.C.) at Boston shows the abduction of Helen: Paris here is a warrior armed with helmet and spear, and he leads Helen by the hand while Eros, the god of love, hovers over them. Among the best-known Pompeian frescoes with representations of Paris is the Judgment of Paris in the Casa di Olconio Rufo.

PARNASSUS [Gr. Parnassos]. The renowned mountain (8,070 ft. high) in Phocis, sacred to Apollo*, Dionysus*,

and the Muses*. It has two peaks, often covered with snow, and is very rough and inhospitable. On the S. slope lies Delphi with the famous oracle at the foot of the Phaedriades rocks, from which temple desecrators used to be thrown. At an altitude of 4,660 ft. lies the Corycian cave, sacred to the nymphs or Muses. Among the springs at the foot of the mountain is the Castalia, whose holy water was used in the temple service. The sanctuary of Apollo lies at a height of about 1,870 ft. and to the S. of the temple yawns the deep chasm of the Plistus.

PARTHAON. King of Calydon, son of Agenor* and father of Oeneus*.

PARTHENON [Gr. Parthenos = virgin]. Large Doric temple at Athens, built on the Acropolis in honor of Athena Parthenos. Pericles, the leader of the Athenian state, commissioned the architect Ictinus and the sculptor Phidias to erect the temple. The work, which was part of the reconstruction of the Acropolis after its destruction by the Persians in 480 B.C., was done between 447 and 432. The temple, of Pentelic marble, has eight columns at each end and seventeen along each flank. The statue of the goddess, sculptured in gold and ivory by Phidias, stood in the eastern part; nothing of it has survived. The building was decorated with 92 metopes, 160 meters of frieze, and two pediments filled with figures, all executed by the best sculptors of the 5th century. Only a small proportion of the sculptures is still in position, most of them being in London (Brit. Mus.). The temple itself became a Christian church and then a mosque; in 1687 the building was largely destroyed during the siege by the Venetians.

PARTHENOPAEUS [Gr. Parthenopaios]. One of the Seven* kings who marched against Thebes (Virg. vi, 480).

PASIPHAE. Daughter of Helius* and Perseis*; wife of King Minos of Crete. She was the mother of Glaucus (4)*, Androgeus*, Phaedra*, and Ariadne*. When Minos had the misfortune to offend Poseidon*, the god filled Pasiphaë with a consuming passion for a bull, as a result of which she became mother of the Minotaur*.

Iconography. She is represented as a serious, thoughtful woman on various Pompeian frescoes, e.g. in the Casa dei Vettii and Casa della Caccia. Some Etruscan reliefs show her with the Minotaur and Minos.

PASITHEA. 1. One of the Graces or Charites*. 2. A Naiad*, married to Erechtheus (1)* and mother of Pandion* by him.

PATROCLUS [Gr. Patroklos]. Son of Menoetius (2)*, the king of Opus in Locris. After causing the death of his friend Clysonymus*, Patroclus, while still young, was taken to Peleus* by Menoetius. He grew up with Achilles and became his bosom friend. He later left for Troy with Achilles as his comrade in arms and was slain by Hector*. His death aroused in Achilles a burning desire for revenge, and the latter did not rest until he had killed Hector and honored Patroclus' memory with solemn funeral games. His heroic exploits at Troy are described in Book xvi of Homer's *Iliad,* called Patrokleia (Hom. Il. i, 307f.; xi, 765f., 729f.; xvi, 126f., 257f., 786f.).

Iconography. A painting famous in antiquity was that of the underworld by Polygnotus, which was placed in the Lesche of the Knidians at Delphi (c. 458-447 B.C.) and on which the figures of Achilles and Patroclus occurred. The work has been lost to us. Patroclus is also seen on many monuments as a warrior, usually with a beard: e.g. on the well-known Attic vase by Sosias (c. 500 B.C.) at Berlin, on which Achilles is shown bandaging Patroclus. The funeral games in honor of the slain Patroclus can be seen on a fragment of a vase by Sophilus (c. 570 B.C.): the crowd on the tribune are watching the races. Patroclus also occurs on mural paintings at Pompeii, e.g. together with Briseis and Achilles in the latter's tent (Casa degli Amorini Dorati). Another representation is found on the Pasquino group (2nd half of 3rd century B.C.) at Rome, which shows Menelaus with the body of Patroclus.

PEGASUS [Gr. Pegasos]. The winged horse born to Medusa and sired by Poseidon. When Perseus* beheaded Medusa, Pegasus sprang from her body and flew up to the heavens, where he became the steed of Zeus. A blow from Pegasus' hoof caused the spring Hippocrene* to gush forth on Helicon*. While the beast was drinking at the spring Pirene on the Acrocorinth or citadel of Corinth, he was captured by Bellerophon*. A.t.o. Pegasus was presented to him by the gods for the battle with the Chimaera. After slaying the monster Bellerophon tried to ascend to heaven on Pegasus, but the horse threw him and continued on its way. It was accorded a place among the stars.

Iconography. Pegasus occurs particularly on coins, being shown on many from Corinth, Corcyra, Syracuse, etc. A terra cotta relief from Melos shows Bellerophon on Pegasus battling against the Chimaera. On a Roman relief Bellerophon is seen watering Pegasus at a spring. The horse is usually represented with wings but occasionally without, e.g. on one of the metopes of temple C at Selinus (early 6th century B.C.), where Medusa, who is being beheaded by Perseus, holds Pegasus in her right arm.

PELASGUS [Gr. Pelasgos]. 1. Mythical ancestor of the Pelasgians, a people considered by Herodotus to be the oldest inhabitants of Greece. 2. King of Argos, who offered Danaus* and his daughters refuge from Aegyptus*.

PELEUS. Son of Aeacus* and Endeis*. He and his brother Telemon* killed their half-brother Phocus* while throwing the discus. They fled from Aegina, took part in the expedition of the Argonauts*, and finally arrived at the court of Eurytion, king of Phthia, who gave Peleus his daughter in marriage and part of his kingdom. Peleus participated in the Calydonian hunt*, where he had the misfortune to kill his father-in-law. He therefore left Phthia and went to Iolcus, where he took part in the funeral games instituted by Acastus* in honor of his father Pelias*. Astydamea*, wife of Acastus, slandered Peleus to her husband, who, in his anger, made an attempt on Peleus' life during a hunt on Mt. Pelion. The gods, however, came to Peleus' aid; he slew Acastus and his wife and obtained the beautiful Nereid Thetis* in marriage from the gods. She bore him Achilles*. It was at the marriage of Peleus and Thetis that the incident of Eris* and her apple of discord took place. Legend has it that upon Achilles' death Peleus was expelled from his kingdom of Phthia, temporarily restored by Neoptolemus*, but dethroned again for good by Orestes*. On his death he was placed in the underworld alongside Aeacus and Achilles, but others say he followed Thetis to the unfathomed depths of the sea and lived on there by her side (Ov. xi, 217f.).

Iconography. Peleus can be seen on many monuments as a hunter, naked or wearing a cloak, and with a sword, club, or hunting knife in his hand. His marriage to Thetis is among the subjects painted on the famous François vase (c. 570 B.C.) at Florence; is also the subject of several Renaissance and Baroque paintings.

PELIAS. Son of Poseidon* and Tyro*, and king of Iolcus in Thessaly. He had gained power illegally by dethroning his stepbrother Aeson*. Later, however, Aeson's son Jason* asserted his rights and claimed the throne of Iolcus from his uncle. Pelias promised to abdicate if Jason brought him back the Golden Fleece* from Colchis. Jason performed the task (see ARGONAUTS), but Pelias refused to keep his promise. Medea*, Jason's wife, succeeded by a ruse in getting Pelias out of the way. She convinced his daughters that she possessed the power to rejuvenate their father: they had to cut him into pieces and boil these with all kinds of herbs, whereupon Medea would bring him forth rejuvenated from the pot. At the critical moment, however, she refused to help. (Ov. vii, 297f.).

Iconography. On the now lost painting of the underworld by Ignotus at Delphi, Pelias was shown seated on his throne. That is how he is also seen on several Greek vase paintings. Sometimes, too, he

leans on a staff while Medea helps his daughters to prepare her revenge.

PELION. Inhospitable and wooded mountain (5,308 ft. high) to the N. of the Gulf of Volos in the E. of Thessaly. In their attempt to storm heaven the Giants* piled Pelion on top of Ossa* and Olympus*.

PELOPEA [Gr. Pelopeia]. Daughter of Thyestes* and mother by him of Aegisthus*.

PELOPS. Son of Tantalus*, husband of Hippodamea (2)* and father of Atreus* and Thyestes*. Wishing to test the gods, Tantalus killed Pelops and served his body to the gods as food. The crime was discovered and Pelops was restored to life. A piece of his shoulder, however, had been absent-mindedly eaten by Demeter* and was now replaced by ivory. At Pisa in Elis he sued for the hand of Hippodamea*, daughter of Oenomaus*. By deceit and murder (see MYRTILUS) he succeeded in making her his wife, after which he ruled over Elis. His reign was glorious and the whole southern peninsula of Greece was named after him (Peloponnesus = island of Pelops). He is one of those to whom the institution of the Olympic Games* is attributed. The curse brought down on his family by Tantalus' crime was fulfilled in Pelops and his sons.

Iconography. On the E. façade of the temple of Zeus at Olympia. Pelops stands with spear and shield, ready for the contest with Oenomaus (sculpture from 1st half of 5th century B.C.). The contest itself is frequently depicted on vases, sarcophagi, and Etruscan cinerary urns. Pelops is sometimes clad in Phrygian garments, sometimes in Greek, e.g. on an amphora at Arezzo (c. 415 B.C., by the Meidias painter): Pelops has his bride beside him in the chariot, holds the reins in his hand, and is driving off at full speed, clothes and hair flying in the wind.

PENATES. See DI PENATES.

PENELEOS. One of the Argonauts*.

PENELOPE [Gr. Penelopeia]. Daughter of Icarius* and Periboea (3)* and wife

of Odysseus*; proverbial even in antiquity as a chaste, faithful wife. During her husband's long absence she remained faithful to him, although many young noblemen sued for her hand and it was rumored that Odysseus was dead. She managed to put off her suitors by saying she would make her choice as soon as she had completed the shroud she was weaving for Laertes*; each night she undid what she had woven during the day. Her ruse was betrayed by a maidservant, and Odysseus came back just in time to save a critical situation. Penelope is a noble principal figure in Homer's *Odyssey* (Hom. Od. ii, 52f., 89f.; xi, 182f., etc.). After the death of Odysseus, Penelope married Telegonus*, by whom she became the mother of Italus*.
Iconography. A statue in the Vat. Museum shows a veiled female figure, seated in an attitude of mourning. Although it is called Penelope, others say it is a sepulchral ornament of the kind also found on tomb reliefs. One side of a red-figured Attic vase (c. 435 B.C.) shows Penelope seated at her loom. The reunion of Odysseus and Penelope is the subject of a fresco at Pompeii.

PENTHESILEA   [Gr.   Penthesileia]. Daughter of Ares* and queen of the Amazons*. After Hector's death she came to the aid of a hard-pressed Troy. She was slain by Achilles*, who at the moment that he killed her was moved by her courage and beauty.
Iconography. A well-known Greek bowl at Munich (c. 460 B.C.) shows Achilles transfixing the queen, and her gaze falling on the hero and moving him. The same scene is also depicted in reliefs on sarcophagi.

PENTHEUS. Son of Echion* and Agave*; king of Thebes. He opposed the introduction of the Dionysiac cult and was torn to pieces by his own mother and other Bacchantes when they mistook him for a wild animal (Ov. 511f.).
Iconography. His death is shown on vases, reliefs, and mural paintings. Pentheus is represented as a young man with a cloak, a Boeotian hat, a sword and hunting

shoes, or completely naked, as on the fresco in the Casa dei Vettii at Pompeii.

PENTHILUS [Gr. Penthilos]. Son of Orestes* and Erigone*. He founded a colony on Lesbos and is the mythological ancestor of the Penthilids, an ancient ruling dynasty on Lesbos.

PERIBOEA [Gr. Periboia]. 1. Wife of Polybus*; she adopted and reared Oedipus* as her own child. 2. Daughter of Hipponous and mother by Oeneus of Tydeus*. 3. A Naiad*, wife of Icarius* and mother of Penelope*. 4. Daughter of Alcathous* and mother by Telamon* of Aiax*.

PERICLYMENUS [Gr. Periklumenos]. 1. Son of Nereus*, took part in the expedition of the Argonauts*. He was renowned for his strength, and Poseidon* also gave him the power of assuming the form of all kinds of animals. He was slain by Heracles at the destruction of Pylos (Ov. xii, 556f.); 2. Son of Poseidon* and Chloris*; one of the defenders of Thebes against the Seven* kings.

PERIERES. King of Messenia, son of Aeolus* and father of Leucippus* and Aphareus*.

PERIGUNE. Daughter of Siris*, the robber slain by Theseus*; she became mother of Melanippus* by Theseus.

PERILAUS [Gr. Perilaos]. Son of Icarius* and Periboea*.

PERIPHAS. King of Attica, famous for his upright character; Zeus changed him into an eagle.

PERIPHETES. An infamous robber, son of Hephaestus*. He lived in the area around Troezen and Epidaurus and killed passing travelers with an iron club. He was put out of the way by Theseus*.

PERO. The exceedingly beautiful daughter of Neleus* and Chloris*. She was married to Bias*, who obtained her hand from her father through the aid of his brother Melampus*.

PERSE or PERSEIS. Daughter of Oceanus* and wife of Helius*. Her children included Aeëtes*, Pasiphaë and Circe*.

PERSEPHONE [Gr., also Persephoneia, Persephassa, or Pherephassa]. Greek goddess of the underworld, daughter of Zeus* and Demeter*. While still a young girl she was plucking flowers in the plain of Enna one day, together with the Oceanids*, when the earth suddenly opened up and Hades*, the ruler of the underworld, came up from the gaping hole in his two-horse chariot and abducted her. No one had noticed the abduction, and only Zeus knew about it. Grief-stricken, Demeter now roamed the world in search of her daughter until Helius*, the all-seeing, revealed to her what had happened. The irate Demeter now withdrew into isolation, with the result that all fertility on earth ceased. Finally Zeus sent Hermes to Hades to ask him to let Persephone return to earth. The god agreed, but before Persephone left he gave her a pomegranate which bound her to Hades and his realm and compelled her to spend three months of the year with him. The remaining nine months she remained with her mother. The myth is a symbol of the death and rebirth of nature. This event was celebrated in honor of Demeter and Persephone in the Eleusinian mysteries*. Persephone was known in the mystic cult as Kore*, and was called Proserpina by the Romans (Ov. v, 341f.).

Iconography. There is a famous Eleusinian relief in which Persephone appears in the company of Demeter and Triptolemus (2nd half of 5th century B.C.): she is shown as a young woman and carries a torch. Her abduction by Hades is occasionally reproduced on vases, mural paintings, and mosaics. Usually, however, she is represented as the queen of the underworld, with a scepter and diadem, ears of corn, a pomegranate, a torch, or a poppy. In this role she occurs on frescoes in Etruscan tombs, e.g. the Tomba del Orco (2nd century B.C.) at Tarquinia, where she is enthroned beside Hades and clad in a rich garment, adorned with jewels, and with serpents in her hair. On a fresco from Pompeii, now at Naples, she is shown veiled and carrying a basket of fruit.

PERSES. 1. Son of Perseus* and Andromeda* and mythical ancestor of the Persians. 2. Son of Helius* and father of Hecate*.

PERSEUS. Son of Zeus* and Danaë*. After Perseus' birth Acrisius*, Danaë's father, wished to kill both mother and child. He had them shut in a chest and thrown into the sea. The chest landed on the island of Seriphos, where Danaë and her child were taken in by King Polydectes. After some time he wanted to make Danaë his wife and to get rid of Perseus. He ordered Perseus to fetch him the head of Medusa*, one of the Gorgons, an extremely dangerous undertaking. Hermes* and Athena* placed Perseus under their protection and took him to the Graeae*, who possessed one eye and one tooth in common. Perseus stole the eye and the tooth, and refused to give them back unless the Graeae showed him the way to the nymphs. These, on his arrival, supplied him with every kind of aid for his task, such as winged shoes and a helmet of invisibility. Athena presented him with a brightly polished shield and Hermes gave him a sickle. Thus armed, he flew to the far west, where the Gorgons had their abode. He found them asleep and approached them very cautiously, for the sight of the face of the monsters turned men to stone. With face averted and using Athena's shield as a mirror, he cut off Medusa's head and escaped the pursuit of the other two Gorgons by putting on his helmet of invisibility. On his way home he rescued Andromeda* and married her. He used Medusa's head to defend himself against the pursuing Phineus*. On his return to Seriphos he turned Polydectes to stone and took Danaë and Andromeda to Argos, where he accidently killed his grandfather Acrisius with a discus. Loath to accept the throne of Argos in these circumstances, he went to Tiryns, from which place he set out to found Mycenae. He was the ancestor of many heroes, including Heracles*, and was venerated as a hero or demigod both in Argos and at Athens; sanctuaries on Seriphos and in Mycenae were also dedicated to him (Ov. iv, 605f.; v, 1f.).

Iconography. Perseus is frequently represented in ancient art as a young hero with his attributes: winged shoes, the helmet of invisibility, and a crooked sword. Some Greek vases show Danaë with young Perseus and the chest in which they were intended to go to their death. Perseus slaying Medusa is seen on a metope of temple C at Selinus (early 6th century B.C.). His rescue of Andromeda is illustrated on vases, coins, gems, frescoes, and reliefs at Pompeii, these include a fresco in the Casa dei Vettii, another in the Casa del Sacerdote Amando, and a stucco relief in the temple of Isis. Marble reliefs in the Capitoline Museum at Rome and the National Museum at Naples also depict Andromeda's rescue. A famous work of a later age is Cellini's "Perseus" in the Loggia dei Lanzi at Florence.

PHAEACIANS [Gr. Phaiakes]. A mythical people, mentioned by Homer in his Odyssey as living on the mythical island of Scheria*, identified in antiquity with Corcyra. When Odysseus was shipwrecked and washed ashore there, he was hospitably entertained by King Alcinous* and his daughter Nausicaä*. The Phaeacians finally brought him home to his native Ithaca in a single night with their speedy ship (Hom. Od. v, 288f.; vi, 201f.; viii, 556f.).

PHAEDRA [Gr. Phaidra]. Daughter of Minos* and Pasiphaë, and wife of King Theseus of Athens. She fell in love with her stepson Hippolytus, who repulsed her. In a rage she denounced him to Theseus, who had the youth killed. Tortured by remorse, Phaedra then put an end to her own life. The Phaedra myth has more than once been treated in literature: Euripides' *Hippolytus*, Seneca's *Phaedra*, and Racine's *Phèdre*.
Iconography. Phaedra is occasionally shown in mural paintings as a lonely, grief-stricken woman whose love is unrequited.

PHAETHON [= shining]. Son of Helius* and Clymene*. He went to the sun-god's palace to ask for a sign by which everyone would recognize him as the son of Helius. His father swore by the Styx that he would grant any wish of Phaethon's. The latter now asked to be allowed to drive the chariot of the sun for one day. Being bound by his oath, Helius un-

willingly consented. Phaethon was unable to control Helius' horses and nearly burned up the earth. The Ethiopians, for instance, were scorched by the heat from the plunging and soaring sun chariot and thus acquired their dark complexions. Zeus was finally compelled to destroy Phaethon with his thunderbolts to avoid still greater evil (Ov. ii, 1f.).
Iconography. Phaethon occurs chiefly on later monuments of the Roman Imperial age, e.g. on a sarcophagus from Ostia (2nd century A.D.), now at Copenhagen. The downfall of Phaethon is a favorite subject of Renaissance and Baroque painters, e.g. Michelangelo, Tintoretto, Brueghel, and Rubens.

PHAETHUSA [Gr. Phaethousa]. Daughter of Helius*. She and his sister Lampetia* grazed their father's flocks.

PHALANTHUS [Gr. Phalanthos]. A Spartan who deserted during the Messenian Wars and went to Italy. He is reputed to have founded Tarentum (now Tarento) and was venerated as a demigod there. Others regarded Hercules* as founder of the city (Virg. iii, 551).

PHANTASUS [Gr. Phantasos]. Son of Hypnos*. The inanimate things that men encounter in their dreams are brought about by him (Ov. xi, 641f.).

PHEMIUS [Gr. Phemios]. Singer at the court of Odysseus* in Ithaca. As his participation in the excesses of Penelope's suitors had been forced upon him, he was spared by Odysseus when he took revenge (Hom. Od. 1, 154f.), 325f.; xxiii, 133f.; xxiv, 439f.).

PHEMONOË. Daughter of Apollo. According to tradition, she was the first Pythia*. She was also said to have invented the hexameter (verse of six measures or feet); at any rate, the oracle's answer was given in that verse form.

PHERECLUS [Gr. Phereklos]. A Greek shipbuilder who made the ship on which Paris* abducted Helen*.

PHERES. 1. Name given to the Centaurs* by Homer (Hom. Il. i, 268; ii, 743f.). 2. Son of Cretheus* and Tyro*; he was the founder of Pherae in Thessaly and father of Admetus*.

PHERUSA [Gr. Pherousa]. One of the Nereids*.

PHILAEUS [Gr. Philaios]. Son of the greater Ajax* and Tecmessa. He was the founder of the great Athenian family of the Philiads, of which Miltiades, the general and victor in the Battle of Marathon, was a member.

PHILAMMON. Son of Apollo*. He was a Thracian singer and musician, and father of Thamyras* and Eumolpus* (Ov. xi, 317).

PHILEMON. A pious, aged Phrygian, husband of Baucis. Despite their poverty, they touchingly gave hospitality to Zeus* and Hermes* when, disguised as travelers, they asked for shelter after rich and distinguished people had shut their doors upon them. The whole district was turned into a swamp, but the hut of Philemon and Baucis was changed into a temple. The old people were allowed to make a wish and Philemon asked that they might both spend the rest of their lives as temple guardians in the service of the gods. When their lives drew to an end Philemon was changed into an oak and Baucis into a linden (Ov. viii, 611f.).

PHILOCTETES [Gr. Philoktetes]. Son of Poeas and king of Meliboea on the E. coast of Thessaly. He was a friend of Heracles* and was given the latter's bow and arrows because he was the only person willing to light the funeral pyre of Heracles. He set sail with seven ships to take part in the Trojan War but was bitten by a serpent on the island of Chryse. The suppurating wound that resulted spread such an unbearable stench that on the advice of Odysseus* and the command of the Atrides* he was left behind on the island of Lemnos, where he spent ten years in isolation and suffering. As an oracular pronouncement said Troy could never be taken without the unerring arrows of Heracles, Odysseus and Neoptolemus* were sent to Lemnos to fetch Philoctetes. On his arrival at Troy his wound was healed by Asclepius* or Machaon*. By slaying Paris* Philoctetes hastened the fall of Troy. Some say that on the way back from Troy he landed in Italy and there founded Petelia (now Strongoli) in Bruttii. He is the subject of tragedies by Aeschylus, Sophocles, and Euripides (Hom. Il. ii, 718, 721f.; Virg. iii, 402; Ov. xiii, 315f.).

PHILOMELA. Daughter of Pandion*, the king of Athens, and sister of Procne*. She was dishonored by her brother-in-law Tereus*, who also cut her tongue out so that his outrage should not be revealed. But Philomela conveyed the story to her sister by weaving it into cloth. Together they now took vengeance on Tereus (see ITYS), and when the women were pursued by Tereus, the gods changed Philomela into a nightingale, Procne into a swallow, and Tereus into a hop vine. Others say Philomela became a swallow and Procne a nightingale. In Roman writers Philomela is sometimes represented as the mother of Itys (Ov. vi, 424f.).

PHILONOË. 1. Daughter of Tyndareus* and Leda* and loved by Artemis*, who made her immortal. 2. Daughter of Iobates and wife of Bellerophon*.

PHILYRA. A nymph, daughter of Oceanus* and mother by Saturn* of Chiron*. She was changed to a linden.

PHINEUS. Brother of Cepheus* and betrothed to Andomeda*. When he objected to his fiancée being given in marriage to Perseus*, he was turned to stone by Perseus with Medusa's* head (Ov. v, 8f.). 2. Son of Agenor* and king of Salmydessus in Thrace. At the urging of his second wife, Idaea, he had his two sons by his first marriage blinded. The gods punished him by striking him with blindness, and he was unceasingly tortured by the Harpies*, who stole or fouled his food. His torment came to an end when the Argonauts* visited him on their travels and Calais* and Zetes* chased the Harpies (Ov. v, 1f.).

Iconography. Phineus, with the Harpies stealing his food, is shown as an old, blind, bearded man, e.g. on a black-figured Greek bowl (c. 520 B.C.), now at Würzburg.

PHLEGETHON or PYRIPHLEGETHON [= burning]. A river of fire which flowed in the underworld (Virg. vi, 265, 551).

PHLEGYAS. Son of Ares* and Chryse* and mythical ancestor of the Phlegyae, a rapacious people of Thessaly. He was also king of the Lapithae* and father of Ixion* and Coronis. When Coronis became mother of Asclepius* by Apollo*, Phlegyas was so enraged that he set fire to the temple at Delphi. In revenge the god killed him, and some say that Phlegyas, on his arrival in the underworld, had to undergo punishment similar to that of Tantalus* or Ixion (Virg. vi, 618f.).

PHOBETOR. Son of Hypnos*. He caused all kinds of animals to appear to human beings in their dreams (Ov. xi, 640).

PHOCUS [Gr. Phokos]. 1. Son of Aeacus* and Psamathe*; he was killed by his two brothers Peleus* and Telamon* (Ov. vii, 477). 2. Son of Poseidon*; moved from Corinth to Phocis, which is named after him.

PHOEBE [Gr. Phoibe]. 1. Title of Artemis*-Diana as moon-goddess. The name is the feminine form of Phoebus (Gr. Phoibos), her twin brother Apollo's* title as sun god. 2. Daughter of Leda* and sister of Helen*. 3. Daughter of Uranus* and Gaea*; she was the mother of Leto* and Asteria*, and is said by some to have occupied the oracle of Delphi before Apollo.

PHOEBUS [Gr. Phoibos = radiant]. Epithet of Apollo* as sun god. The Romans in particular honored him under the double name of Phoebus Apollo.

PHOENIX [Gr. Phoinix]. 1. Son of Agenor* and king of Tyre (now Sûr) in Phoenicia. He was the father of Europa's* brother, and mythical ancestor of the Phoenicians. 2. Son of Amyntor*. Cursed by his father because they both had the same mistress, he fled to Peleus*, at whose court he became the tutor and friend of the young Achilles*. In the war against Troy he was one of the leaders of the Myrmidons* (Hom. Il. ix, 168, 223, 427, 690f.). 3. A mythical bird of the Egyptians, also mentioned by Greek and Latin writers (e.g. Herod. ii, 73; Ov. xv, 392f.). The Egyptians spoke of it as a

heron, classical literature as a peacock or eagle. Several versions of its death were current. A.t.s. the wonder bird came to Egypt every 500 or 1,461 years, built its nest, and died in it; a new Phoenix rose from its dead body. A.t.o. the new Phoenix arose from the blood the dying bird drew from its breast. The most familiar version is that the bird was consumed by fire in its nest and rose rejuvenated from the ashes. The numbers 500 and 1,461 have an astrological significance. *Iconography.* The Phoenix is seen on late Roman coins (2nd century A.D.). It appears especially in Christian art on sarcophagi and mosaics as a symbol of the Resurrection. The Phoenix was similarly used in later times, but mainly as a symbol of resurrection in a secular sense.

PHOLUS [Gr. Pholos]. A Centaur*, son of Ixion*, who, unlike the other Centaurs, offered Heracles* hospitality. In the struggle that arose between Heracles and the Centaurs, Pholus too was unfortunately killed by the hero (Ov. xii, 306). *Iconography.* One of the archaic metopes on the Thesaurus at Paestum (first half of 6th century B.C.) shows Pholus making a gesture of friendship toward Heracles.

PHORBAS. A Thessalian who was called to Rhodes by the inhabitants of the island to free them from a plague of serpents. He cleared the island and was afterwards venerated as a hero.

PHORCUS. See PHORCYS.

PHORCYS or PHORCUS [Gr. Phorkus or Phorkos]. 1. Greek sea god, son of Pontus* and Gaea*. He was the father of the Hesperides*, the nymphs Thoösa* and Scylla (1)*, and various monsters, such as the Gorgons*, the Graeae*, and the dragon Ladon*. The Cyclops Polyphemus* was his grandson (Hom. Od. i, 72; xiii, 96, 345). 2. A leader of the Phrygians in the Trojan War. He was slain by Ajax (Hom. Il. xvii, 218, 312, 318).

PHORONEUS. Son of the river god Inachus* and the Oceanid Melia*. He was king of Peloponnesus and introduced the worship of Hera* there. He is also said to have induced his people to live together in cities and to have brought civilization, e.g. by teaching people the use of fire. He was accorded divine honor, especially in Argos.

PHRIXUS [Gr. Phrixos]. Son of Athamas* and Nephele*. When his stepmother Ino tried to take his life, he and his sister were miraculously rescued by Nephele (see HELLE). Having duly hung up in the sacred wood of Ares the golden fleece of the ram that had brought him to Colchis, he married Chalciope, daughter of the king of Colchis, Aeëtes*.

PHTHIA [Gr. Phthiotis]. A district in the S.E. of Thessaly with a city of the same name; abode of Peleus* and Achilles*.

PHYLACUS [Gr. Phulakos]. Father of Iphicles*. He was the founder of the city of Phylace in Thessaly which later became the residence of Protesilaus*.

PHYLEUS. Son of King Augias*. When Heracles* undertook his punitive expedition against Augias, Phyleus sided with him and was expelled by Augias. Upon Augias' death Heracles gave his kingdom to Phyleus.

PHYTALUS [Gr. Phutalos]. A hero honored at Eleusis*. He entertained Demeter* hospitably when she roamed around in search of her daughter Persephone*.

PICUMNUS. Old Italian god of the crops. He was credited with having discovered the use of dung for fertilizing arable land, and in that capacity he was called Sterquilinus* (or a.t.o. Stercutus; stercus = dung). He and his brother Pilumnus* were also protectors of newborn babies: Pilumnus warded off children's diseases and Picumnus promoted growth.

PICUS [Lat. = woodpecker]. Old Roman rural deity, son of Saturn* and father of Faunus*. He was married to Pomona* or the nymph Canens. When Circe's passion for him remained unrequited, she changed him into a woodpecker (Virg. vii, 48, 171, 189; Ov. xiv, 320f.).

Iconography. Picus was represented as a woodpecker perched on a pillar, later as a youth with a woodpecker on his head.

PIERIA. A district on the borders of Macedonia and Thrace, the birthplace of the worship of the Muses*, who were consequently also called the Pierides*.

PIERIDES. Another name for the Muses, derived from the district of Pieria* in Thessaly, on the eastern slope of Olympus*, which was one of the centers of the Muse cult. The area had many fast-flowing brooks, the sound of which led to the belief that the fountain nymphs were also goddesses of the art of singing. In earliest Greek mythology the Muses are only goddesses of song; not until later were they regarded as patronesses of poetry and the other arts and sciences.

PILLARS OF HERCULES [Lat. Columnae Herculis]. The two rocks on either side of the Strait of Gibraltar at its eastern end, one of which is now known as the Rock of Gibraltar. Hercules* is said to have created the strait by pulling the two rocks apart.

PILUMNUS. Ancient Roman rural deity who taught man to pound or grind corn. He and his brother Picumnus* protected young children from the maladies of infancy. In the living room of houses where there was a newborn baby, it was the custom to make up a bed for Picumnus and Pilumnus. Virgil says Pilumnus was the husband of Danaë* and the great grandfather of Turnus* (Virg. ix, 4; x, 76, 619; xii, 83).

PIRENE [Gr. Peirene]. A sacred spring, dedicated to the Muses*, on the acropolis of Corinth. It was here that Pegasus* was quenching his thirst when he was caught by Bellerophon*.

PIRITHOUS [Gr. Peirithoös]. Son of Zeus* or Ixion*, and king of the Lapithae*. At his wedding to Hippodamea (1)* a violent battle between the Lapithae and the Centaurs* broke out after the latter had tried to abduct the bride and other women. Pirithous helped his friend Theseus* to abduct Helen* and was accompanied by him when he himself went down into the underworld to kidnap Persephone*. Hades, however, chained the two to a rock, and only Theseus was later freed by Heracles* (Ov. viii, 302f.).

Iconography. On many vase paintings Pirithous occurs as a warrior, naked or in a fluttering cape, taking part in the battle against the Centaurs. His escapades with Theseus (descent to the underworld, abduction of Helen) are shown on many monuments.

PISIDICE [Gr. Peisidike]. One of the daughters of Pelias*.

PISISTRATUS [Gr. Peisistratos]. Nestor's* youngest son. He accompanied Telemachus on his journey from Pylos to Sparta (Hom. Od. iii, 36f., 400f.).

PITTHEUS. King of Troezen; son of Pelops*. His daughter Aethra* made him grandfather of Theseus* (Ov. viii, 622).

PITYS [Gr. Pitus = pine tree]. A Greek nymph who was changed into a pine tree by the gods to save her from the amorous attentions of Pan*.

PLEIADES. The seven daughters of Atlas* and Pleione*: Electra (3)*, Halcyone, Celaeno, Maia*, Sterope, Taygete*, and Merope (2)* They were set in the heavens as the stars of the same names in order, some say, to free them from pursuit by Orion or, a.t.o., after they had killed themselves for grief at the death of their sisters the Hyades* (Ov. xiii, 293).

PLEIONE. Daughter of Oceanus* and Tethys* and mother by Atlas* of the Pleiades*.

PLISTHENES [Gr. Pleisthenes]. Son of Pelops* and brother of Atreus* and Thyestes*. A.t.s. he was the father of Agamemnon* and Menelaus*, whom he had brought up by Atreus*. A.t.o. he was Atreus' son.

PLUTO or PLUTON [Gr. Plouton]. Ancient Greek deity, probably god of the spaces under the earth from which he supplied the crops with food. Hence god of the lower world and identified with Hades*. Sometimes also identified with Plutus* (= riches).

PLUTUS [Gr. Ploutus = riches]. Greek personification of wealth. He was regarded as the son of Demeter*, since a large stock of grain is a symbol of wealth. Pluto(n), the other name for Hades, is also derived from *ploutos*.
Iconography. Plutus is usually represented as a youth with a cornucopia or a basket of ears of grain in his hand. A wellknown marble group by Cephisodotus (c. 375 B.C.), of which there is a copy at Munich, shows Irene (= peace) with young Plutus in her arm.

PLUVIUS [Lat. = causing rain]. Title by which the Romans invoked Jupiter* in long periods of drought. Also an epithet of the Hyades*.

PODALIRIUS [Gr. Podaleiros]. Son of Asclepius* and, like his brother Machaon*, a famous physician (Hom. Il. ii, 732; xi, 833).

PODARCES [Gr. Podarkes]. Son of Iphicles*. When his brother Protesilaus* died, he became leader of the men from Phylace who fought for Troy (Hom. Il. ii, 704).

PODARGE. One of the Harpies*, mother by Zephyrus* of Xanthus and Balius, the horses of Achilles (Hom. Il. xvi, 150).

POEAS [Gr. Poias]. One of the Argonauts*, friend of Heracles* and father of Philoctetes*. Some say it was not Philoctetes but Poeas who lit Heracles' funeral pyre and received the hero's bow and arrows.

POLITES. 1. Son of Priam; famed for his fleetness of foot. He was slain by Neoptolemus* at the fall of Troy (Hom. Il. ii, 791f.; xiii, 533f.). 2. A companion of Odysseus (Hom. Od. x, 224).

POLLUX. Latin name for Polydeuces; see DIOSCURI.

POLYBUS [Gr. Polubos]. 1. King of Corinth by whose shepherd the infant Oedipus was found and who reared the foundling at his court. 2. King of Thebes in Egypt, at whose court Menelaus* stayed for a long time after the end of the Trojan War. 3. King of Sicyon and grandfather of Adrastus*.

POLYDAMAS. A wise Trojan hero who possessed the gift of prophecy. He was a friend and adviser to Hector*.

POLYDEUCES [Gr. Poludeukes]. Twin brother of Castor; see DIOSCURI.

POLYDORA. Daughter of Meleager*.

POLYDORUS [Gr. Poludoros]. 1. Son of Cadmus* and Harmonia*, father of Labdacus*. 2. The youngest son of Priam*. Toward the end of the Trojan War his father entrusted him to the Thracian king Polymestor*, who killed Polydorus to obtain possession of the treasures Priam had given him (Virg. iii,

45; Ov. xiii, 530). Hecuba* is said to have avenged the murder later. 3. Son of Hippomedon and one of the Epigoni*.

POLYHYMNIA or POLYMNIA [Gr. Polumnia]. The Muse of serious poetry, of hymns, and also of eloquence. *Iconography.* She is represented as a serious woman, with a thoughtful countenance and a pensive look in her eyes. She is clad in a long mantle and usually rests one elbow on a pillar. Sometimes she holds a finger to her mouth; there is a well-known statue of her in the Vatican Museum.

POLYMESTOR or POLYMNESTOR. A Thracian king to whom Priam* entrusted his son Polydorus*. After the fall of Troy he killed the boy and threw him into the sea.

POLYMNIA. See POLYHYMNIA.

POLYNICES [Gr. Poluneikes]. Son of Oedipus* and Jocasta* and brother of Eteocles*. After their father's abdication they agreed to rule Thebes in alternate years. Eteocles broke the agreement by refusing to make way for his brother at the end of the year. Polynices then marched with six allies against Thebes (see SEVEN AGAINST THEBES). Each brother died by the other's hand.

POLYPEMON. See PROCRUSTES.

POLYPHEMUS [Gr. Poluphemos]. 1. A Cyclops*, son of Poseidon* and Thoösa*. When Odysseus in his wanderings landed near his cave, Polyphemus shut him and some of companions up in it. By a ruse Odysseus succeeded in blinding the Cyclops' one eye and ecaping from the cave. The enraged Polyphemus called down the wrath of his father Poseidon on the escaping Greeks, and Odysseus was pursued by storms for the rest of his voyage (Hom. Od. i, 70; ix, 106f.; Virg. iii, 618f.; Ov. xiii, 765). Another myth tells of the love of Polyphemus for the nymph Galatea, which resulted in the death of Acis*. 2. A friend of Heracles* who took part with him in the voyage of the Argonauts*. The two of them were left behind in Mysia where Polyphemus founded the city of Cius (now Gemlik). *Iconography.* The blinding of Polyphemus by Odysseus' companions is a frequently recurring theme, particularly on ancient Greek pottery, where the Cyclops is shown as a naked bearded giant with satyr's horns. In vase paintings two normal human eyes are sometimes sketchily indicated in addition to the single eye in his forehead. Some show a row of men carrying a long pole and pushing its pointed end into the giant's eye, e.g. a krater by Aristonothus from Argos (7th century B.C.), now at Rome, and a Chalcidian amphora (c. 530 B.C.), at London. On a Laconian kylix (c. 550 B.C.) at Paris, Odysseus is seen handing the Cyclops a glass of wine, while the giant holds in his hand some limbs of men he has been eating. Wall paintings sometimes depict his love for Galatea, e.g. one in the Casa del Sacerdote Amando at Pompeii: the nymph, seated on a dolphin, is being watched by Polyphemus, represented as a shepherd. There is also the fresco in the house of Augustus on the Palatine at Rome (the "Casa di Livia"), which shows Polyphemus up to his waist in water gazing amorously at the nymph as she sails past on a sea horse. Two other nymphs also watch, and a little Cupid stands on the Cyclops' shoulders, manipulating the reins around the latter's neck.

POLYPOETES [Gr. Polypoites]. Son of Pirithous* and Hippodamea*, leader of the Thessalians in the Trojan War (Hom. Il. ii, 740).

POLYXENA [Gr. Poluxene]. Daughter of King Priam*. The hero Achilles* is said to have been in love with her or, a.t.o., she with him. On the fall of Troy she was sacrificed by Neoptolemus* on Achilles' grave or, a.t.o., she committed suicide on it (Ov. xiii, 848f.).

POMONA [Lat. *pomum* = fruit]. Roman goddess of tree fruit. With her beauty she attracted the interest of wood and field gods; finally Vertumnus, disguised as an old woman, persuaded her to accept his proposal, and she became his wife. A special priest, called the Flamen Pomonalis, was in charge of her worship at Rome (Ov. xiv, 623). *Iconography.* Pomona was represented with a pruning knife in her hand, mainly by Renaissance and Baroque painters.

PONTUS [Gr. Pontos = the sea]. Greek personification of the sea, son of Aether* and Gaea*; also father by Gaea of Nereus*, Phorcys* and other marine deities.

PORTUNALIA. See PORTUNUS.

PORTUNUS. Old Roman deity, prob. a god of keys and doors (cf. JANUS), who protected grain barns, especially at harvest time, and hence also the patron of the port of Rome. His festival, the Portunalia, was celebrated on Aug. 17. Possibly he was sometimes identified with the river god Tiberis*, for some authors call the festival on Aug. 17 the Tiberinalia. It is perhaps significant in this connection, that Rome's grain silos were situated along the Tiber and that the port and river played a great part in the import of grain. Portunus was also later identified with the Greek Palaemon* or Melicertes*. There was a temple of Portunus at Portus, the port of Rome, and one in the city itself near the Tiber. The rectangular temple still standing on the Forum Biarium (now the Piazza della Verità) is thought by some experts to be that of Portunus, while others consider Portunus' temple to be the circular one on the same square.

Iconography. The god is represented with a key in his hand.

POSEIDON. Greek god of the sea and water. Originally a deity of somewhat different character, being a.t.s. the ruler of the water sources in the innermost part of the earth and a.t.o. the god of horses. In historical Greek times he was regarded as the son of Cronus* and Rhea* who was given dominion over all waters when the universe was divided up. He lived with his wife Amphitrite* and their offspring in his golden palace at the bottom of the sea, where he controlled all marine phenomena with his trident: he raised storms and made them subside again, he caused islands to rise from the sea, and all sea deities were subject to him. He also generated earthquakes, and one of his titles means "earthshaker." He split rocks and caused springs to gush forth, and he was associated with every kind of volcanic activity. Everything to do with the sea, such as fishing, shipping, ports, etc., was under Poseidon's protection. Sailors prayed to him for a safe voyage, and anyone who incurred his wrath could expect storms and shipwreck. That was the experience of Odysseus*, for instance, who had blinded his son, the Cyclops Polyphemus* (Hom. Od. i, 20f.). The horse, in particular, was sacred to Poseidon. In his contest with the goddess Athena* for dominion over Attica Athena had presented the olive to the country; Poseidon's gift was the horse. He was also the father of the horse Pegasus. Poseidon is associated with countless myths, e.g. the adventures of Perseus and those of Odysseus. He was credited with the paternity of the giant Antaeus*, Procrustes*, Cercyon*, Triton*, Nereus*, Pelias*, and the Aloadae*. He was the father of Polyphemus* by Thoösa*. Many cities regarded him as their founder and protector; e.g. he was supposed to have built the walls of Troy together with Heracles (Hom. Il. vii, 452f.). Although Poseidon was a brother of Zeus, he was inferior to him in power; nevertheless, he was bold enough to conspire with Hera and Athena to attack Zeus (Hom. Il. i, 400f.). One of the chief places where he was worshiped was the Isthmus of Corinth, where the national festival, known as the Isthmian Games*, was held in his honor. His temples were often situated on promontories, e.g. at Sunium, Mycale, and Taenarum. In addition to the horse, the dolphin and the pine tree were sacred to him, the latter because it was used for shipbuilding. The sacrifices offered to Poseidon consisted of horses, black bulls, rams, and wild boars. The Romans completely indentified their god Neptune with Poseidon.

Iconography. In the archaic period Poseidon is seen on black-figured Greek vases as a bearded figure in a long garment and mantle, with a wreath or diadem on his head. Occasionally, e.g. in the fight against the Giants, he wears a short coat of mail and carries a sword. His attribute, the trident, also figures in vase paintings. From the 5th century B.C. on, the god is usually shown only partly clothed or quite nude. Among the known sculptures of

Poseidon are those on the frieze of the Parthenon and the magnificent bronze statue found at Artemisium, which represents the god completely nude in a standing attitude, with his left hand stretched straight out in front and his right ready to hurl the trident (c. 460 B.C.). Some scholars, it is true, are of the opinion that this statue represents Zeus, but others have strong arguments to support their view that it is a figure of Poseidon. Hellenistic representations of Poseidon sometimes show him with a dolphin or other creatures of the sea, and with one leg resting on a mound of earth. Among the representations of the god on coins, the best-known are those from the city named after him, Poseidonia (Lat. Paestum) on the Gulf of Salerno in southern Italy. The representations of Poseidon-Neptune on Roman mosaics are countless; a floor mosaic in the thermae on the Decumanus Maximus at Ostia shows Neptune driving a team of four sea horses surrounded by Nereids, Tritons, dolphins, etc. The god is also frequently depicted on frescoes at Pompeii and Herculaneum. In Renaissance and Baroque painting and sculpture the figure of Neptune is a favorite subject, and statues of the god occur particularly in gardens, parks, and ornamental fountains.

PRIAM [Gr. Priamos]. Son of Laomedon* and king of Troy. When Heracles captured the city, he was taken prisoner, but he was later ransomed by his sister Hesione. He was the last king to reign over Troy. He was married first to Arisbe and later to Hecuba*. His offspring were extremely numerous; his sons included Hector*, Paris*, Helenus*, Deiphobus*, and Polites*. The best-known of his daughters were Cassandra* and Creusa*. During the siege of Troy he lost many of his sons, among them the beloved Hector. To redeem the latter's body from the enemy he went personally to the Greek camp and begged Achilles to return it (Hom. Il. xxiv, 143f.). When the city fell, Priam was slain in his palace by Neoptolemus* (Virg. ii, 501f.).

Iconography. The king occurs in many scenes from the Trojan War. He is shown as a graybeard, sometimes leaning on a stick. His death is seen on—*inter alia*—an Attic hydria by the Cleophrades painter (c. 485 B.C.), now at Naples: the king has sought asylum on an altar and the blood-covered body of the murdered Astyanax* lies on his knees. Priam's visit to Achilles is illustrated on a magnificent frieze comprising a white stucco relief on a blue background in the Casa del Larario at Pompeii.

PRIAPUS [Gr. Priapos]. God of fertility, orginally venerated mainly at Lampsacus (now Lapseki) on the Hellespont. From Asia Minor his worship spread in the Hellenistic period over Greece and Italy, where he was chiefly regarded as the patron of horticulture and viticulture. Worshipers offered him the first fruits of the fields, milk, honey, and asses. His statue in the form of a rough herma* was found in gardens and vineyards everywhere.
Iconography. Priapus is represented in a long garment tucked up in front. He was bearded and had a sickle in his right hand. He usually occurred on hermae but is also found in mural paintings and on gems and coins.

PROCAS. King of Alba Longa*, father of Amulius* and Numitor* (Virg. vi, 767; Liv. i, 3, 9).

PROCLEA [Gr. Prokleia]. Daughter of Laomedon*.

PROCNE [Gr. Prokne]. Daughter of Pandion (1)*, wife of Tereus* and mother of Itys*. Together with her sister, she took a terrible revenge on Tereus (see PHILOMELA).

PROCRIS [Gr. Prokris]. Daughter of the Athenian king Erechtheus* and wife of Cephalus*.

PROCRUSTES [Gr. Prokroustes = stretcher-out]. Nickname of a Greek robber whose real name was Damastes or Polypemon. He lived near Eleusis and captured passing travelers in order to fit them into one of his two beds. One bed was short and the other long. He placed short prisoners in the long bed and racked them out until they fitted it; from long

men he cut off enough to make them fit
the short bed. Theseus* put an end to his
gruesome enjoyment (Ov. vii, 438).
PROETUS [Gr. Proitos]. Son of Abas
(1)*; king of Argos. Expelled from
Argos by his brother Acrisius*, he later
became king of Tiryns. He was married
to Antea* (Ov. v, 238f.).
PROMACHUS [Gr. Promachos]. 1. One
of the Epigoni*. 2. Son of Aeson*.
While his brother Jason* was away with
the Argonauts* in quest of the Golden
Fleece*, Promachus and his father were
put to death by Pelias*. 3. Title of
honor under which Pallas Athena was
venerated at Athens as protectress of
that city (*promachos* = who precedes into
battle).
PROMETHEUS [Gr. = forethought].
One of the Titans*, son of Iapetus* and
Clymene. In Greek mythology he was
a benefactor of humanity: when Zeus*
desired to destroy mankind with a flood,
Prometheus advised his son Deucalion*
to build a ship and thus save himself.
A.t.s. Prometheus created man of earth
and water before or after the flood. In
disobedience to Zeus he stole fire from
heaven and brought it back to earth,
hidden in a reed stalk. He also taught
men numerous arts and brought them
civilization. Zeus punished mankind
through Pandora* and chained Prometheus to a rock where an eagle daily
ate his liver, which immediately grew
again. Heracles finally killed the bird,
and Zeus admitted Prometheus to Olympus. Many myths arose around Prometheus, all of which characterize him as
the man who dared oppose Zeus in order
to bring progress and civilization to humanity. As a counterpart to Prometheus
the Greeks invented his brother Epimetheus (= afterthought), who married
Pandora despite Prometheus' warning.
Aeschylus' tragedy *Prometheus Bound* is
renowned.
Iconography. Prometheus is represented
in early Greek art as a beardless young
man, later as an older, bearded man.
His punishment, and his delivery in particular by Heracles, are the subjects of
many Greek vase paintings. In Roman
art he is more often seen as the creator
of man. Later art regards Prometheus
principally as the hero who stole fire
from heaven for man's sake.
PROPOETIDES. Girls from Amathus,
a city on the S. coast of Cyprus with
a famous sanctuary of Aphrodite*. They
denied the divinity of the goddess and
were punished by being changed to stone
(Ov. x, 238f.).
PROSERPINA. Latin name for Persephone*.
PROTESILAUS [Gr. Protesilaos]. Son
of Iphicles* from Thessaly. He was the
first Greek to die at Troy, thus fulfilling
an oracular pronouncement that the first
man to jump ashore from the Greek
invasion fleet would also be the first to
be killed. His wife Laodamia (2)* committed suicide (Ov. xii, 68).
PROTEUS. Greek sea god who tended
Poseidon's seals. He possessed the gift
of prophecy and also the power to assume any form he wished. His usual
abode was the island of Pharos off the
coast of Egypt. A.t.s. Psamathe* was
his wife (Hom. Od. iv, 384f., 450f.).
Iconography. The scene from Hom. Od.
iv, 384, in which Menelaus asks Proteus for news of Odysseus' fate, was
illustrated on the so-called throne of
Amyclae (late 6th century), a seat made
by Bathycles of Magnesia for a statue
of Apollo. Practically nothing of the
work has survived.
PROTOGENEA   [Gr.   Protogeneia].
Daughter of Deucalion* and Pyrrha*.
PSAMATHE. 1. A Nereid*, mother of
Phocus* by Aeacus* (Ov. xi, 398). 2.
Daughter of Crotopus, king of Argos.
She became mother of Linus* by Apollo, for which she was killed by her
father.
PSYCHE [Gr. = breath, soul]. Greek
personification of the human soul. In the
well-known fable by the Roman writer
Apuleius (c. 125–c. 180 A.D.) Psyche was
the youngest of three princesses and so
beautiful that she excited the jealousy of
Aphrodite, who had Cupid (Amor*)
make her fall passionately in love with a

terribly ugly man. The god himself, however, fell in love with her and visited her every night, but always in complete darkness, so that she did not know who her lover was. Incited by her sisters, she tried to discover her lover's identity by lighting a lamp so that she could see his face as he lay asleep. However, a drop of oil from her lamp fell on him and he woke up, saw what she was trying to do, and left her. Psyche now roamed all over the world in search of Cupid and was finally united with him.

Iconography. On older Greek vases Psyche is represented in the shape of a bird with a human head, sometimes bearded. Later she is shown as a cock, butterfly, or small winged human figure. As Cupid's lover she is a beautiful young woman, often with butterfly's wings. There is a well-known Cupid and Psyche group (3rd century B.C.) in the Capitoline Museum at Rome. In later times there are, among others, Raphael's painting in the Farnesani at Rome and sculptures by Canova and Thorwaldsen.

PTAH. Egyptian deity, the local god of Memphis. He was the patron of artists and craftsmen. The high priest of Ptah bore the title "Supreme Chief of Artists." *Iconography.* The god is represented as a mummy of small proportions; the hands folded in front of the body hold a scepter or a whip.

PTOLIPORTHUS [Gr. Ptoliporthos = city-destroyer]. Epithet used of Ares*, Achilles*, Odysseus*, and others.

PYGMALION. 1. King of Cyprus who fell in love with the ivory statue of a woman he had made. He begged Aphrodite to breathe life into her, and when she did so he married his own creation (Ov. x, 243f.). 2. King of Tyre, brother of Dido. He murdered her husband Sychaeus (Virg. i, 347).
Iconography. Pygmalion's love for the nude statue of a woman is a theme employed by many Renaissance and Baroque artists, e.g. Bouchet and Falconet.

PYLADES. Son of Strophius. He was the faithful friend of Orestes* and married the latter's sister Electra (1)*. Orestes and Pylades are the David and Jonathan of classical mythology.
Iconography. Pylades is shown on vases, reliefs and wall paintings, e.g. in the Casa di Olconio Rufo and Casa di Sirico at Pompeii, but only in the adventures common to him and Orestes.

PYRACMON [Gr. Purakmon]. A Cyclops (Virg. viii, 425).

PYRACMUS [Gr. Purakmos]. One of the Centaurs* at the wedding of Pirithous* (Ov. xii, 460).

PYRAMUS [Gr. Puramos]. A young man of Babylonia. He and the extremely beautiful Thisbe formed a perfect pair of lovers. They were kept apart by their parents and only spoke to each other through a chink in the wall between their respective houses. They finally arranged a secret meeting, and Thisbe arrived first at the appointed place. Terrified by a lion that chanced to appear, she fled, leaving behind her veil. The animal's blood-covered mouth left stains on the veil, and when Pyramus found these traces later he thought his beloved had been devoured by the lion, and in despair he took his own life. On finding his body Thisbe did likewise (Ov. iv, 55f.).
Iconography. This story is seldom if ever illustrated in antiquity but is extremely popular in Renaissance and Baroque art, in paintings, pen drawings, and prints.

PYRGO. The nurse of Priam's children (Virg. v, 645).

PYRIPHLEGETHON. See Phlegethon.

PYRRHA. Daughter of Epimetheus* and wife of Deucalion* (Ov. i, 350f.).

PYRRHUS [Gr. Purrhos]. Original name of Achilles'* son; he was later called Neoptolemus*.

PYTHIA. Name of the priestess of Apollo's sanctuary at Delphi*. Seated on a tripod over a cleft in the ground, she was sent into a trance by the overpowering fumes that rose from the cleft and by chewing laurel leaves. From the incoherent sounds she uttered in her ecstasy the attendant temple priests formulated the oracular pronouncement (see ORACLE).

Iconography. On a bowl by the Codrus painter (5th century B.C.), now at Berlin, we see Aegeus standing before the Pythia; she is sitting on the sacred tripod, with her head shrouded, and holds a bowl in her left hand and a laurel branch in the other.

PYTHIAN GAMES or PYTHIA. National contests of the Greeks, held in the plain of Crissa near Delphi in honor of Apollo, originally every eight years but later every four. The god himself is said to have instituted the games, but their history begins about 582 B.C. The Pythia originally consisted of contests in music, singing, drama, and verse recitation. In imitation of the celebrated Olympic Games, athletic contests and chariot racing were added later. The athletic events were held in the stadium that can still be seen at the foot of Parnassus*, while the chariot races took place in the plain of Crissa. The prize was a victor's wreath of laurels, the tree sacred to Apollo. The Pythian Games were highly regarded and continued to be celebrated until well into Roman Imperial times.

PYTHIUS [Gr. Puthios]. Epithet applied to Apollo* as the slayer of the dragon Python*.

PYTHON. A monstrous dragon that arose from the mud of the Deluge. It devastated the region around Delphi* until it was slain by Apollo*, who thereby acquired the title Pythius (Ov. i, 430f.).

Q-R

QUIRINALIA. See Quirinus.

QUIRINUS. Ancient Roman deity whose origin and significance are not clear. Romulus* was identified with him in late Republican times (Virg. i, 292). Quirinus is also another name for Mars*, and as such he was worshiped on the hill of Rome that was named after him: the Quirinal. A special priest, the Flamen Quirinalis, was in charge of the worship of Quirinus. The priestly college of the Salii Agonenses or Quirinales was also concerned in his cult, of which little else is known with certainty. The festival of Quirinalia in his honor was held on Feb. 17.

RA or RE [Eg. = sun]. The Egyptian sun god, worshiped particularly at Heliopolis (= sun city). He was associated with various other gods, such as Ammon*, Atum, Harakhte, etc.

Iconography. Ra is represented as a man with the head of a falcon (association with Horus) or a ram (association with Ammon). He often has the sun's disk on his head, and he is shown standing in a boat in which he sails through the sky or the underworld.

RAPE OF THE SABINE WOMEN. A legend from the earliest history of Rome relates that Romulus' settlement on the Palatine hill consisted of nothing but men. To rectify the shortage of women the Latins had recourse to a stratagem. They invited the members of the Sabine settlement on the nearby Quirinal hill to a festival and kidnaped the Sabine women (Liv. i, 9, 6f.).

REMULUS. A Rutulian married to a sister of Turnus*. He was slain by Ascanius (Virg. ix, 593, 633).

REMUS. Twin brother of Romulus*, who killed him in a quarrel (Liv. i, 5f.).

RHADAMANTHYS or RHADAMANTHUS [Gr. Rhadamanthus]. Son of Zeus* and Europa*; king of Knossos*. Driven from Crete by his brother, he settled in Boeotia and married Alcmene*. Upon his death he was placed in the underworld as a judge (Virg. vi, 566; Ov. ix, 436).

RHAMNUSIA. See NEMESIS.

RHEA [Gr. Rhea or Rheia]. Daughter of Uranus* and Gaea*; wife of Cronus*. She was the mother of several of the Olympian gods—Zeus, Hades, Poseidon, etc.—and was worshiped as the Magna Mater, the Great Mother Goddess. On Crete, where Zeus* was born, she enjoyed special veneration (Magna Mater Idaea = Great Mother of Mt. Ida), and she was probably originally a Cretan deity. She was completely identified with Cybele both in Crete and elsewhere, and the worship of Rhea-Cybele extended over the entire Greek world and later over the Roman.

Iconography. On a Roman altar relief at Rome, Rhea is shown with a naked torso and her head enveloped in a cloak. On Syrian coins she stands between two Corybantes and with young Zeus on her arm.

RHEA SILVIA or ILIA. Daughter of King Numitor* of Alba Longa*. She was dedicated to the service of Vesta by her uncle Amulius*, so that she would have to remain a virgin. However, she became mother of Romulus* and Remus by Mars*. A.t.s. Amulius threw her into the Tiber, where she became the wife of the river god (Liv. i, 3).

Iconography. A Roman sarcophagus (c. A.D. 210) in the Vatican Museum shows Rhea Silvia resting by the river Tiber, while Mars, dressed as a warrior, approaches her. The girl, who is naked from the waist up, turns uncertainly from the god, with her mantle raised protectively.

RHESUS [Gr. Rhesos]. Thracian king

who came to the help of Troy when it was besieged. Diomedes* and Odysseus* penetrated into his camp secretly, killed the king, and stole his famous horses (Hom. Il x, 435f.).

RHODOPE. A Greek fountain nymph from Thrace, wife of Haemus*. She was changed into the mountain of the same name (now Despoto).

ROBIGALIA. See ROBIGUS.

ROBIGUS [Lat. = rust]. Old rural Roman god who protected the grain from rust, or mildew. Ovid mentions a goddess Robiga. Robigus' festival—the Robigalia—was held on April 25.

ROMA. Roman personification of the city of Rome, venerated as a goddess. *Iconography.* Roma is represented as a female figure wearing a helmet. The helmet is generally decorated with the head of a griffin and wings. She is usually seated on a throne, with a spear in her hand and a shield resting against the throne. Her image occurs on many coins and reliefs. The temple of Venus and Roma on the Velia hill at Rome is renowned. It was begun by Hadrian in A.D. 121 and was consecrated about 140 in the reign of Antoninus Pius. Considerable portions of the temple still survive.

ROMULUS. Legendary founder and first king of Rome; son of Mars* and Rhea Silvia*, and twin brother of Remus. The twins were thrown into the Tiber in a basket by their uncle Amulius*. The river had just overflowed its banks, and the basket stuck in the mud at the foot of the Palatine* hill near the Lupercal, a cave sacred to Faunus* Lupercus. A wolf suckled the children in the shadow of a fig tree in front of the Lupercal (the so-called Ficus Ruminalis), where they were later found by the shepherd Faustulus*, who reared them. When Remus was captured by robbers and taken before Numitor*, the latter recognized him as his grandson. When Numitor revealed their origin, the twins, who had meanwhile grown up, killed Amulius and founded a settlement on the Palatine. A quarrel now arose between the brothers

about the name to be given to the city, and Remus insulted his twin by laughing at the settlement's low walls and jumping over them. Romulus finally slew his brother and ruled over the incipient city, which was as yet inhabited only by men. This situation was remedied by the Rape of the Sabine Women*, after which Romulus shared the throne with the Sabine king, Titus Tatius. After the latter's death Romulus ruled alone. At the end of his reign Rome's first king was taken up to heaven by the god Mars, after which he was accorded divine honor under the name of Quirinus*. One of the 8th–6th century B.C. structures discovered on the Palatine was given the name "Hut of Romulus." Finally, there stands on the Forum Romanum the Lapis Niger (= black stone), the oldest monument in Rome. According to some ancient authors, this spot had been set aside for Romulus' grave. But when Romulus was taken up into heaven, the shepherd Faustulus was buried there instead. Other old texts state that Romulus was in fact buried on the Forum (Liv. i, 4f.; Virg. i, 275; vi, 778, 781; viii, 342; Ov. xiv, 772f.).

Iconography. The representation of the wolf suckling Romulus and Remus first appears on Roman-Campanian coins c. 300 B.C. The twin brothers are also seen on many Roman monuments, the best known of which is the famous she-wolf of the Capitol (prob. Etruscan, 5th century B.C.). The figurines under the animal, however, are 16th century additions. Statues of Romulus which adorned the Forum Romanum at Rome, the Eumachia at Pompeii, etc. have been lost. His image has been better preserved on frescoes: in the Casa di Polybio at Pompeii, for instance, he is shown as a victor, with a trophy in his hand. From a later age is the fountain of Perugia with the figures of Romulus and Remus, by the brothers Pisano. Rubens, too, has perpetuated the brothers in his paintings.

RUMINA. Roman goddess, protectress of nursing mothers. Her temple stood near the Fiscus Ruminalis (see Romulus).

S

SABAZIUS [Gr. Sabazios]. Phrygian or Thracian deity whose worship spread over Greece in the 5th century B.C. In the Greek world the god was equated with Dionysus* and sometimes also with Zeus*. In the Roman Empire Sabazius became an epithet for Bacchus*. The god was also associated with the cult of Rhea*-Cybele.

SABUS. Son of Sancus, the oldest king of the Sabines, by whom he was worshiped as their national god.

SABINE WOMEN. See RAPE OF THE SABINE WOMEN.

SALACIA. Roman sea goddess, wife of Neptune*.

SALII. Roman college of priests, divided into two sections: the Salii Palatini, who administered the cult of Mars* on the Palatine* Hill, and the Salii Aginenses, Collini, or Quirinalis, who were consecrated to the worship of Quirinus* on the Quirinal.

SALMACIS [Gr. Salmakis]. Nymph of a very clear spring in Caria (Asia Minor), the water of which made the user effeminate (see HERMAPHRODITUS).

SALMONEUS. Son of Aeolus* and Enarete*; king of Elis. In a frenzy of arrogance he tried to equal Zeus by driving around in a bronze chariot and imitating the god's thunder and lightning. He also ordered people to make sacrifices to him. He paid for his arrogance with his life: he was slain by the supreme god's shafts of lightning (Virg. vi, 585f.).

SALUS [Lat. = health]. Roman goddess of the public weal, including both of the individual and that of the state. As goddess of health, she is identified with Hygeia*. The temple of Salus Publica Populi Romani (= goddess of the public weal of the Roman people) was consecrated on the Quirinal at Rome in 302 B.C. (Liv. x, 1, 9). The fact that in 180

B.C. sacrificial ceremonies were performed in honor of Apollo*, Asclepius*, and Salus* suggests that even at that time the goddess' chief function was rather that of protectress of personal health (Liv. xl, 19).

SARPEDON. 1. Son of Zeus* and Europa*. Expelled by his brother Minos, he went to Asia Minor and became king of the Lycians; he lived for three generations of men. 2. Son of Zeus and Laodamia (1)* and king of the Lycians. During the siege of Troy he came to Priam's assistance. He was slain by Patroclus*, and Zeus had his body taken back to Lycia by Apollo (Hom. Il. v, 471f.; xvi, 419f., 666f.).

SATURN [Lat. Saturnus]. Old Italic god of agriculture, married to Ops*. He was venerated as the benefactor of humanity and bringer of prosperity and civilization. He was later identified with the Greek god Cronus* and regarded as the father of Jupiter*, Ceres*, Juno*, etc. Jupiter is said to have dispossessed him, and the god Janus* received him hospitably in Italy, where he introduced agriculture and wine growing and where his reign meant a period of prosperity and undisturbed happiness, the so-called Golden Age*. Part of his temple at the foot of the Capitoline Hill can still be seen. As a Latin god Saturn was never popular. Only his identification with Cronus gave his name some prominence, and his name survived principally in the festival of the Saturnalia (Virg. viii, 319).

SATURNALIA. Festival of Saturn*, the most popular in the Roman calendar, originally celebrated on Dec. 17 but soon extended by a few holidays. These were limited to three by Augustus but increased to five again later. On Dec. 17 an official sacrifice was offered at the temple of Saturn on the Forum Romanum, followed by public festivities, with a banquet for senators and notables. The next few days were passed in a general spirit of gaiety with visits to friends and relatives and exchanges of gifts and good wishes. A favorite form of present was one of the small clay figurines baked specially for the festival in the days that preceded it. While the festival lasted, slaves were served by their masters and treated as equals. Perhaps remembrance of the Golden Age* of Saturn had something to do with these various practices, though more probably the festival was inspired by the need to give each other pleasure around the winter solstice. The wax candle was another feature of this festival, being a symbol of the returning sunlight. Various aspects of the Saturnalia are still recognizable in the folklore and religious customs of the Christianized world.

SATYR [Gr. Saturos]. A Greek wood demon, half man and half animal, with shaggy hair, goat's feet, horns, and a tail. The Satyrs form part of Dionysus' retinue and personify the coarse sensual instincts. Drinking, playing, and pestering nymphs were their favorite pastimes. The Romans identified them with the Fauns.
Iconography. The satyr is shown extremely often on Greek vases as a human being with more or less animal-like characteristics. The tail in particular, is seldom absent. The face is typified by a blunt nose and mischievous eyes. Satyrs are generally shown in sensual and occasionally obscene settings. The attributes of Dionysus—ivy, flute, etc.—are also used for them. They are often shown in the company of nymphs or Maenads*, whom they boisterously pursue. In sculpture they are given a quieter and more human appearance. There is a famous satyr by Praxiteles (4th century B.C.), now at Rome: with his flute in one hand and his other hand on his side, he lolls against a tree trunk. The Barberini satyr at Munich is a Hellenistic work; it shows a drunken satyr sleeping off his hangover. Also well known is the bronze dancing satyr from the Casa del Fauno

at Pompeii, now at Naples (Mus. Nazionale). Innumerable satyrs are shown on frescoes, coins, and cameos.
SCAEVOLA. See MUCIUS SCAEVOLA.
SCAMANDER [Gr. Skamandros or Xanthos]. River near Troy and the god of that river. The river god was the father of Teucer (1)* and during the siege of Troy sometimes took part in the battle (Hom. Il. xx, 73f.; xxi, 1f., 120f.).
SCAMANDRIUS [Gr. Skamandrios]. See ASTYANAX.
SCHERIA. In Homer, the island of the Phaeacians* where Odysseus* was shipwrecked and washed ashore. Corfu has sometimes been fancifully identified with this fairy-tale island.
SCHOENEUS [Gr. Schoineus]. Son of Athamas* and Themisto*, king of Boeotia and father of Atalanta*.
SCIRON [Gr. Skeiron]. A cruel robber who dwelt on a rock on the border of Megaris. He forced travelers to wash his feet and, as they did so, kicked them over the steep rocks into the sea. Theseus made him undergo the same fate (Ov. vii, 444).
SCYLLA [Skulla]. 1. Daughter of Phorcys*; she was changed into a monster by the jealous Circe* (Ov. xiv, 52f.). 2. Daughter of Poseidon*, a monster with the body of a dog and six heads; she lived in a cave by the Strait of Messina, opposite Charybdis* (Ov. vii, 65). When Odysseus* was sailing through the strait and came too close to her cave, she seized six of his crew and devoured them (Hom. Od. xii, 80f.; 223.; 430f.). On his travels Aeneas, too, came close to Scylla (Virg. iii, 424). 3. Daughter of Nisus*, the king of Megara. In her love for Minos* she betrayed her father to him. Minos thought her action abominable and drowned her. A.t.o. she jumped into the sea of her own accord and was changed into a bird (Ov. viii, 6f.).
Iconography. Scylla (3) is shown handing Nisus' golden hair over to Minos on a mural painting in the Casa di Castore e Polluce at Pompeii.
SELENE [Lat. Luna = moon]. The Greek moon goddess, daughter of Hyperion* and twin sister of Helius*. At

night she rose from the ocean driving her chariot drawn by four white horses or oxen. She was often identified with Artemis*, Persephone*, or Hecate*. The legend of her love for Endymion* is well known. The goddess Luna who was her Roman counterpart was held in greater veneration.

Iconography. In art Selene was represented in much the same way as Artemis, but was distinguished by the veil around her head, which was adorned by a halo or a crescent moon. Her attribute is a torch. Her love for Endymion is a favorite theme in art.

SEMELE. Daughter of Cadmus* and Harmonia*, and mother by Zeus of Dionysus*. Zeus had promised her, as his beloved, to grant any wish she cared to make. On the advice of the jealous Hera*, she asked him to appear to her in might and majesty under his true form. When the god appeared to her with thunder and lightning, she was overcome by the sight and by the heat of his thunderbolts and died. Zeus hid her unborn child, Dionysus, in his thigh (Ov. iii, 293).

SEMENTIVAE. See TELLUS.

SEMONIA. Roman goddess of sowing.

SERAPIS. The state god in Egypt under the rule of the Ptolemies. Ptolemy I (Soter) introduced the worship into Egypt. The Egyptians regarded Serapis as a combination of Apis* and Osiris*. His worship also became widespread in Hellas and Rome, where he was venerated as an amalgam of Zeus* and Hades*. As a god of health and sickness he was sometimes identified with Asclepius*. The most famous temple of Serapis was in Alexandria; it was destroyed in 391 by the Christians.

Iconography. In Greek art Serapis is an elderly man with curly hair and beard. His head shows a strong resemblance to that of Zeus. On his head Serapis wore the bushel, a basket filled with objects used in the mystery service. The statue of Serapis for the chief temple at Alexandria is attributed by tradition to the sculptor Bryaxis.

SERESTUS. A companion of Aeneas who sometimes acted as his deputy (Virg. i, 611; ix, 171).

SERGESTUS. One of Aeneas' companions. He was the founder of the Sergias, an important patrician family at Rome, of which Catalina, for example, was a member (Virg. iv, 288).

SEVEN AGAINST THEBES. When Polynices* was expelled from Thebes by his brother Eteocles*, Adrastus*, at whose court the exile found refuge, organized a war expedition by seven heroes against Thebes, the city with the seven gates, in order to restore Polynices to his rightful position. All the heroes died except Adrastus.

SIBYL. In Greek and Roman mythology, the name given to a woman who was inspired by Apollo* and prophesied in an ecstasy. Originally there was considered to be only one Sibyl, but later the number became ten or twelve. The best known is the Sibyl of Cumae (in southern Italy), who came from the east, was very old, and foretold the future to many, including Aeneas. She also guided him on his visit to the underworld (Virg. vi, 10, 77, 83, 258). The cave in which she dwelt is still pointed out near Cumae (now Cuma). The Sibylline books* are ascribed to the Cumaean Sibyl. The best known Sibyl in Greece was that of Erythraea.

Iconography. Sibyls are often depicted in medieval and later art, e.g. on choir stalls, in glass windows, and on carpets. Michelangelo's paintings in the Sistine Chapel, in which he portrays five Sibyls, are renowned. Medieval art transformed the pagan prophetesses and sometimes placed them beside the Jewish prophets.

SIBYLLINE BOOKS. A collection of old Roman oracular pronouncements which were attributed to the Cumaean Sibyl. One of Rome's kings, Tarquinius Priscus, is said to have bought the books. They were kept in the crypt of the Capitol and consulted in times of danger to the state by a college of two, later ten or fifteen, men (Liv. xxxviii, 45, 3).

SIDERO. Wife of Salmoneus* and stepmother of Tyro*. Because of her cruel treatment of Tyro she was killed by Tyro's sons Pelias* and Neleus*.

SILENI [Gr. Seilenoi]. Greek wood-demons, closely related to the satyrs. Like satyrs, fauns, etc. they form part of Dionysus' retinue.

Iconography. Sileni are represented innumerable times, particularly on Greek vases. They are shown as human beings with a flat nose, thick lips, and a horse's ears and tail (see also SATYR).

SILENUS [Gr. Seilenos]. Son of Hermes* or Pan*, tutor of the young Dionysus* and his faithful companion. He was an inveterate wine drinker and lived in a permanent state of intoxication, so that other satyrs had to support him or transport him on an ass. Midas* once received a princely reward from Dionysus for his hospitality to Silenus when the latter in a befuddled state had become detached from the god's retinue (Ov. xi, 85f.).

Iconography. In art Silenus is represented as a merry, pot-bellied, bald old gentleman, although there are also sculptures which show him as a well-built, dignified man and noble guardian of the youthful Dionysus, e.g. a statue in the Louvre.

SILVANUS [Lat. *silva* = wood]. Roman forest god, protector of plants, trees, and herds. He has features in common with Faunus* and Pan*. Like the latter, he was well disposed toward mankind but was occasionally mischievous, being fond, for instance, of causing the lonely traveler sudden terror. He was also reputed to be the guardian of landed property, a function he shares with Terminus*. There is also a connection between Silvanus and Mars, for Mars Silvanus was invoked to protect cattle. The first fruits of the fields were sacrificed to Silvanus, women being excluded from the ceremony. Statues of the deity were likewise set up in places to which women were not admitted.

SILVIUS. Son of Aeneas* and Lavinia*. He succeeded Ascanius* as king of Alba Longa* (Virg. vi, 763).

SINIS. A robber who dwelt on the Isthmus of Corinth. He tied his victims between two pine trees which he had bent together. He then released the trees so that the unfortunate traveler was torn asunder. He himself suffered the same fate at the hands of Theseus (Ov. vii, 440).

SINON. A Greek spy who cunningly managed to gain the besieged Trojans' trust and persuaded them to take the Wooden Horse* into the city (Virg. ii, 77f.).

SIRENS [Gr. Seirenes]. In Greek mythology, creatures with bodies like birds' and heads like women's. They lived on an island and with their bewitching song irresistibly lured passing sailors to the coast, where they suffered shipwreck. Odysseus managed to escape their influence by plugging his crew's ears and having himself tied to the mast (Hom. Od. xii, 39f., 158f.). The song of the Sirens also failed to affect the Argonauts* as they passed, because the even lovelier voice of Orpheus reduced the Sirens to silence. Homer speaks of two Sirens, later authors of three or four. They were thought of as daughters of Phorcys* or the river god Achelous*. Ovid describes them as nymphs and playmates of Proserpina* who were present at her abduction. As they made no attempt to prevent the crime, Ceres* (Demeter) changed them into birds with women's faces (Ov. v, 551f.). Latin authors specify their abode as the *Sirenum scopuli,* three small rocky islands between Sorrento and Capri (Virg. v, 864; Ov. xiv, 88).

Iconography. The adventure of Odysseus with the Sirens is depicted several times, e.g. on a Corinthian aryballos (c. 570 B.C.), in Boston. Several Sirens are here represented entirely as birds of prey. The more normal representation of the Sirens as large birds with women's heads is found on the well-known Attic vase by the "Siren Painter" (c. 475 B.C.), now at London: it shows Odysseus' ship, with the hero lashed to the mast, passing at full speed between two rocks on which the Sirens are perched. One of the monsters is plunging into the sea because her plans have been thwarted.

SISYPHUS [Gr. Sisuphos]. Son of Aeolus* and Enarete*. He was the founder and king of Corinth and was supposed to have instituted the Isthmian Games*. Tradition attributed all kinds of crimes to him; as a brigand he was a danger to the surrounding area; he betrayed the secrets of the gods; he murdered travelers and even, by his cunning, managed to capture Death, so that he was immortal until Hades* personally intervened. In the underworld, as punishment for his crimes, he had to roll a huge rock up a mountain. Each time, just before he reached the summit, it rolled down again. Some say that he was the father of Odysseus* by Anticlea* before she married Laertes* and that Theseus was the hero who rid the country of Sisyphus.

Iconography. The punishment of Sisyphus is shown on many Greek vases. He is represented nude or with a skin over his shoulders. In the Lesche at Delphi there was a painting, famous in antiquity, by Polygnotus (5th century B.C.), which showed Sisyphus rolling his rock up the mountain.

SMINTHEUS. Epithet of Apollo*, derived from Smintha, a city in the Troad, or from *sminthos* (Gr. = mouse) to mean the "destroyer of mice."

SOL [Lat. = sun]. The Roman sun god, completely identified with the Greek god Helius*. Sacrifices were offered to Sol Indiges on the Quirinal at Rome on August 8. In later Imperial times the cult of Sol Invictus was introduced from Syria to Rome by Heliogabalus (218-222), who was priest of the temple of the sun at Emesa (now Homs) in Syria. *Iconography.* See HELIUS.

SOMNUS [Lat. = sleep]. Roman personification of sleep, equivalent to the Greek Hypnos*. Somnus caused the death of Palinurus*. (Virg. v, 838).

SORANUS. Sabine deity who was worshiped on Mt. Soracte to the N. of Rome. Virgil (xi, 783) speaks of Apollo Soranus, venerated on Soracte, where his devotees, the "Hirpi Sorani" (= wolves of Soranus), walked barefoot through fire.

SPARTI. The armed men who sprang from the dragon's teeth sown by Cadmus* (Gr. *spartos* = sown). They slaughtered each other until five were left; these became the forefathers of the Thebans.

SPERCHEUS [Gr. Spercheios]. God of the river of the same name in Thessaly, son of Oceanus* and Gaea*.

SPHINX [Gr. *sphinggein* = to throttle]. Greek demon of ruin and misfortune, who captured people and killed them. She was also a soothsayer. The myth of the unsolved riddle and the associated plague forms part of the Oedipus* legend, in which a Sphinx ravages the district round Thebes. "Sphinx" was also the Greek designation for the lioness "couchant" with a queen's head which is familiar from the Egyptian world.

Iconography. In Egyptian art the Sphinx is a statue of a lion with the Pharaoh's head; the Sphinx of Giza, for instance, is a kind of statue of the Pharaoh Khafre. In Greek art the Sphinx is a female creature allied to the Harpies: the body of a lion with the head of a woman. The scene between Oedipus and the Sphinx is painted on a vase (1st half of 5th century B.C.) in the Vatican Museum.

STATA MATER. Roman goddess who gave protection against fire. Her statue stood on the Forum Romanum, and she was closely associated with Vulcan* and Vesta*, being sometimes identified with the latter.

STATOR. Epithet applied to Jupiter* as the god who turned flight into a resistance (Lat. *stare* = to stand). There were two temples to Jupiter Stator at Rome; the older, according to tradition, was founded on the Velian Hill by Romulus* during the Sabine War, in which the Romans were forced to retreat (Liv. i, 12, 3f.). Romulus' simple shrine was replaced in 294 B.C. by a proper temple (Liv. x, 36, 11; x, 37, 15).

STENTOR. One of the Greek heroes at the siege of Troy. He was famed for his powerful voice, which was as loud as that of fifty men.

STERCUTUS [Lat. *stercus* = dung]. Roman god whose task it was to ensure that arable land was fertilized; another name for Saturn* or, others say, Picumnus*.

STEROPE. One of the Pleiades*.

STEROPES. One of the Cyclopes. It was his task to forge the shafts of lightning.

STERQUILINUS. Another name for Picumnus* as the Roman god who fertilized agricultural land.

STHENELUS [Gr. Sthelenos]. 1. Son of Capaneus* and Evadne* and one of the Epigoni*. In the Trojan War he and Diomedes* led the men from Argos (Virg. ii, 261). 2. Son of Perseus* and Andromeda*, king of Mycenae and father of Eurystheus*. 3. Son of Androgeus* and companion of Heracles* on his expedition to the Amazons*. 4. King of Liguria and father of Cycnus*.

STIMULA [Lat. = she who excites]. Roman goddess who generated passion in women; later identified with Semele*. The Bacchanalia* were celebrated under her auspices.

STRENIA. Sabine goddess, venerated at Rome at the beginning of the new year. Her sanctuary stood on the Via Sacra.

STROPHIUS [Gr. Strophios]. King of Phocis, father of Pylades* and brother-in-law of Agamemnon*.

STYMPHALIAN BIRDS. Voracious man-eating birds of prey which haunted Lake Stymphalus, near the city of the same name in Arcadia (now Kionea). They were dispersed by Heracles*.

STYX. The main river in the Greek and Roman nether regions. The gods swore their most binding oaths by it, and if such an oath was broken it was punished by the loss of immortality. "Styx" is also a poetical name for the underworld itself (Virg. vi, 154, 439; Ov. xii, 322).

SUMMANUS. Ancient Roman deity of, some say, Etruscan or Sabine origin. He was the god of nocturnal storms (submanus = the god who sends lightning before dawn) and a counterpart of Jupiter, the god who fired his shafts of lightning in the daytime. His temple at Rome stood on the Circus Maximus, where a sort of cake (Summanalia) was offered to him on June 20.

SYCHAEUS. King of Tyre and husband of Dido*; murdered by his brother-in-law Pygmalion* (Virg. i, 343f.).

SYMPLEGADES [Lat. Cyaneae insulae]. Two small, rocky islands near the mouth of the Bosporus in the Black Sea, which, according to a Greek myth, continually struck together, preventing safe passage by ships. Not until the passage of the Argo* did they become fixed (Hom. Od. xii, 61; Herod. iv, 85, 1).

SYRINX. Greek nymph, pursued by Pan and at her own request changed into a reed by the gods. Pan made his flute from this reed; it consisted of several different lengths of reed placed side by side (Ov. i, 698f.).

T

TAGES. A genius*, grandson of Jupiter*. When an Etruscan farmer Tarchon was plowing his land in the vicinity of Tarquinia, Tages suddenly appeared from the furrow in the form of a boy and taught the art of *haruspicia,* i.e. how to divine the future by inspecting the entrails of a sacrificial animal, to the Etruscans who had rushed up to watch. This peculiarly Etruscan art of prophecy, which was later practiced by the Romans, was recorded in the Libri Tagetici, Haruspicini, or Acherontici (Ov. xv, 558). *Iconography.* On a bronze Etruscan mirror from Tuscany, now in Florence (Museo Archeologico), Tages is shown instructing Tarchon, while several gods stand around, watching.

TALASSIO, TALASSIUS, or TALASSUS. Old Roman or Etruscan marriage deity, invoked as the bride was led to the bridegroom's house. He was said to have been a friend of Romulus* and to have been involved in the Rape of the Sabine Women*. The cry of "Talassio" was traditionally raised as the bride set foot in her new home (Liv. i, 9, 11).

TALAUS [Gr. Talaos]. Son of Bias* and Pero*; king of Argos and father of Adrastus* and Eriphyle*.

TALOS. A bronze giant made by Hephaestus* and presented to Minos* to guard Crete. When he saw strangers he turned red-hot and killed them in his arms. When the Argonauts* landed in Crete, Medea rendered the giant harmless by removing the pin that stoppered his single vein. *Iconography.* Talos' death is shown on a voluted krater (c. 400 B.C.) at Ruvo. Marked out in white paint and raised contours, the metal giant is seen just as he is about to sink to the ground.

TALTHYBIUS [Gr. Talthubios]. King Agamemnon's herald in the Greek army

before Troy (Hom. Il. i, 320; iv, 192f.).

TANTALUS [Gr. Tantalos]. 1. Son of Zeus*, king of Phrygia or Lydia, and father of Pelops* and Niobe*. He was very rich and so highly regarded by the gods that he was allowed to be present at their meals. His success went to his head, and he sinned either by stealing nectar* and ambrosia* or by betraying the gods' secrets. He is even said to have served his son Pelops to them as food. He was subjected to a terrible punishment in the underworld. He was compelled to stand in water up to his chin, with a branch heavy with fruit just above his head. When he tried to drink, the water receded, and when he reached for the fruit, the branch rose out of his reach, so that he suffered eternal hunger and thirst. The curse that Tantalus brought down upon himself by his arrogance also fell upon his descendants, such as Atreus* and Niobe* (Ov. x, 41). 2. Son of Thyestes*, killed by Atreus*. 3. Son of Amphion* and Niobe (Ov. vi, 240). *Iconography.* Tantalus (1) is seen on several Greek vases, including an Apulian krater at Munich, on which he is dressed in theatrical costume with a scepter in his hand. The punishment of Tantalus is also depicted in Baroque art.

TAPHIUS [Gr. Taphios]. Son of Poseidon* and Hippothoë. He was reputed to have founded the city of Taphos on the island of the same name.

TARAS. Son of Poseidon*. He came from Peloponnesus to southern Italy, where he founded Tarentum (Gr. Taras, now Taranto). Others say the city was founded by Heracles (Virg. iii, 551).

TARCHON. Etruscan hero. Together with his brother Tyrrhenus*, he founded the Etruscan League, of which twelve cities were members: Tarquinii (Tarquinia-Corneto), Caere (Cerveteri),

Vulci (Volci), Rusellae (Roselle), Vetulonia, Populonia, Volsinii (Bolsena), Clusium (Chiusi), Arretium (Arezzo), Perusia (Perugia), Volaterrae (Volterra), and Faesulae (Fiesole) or Cortona. Tarchon gave his name to the city of Tarchonium, later called Tarquinii. He supported Aeneas* in his fight against Turnus* (Virg. x, 153, 290; xi, 727, 746).

TARTARUS [Gr. Tartaros or Tartara]. The most terrible section of the underworld of the Greeks and Romans, a bottomless pit under the earth, where Zeus shut up the Titans* and others. Tartarus was also the place where the Cyclopes*, Danaids*, Sisyphus*, Tantalus*, Ixion*, etc., underwent the punishment for their crimes. It was the realm of eternal darkness. See HADES.

TAURIS. The peninsula now known as the Crimea, called Chersonesus Taurica by the Romans.

TAYGETE. Daughter of Atlas*; one of the Pleiades* and companion of Artemis*. She was the mother of Lacedaemon by Zeus. Some say she was turned into a hind by Artemis.

TEIRESIAS. See TIRESIAS.

TELAMON. Son of Aeacus* and Endeis*. He became king of Salamis, took part in the expedition of the Argonauts* and the Calydonian hunt*, and helped Heracles* in the struggle against the Amazons* and against Laomedon* of Troy. As his reward he received Laomedon's daughter Hesione* in marriage. He was the father of Ajax* and Teucer* by Eriboea (Hom. Il. viii, 283f.).

TELCHINES. A mythical priestly family that migrated in earliest times from Crete to Rhodes via Cyprus. They were reputed to have been Poseidon's* tutors and were specially skilled in metalwork. They were sometimes identified with the Cyclopes*, Dactyls*, or Curetes*. When they degenerated into wicked magicians they were killed by the gods.

TELEGONUS [Gr. Telegonos]. Son of Odysseus* and Circe*. On his mother's orders Telegonus set out in search of Odysseus, landing finally in Ithaca. There he was regarded as an interloper, and in the ensuing struggle he killed his father

without recognizing him. Later he married Penelope*, who bore him a son Italus*. He went to Italy where he founded Tusculum (now Frascati) and Praeneste (now Palestrina).

TELEMACHUS [Gr. Telemachos]. Son of Odysseus* and Penelope*. When his father went off to the Trojan War, Telemachus was still a child, but he grew up into a fine young man, standing by his mother in her resistance to the importunate suitors. On Athena's advice he visited Menelaus and Nestor to inquire about his long-absent father. When he returned to Ithaca he escaped an attempt on his life planned by the suitors. He finally met his father at Eumaeus' house and helped him to revenge himself on the suitors (Hom. Od. i, 113f., 296f.; iv, 600f., 768; xvi and xvii, passim). After the death of Odysseus he married Circe or her daughter. A.t.o. he was married to Nausicaä* or Policasta, who bore him Ptoliporthes.

Iconography. Telemachus is seen on many Greek vase paintings referring to Odysseus' adventures. An Attic skyphos (c. 435 B.C.) shows him comforting Penelope, who is sitting sadly at her loom.

TELEMUS [Gr. Telemos]. A Cyclops* who was a soothsayer.

TELEPHASA. Wife of Agenor* and mother of Cadmus* and others.

TELEPHUS [Gr. Telephos], Son of Heracles* and Auge*. As a child he was exposed, but was found by shepherds. On the advice of an oracle he went to Mysia, where he became king. When the Greeks, on the way to Troy, attacked Mysia, they were repulsed by Telephus, who was, however, wounded by Achilles' * spear. Although the Greeks asked him to join them and march against Troy, he refused. The siege of Troy did not prosper because, as an oracle had told Agamemnon*, the city could not be taken without the help of Telephus. The latter's wound would not heal and—once more on the advice of an oracle—he went to Achilles because only he who had inflicted the wound could heal it. A little rust from Achilles' spear cured the wound immediately. In gratitude Telephus gave the

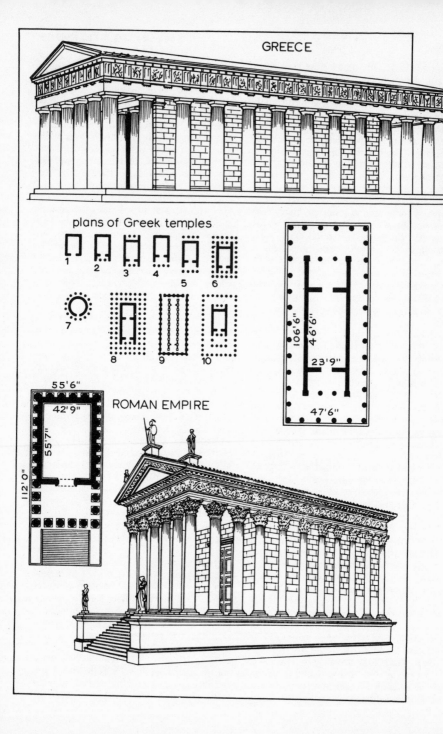

GREECE

plans of Greek temples

1
2
3
4
5
6
7
8
9
10

106'6"
46'6"
23'9"
47'6"

55'6"
42'9"
112'0"
55'7"

ROMAN EMPIRE

Greeks much advice on how to capture Troy, but without personally taking part in the fighting (Ov. xii, 112).

Iconography. The adventures of Telephus are often depicted in ancient art, e.g. on the "Telephus frieze" of the Pergamum altar (c. 150 B.C.). His battle against the Greeks is recorded by Scopas on the W. façade of the temple of Athena at Tegea (c. 360 B.C.). Scenes from his life are also illustrated on cinerary urns, gems, coins, vases, and wall paintings. He is usually shown as a bearded man. nude or wearing a cloak, and tortured by his wound. He occurs as a small child, suckled by a hind, in the well-known mural painting in the Basilica of Herculaneum: sitting on a throne in front of Telephus is Arcadia, a personification of the province, and Heracles stands at the side, looking around and recognizing his son.

TELESPHORUS [Gr. Telesphoros]. A Greek god of healing, son of Asclepius* and brother of Hygeia*. The cult of Telesphorus originated at Pergamum in Hellenistic times (c. 200 B.C.).

Iconography. Telesphorus is represented in a wide cloak with a hood hanging down, sometimes with a Phrygian cap on his head. He is found on terracotta, reliefs, and coins from Asia Minor.

TELLUMO. Roman deity, the male counterpart of Tellus* and personification of the alimentary power of nature.

TELLUS [Lat. = earth]. Roman goddess of the earth, equivalent to the Greek Gaea*. As the fertilizing force that causes the crops of the field to grow, she was also identified with Ceres*. At the Fordicia festival on April 15, cows in calf were sacrificed to her. On January 24-26 the Sementivae were celebrated in honor of Ceres and Tellus to beseech their protection for the seed and the sower. Cakes and a sow were offered, and the teams of oxen were festively decked out on that day. The temple of Tellus at Rome stood on the Forum Pacis.

TEMPLE [Lat. *templum* = a space marked out]. The Greek and Roman temple was exclusively the building in which the statue of the deity was erected, and not a place in which the masses of the faithful assembled for worship. Sacrifices were offered on the altar that stood outside and in front of the temple. The Greek temple was a richly sculptured shrine for the deity. The edifice had no actual façade and stood on a low podium consisting of three steps. The Roman temple stood on a high podium and is distinctly frontal in appearance. The front portal was deep and frequently the columns extended only along three sides, leaving a blank wall at the rear. Both the rectangular and the circular temple were known to Greeks and Romans alike; Greek circular temples are always surrounded by columns, whereas Roman ones are sometimes so surrounded (e.g. the temple of Vesta at Rome) and sometimes not (e.g. the Pantheon at Rome).

TENES. Son of Cycnus (2)*, falsely accused to his father by his stepmother. Cycnus had him put in a chest and thrown into the sea, but the chest came ashore on the island of Tenedos, where Tenes became king. He was venerated as a hero on the island.

TERES. Son of Ares* and husband of Procne* (see PHILOMELA).

TERMERUS [Gr. Termeros]. A brigand in Thessaly, put to death by Heracles*.

TERMINALIA. See TERMINUS.

TERMINUS [Lat. = boundary]. Roman god who protected the boundaries between fields. At the festival of Terminalia, on February 23, neighbors offered

---

TEMPLES

TOP: the Hephaesteum at Athens, formerly known as the Theseum (*c.* 403 B.C.), with floor plan at right below it;
CENTER: floor plans of ten types of Greek temple: (1) megaron; (2) distyle in antis; (3) distyle in antis (both ends); (4) prostyle; (5) amphiprostyle; (6) peripteral; (7) tholos; (8) dipteral; (9) pseudoperipteral; (10) pseudodipteral;
BOTTOM: the *Maison Carrée* at Nimes (16 B.C.), one of the best-preserved Roman temples, with floor plan at left.

sacrifices at their common boundary stone and joined in a banquet. In fact, the stone itself was a sacred object, endowed with divine power, and this power was renewed annually by the wreaths placed on the stone and the sacrificial blood spilled upon it. Not until later was the stone regarded as a personal god. Sacrifices were also offered by the state at the boundary stone on the Via Laurentina, which marked the limit of the "ager Romanus" (the district round Rome). Jupiter, also a protector of boundaries, was closely associated with Terminus and was worshiped under the title of Jupiter Terminus or Terminalis. According to legend, Terminus was the only deity who did not give way to Jupiter when the latter took possession of his temple on the Capitol*. A stone in this temple was honored as the boundary stone of Terminus (Liv. i, 55, 3).

TERPSICHORE. The Muse* of choral dancing and choral singing.
Iconography. She is represented with a lyre in her hand.

TETHYS. Daughter of Uranus* and Gaea*. She was the sister and wife of Oceanus* and mother of countless sons and daughters, who were river gods and sea nymphs.

TEUCER [Gr. Teukros]. 1. Son of the river god Scamander* and the nymph Idaea*. He was the first king of the Trojans, who were also called Teucrians after him. He bestowed his land on Dardanus* and gave him his daughter Arisbe* in marriage. He brought the cult of Cybele* from Crete to Asia Minor (Virg. i, 235; iii, 108). 2. Son of Telamon* and Hesione*; the most famous archer among the Greeks at Troy. He was supposed to be the founder of Salamis in Cyprus (Hom. Il. viii, 266f.; 300f.).

TEUCRUS [Gr. Teukros]. Other name for Teucer (1)*.

THALIA 1. [Gr. Thaleia]. The Muse* of comedy. 2. [Gr. Thalia]. One of the Charites*.
Iconography. Thalia the Muse is represented with a comic mask in one hand and a pedum, or shepherd's crook, in the other.

THALLO. Name under which one of the Horae* was venerated at Athens.

THAMYRAS or THAMYRIS [Gr. Thamuras or Thamuris]. Legendary Greek poet from Thracia who was so vain of his numerous victories that he challenged the Muses to a contest. For this act he was struck blind.

THANATOS [Gr. = death]. Greek personification of death, twin brother of Hypnos*. Neither was of great religious significance.
Iconography. Thanatos is represented as a youth holding a torch upside down in one hand and a wreath or butterfly in the other. He often appears together with Hypnos on Attic sepulchral vases or lekythi. On a sculptured column drum from the temple of Artemis at Ephesus (4th century B.C.) Thanatos has two large wings and is girt with a sword.

THAUMAS. Greek sea god, son of Pontus* and Gaea*, father by the Oceanid Electra of Iris*, the messenger of the gods.

THEA [Gr. Theia]. Daughter of Uranus* and Gaea*; mother, by her brother Hyperion*, of Helius*, Eos*, and Selene*.

THEMIS. Greek goddess of law and order, daughter of Uranus* and Gaea*, and mother by Zeus* of the Moirae* and the Horae*. She was an oracular goddess, the oracle at Delphi being hers before it was Apollo's (Ov. i, 321). She was called Justitia by the Romans.
Iconography. Themis is represented as a blindfold woman with a stern countenance. Her attributes are scales, a sword, a horn of plenty, and a palm branch. Apart from Roman Imperial coins, she is shown particularly often in Baroque and Renaissance art.

THEMISTO. Daughter of Hypseus and third wife of Athamas*. When the latter took back his second wife Ino*, Themisto planned to kill Ino's children at night. To make no mistake she dressed them in black and her own children in white. Ino, however, interchanged the garments, so that Themisto murdered her own offspring.

THERAS. Descendant of Polynices*, who founded a colony on the island of

Calliste, which was thenceforth called Thera (now Santorin).

THERSANDER [Gr. Thersandros]. Son of Polynices*, one of the Epigoni*. He set off with the Greeks for Troy, but on the way he was killed by Telephus in Mysia, where he was later worshiped as a hero.

THERSITES. The ugliest man in the Greek army at Troy, generally hated for his insolent remarks and seditious language. He was killed by Achilles when trying to violate Penthesilea's dead body. Odysseus, too, had had a violent quarrel with him (Hom. Il. ii, 212f.).

THESEUS. The legendary national hero of Athens and Attica, son of the Athenian king Aegeus* and Aethra*, a princess from Troezen. Theseus was born in Troezen and spent his youth there. Aegeus had hidden his sandals and sword under a rock and forbidden Theseus to come to Athens until he could move the stone aside and bring his father's sword. When Theseus was sixteen his mother took him to the rock, which he removed without difficulty. The young hero then went to Athens, experiencing numerous adventures on the way: he killed many bad characters, such as Periphetes*, Sinis*, Sciron*, Cercyon*, and Procrustes*, and rid the region of a monstrous boar. He arrived in Athens to find his father ensnared in the toils of the sorceress Medea*, who now tried to poison Theseus. When Theseus drew his sword, his father recognized him and Medea was expelled. Next the hero slew the Pallantids, nephews of his father who had designs on the throne of Athens. Then came his most famous exploit: slaying the Minotaur* in Crete, an act which freed Athens from the terrible disgrace of being subject to the whims of the Cretan king Minos*. When the latter's son Androgeus had been killed by the Athenians, Minos had mounted a punitive expedition against Greece. With the aid of Scylla*, daughter of King Nisus*, he captured Megara. Athens, too, was taken, and the city was compelled to send seven youths and seven maidens to Crete every eight or nine years as food for the

Minotaur. Theseus voluntarily embarked with the victims and landed in Crete, where the king's daughter Ariadne fell in love with him. She gave him a ball of thread which enabled him to mark his path through the Labyrinth*, where the Minotaur lived, so that he could retrace his steps. After slaying the monster, Theseus fled from Crete with Ariadne but abandoned her on Naxos. There she became the wife of Dionysus*. After instituting the festival of Delia on Delos, the hero returned to Athens, where various festivals were founded in gratitude for the liberation. Unfortunately, Theseus had, on approaching the coast of Greece, forgotten the promise he had given his father: that if his voyage was successful he would hoist white sails instead of the black ones that the ship bearing the sacrifices usually carried. Aegeus, seeing the ships approaching under black sails, assumed the worst and threw himself into the sea, since when it has been known as the Aegean. Theseus succeeded his father, united the tiny states of Attica into a single state with Athens as its capital, and instituted the Panathenaea*. Among the many dangerous exploits in which he took part were the expedition of the Argonauts* and the Calydonian hunt*. He accompanied Heracles on his expedition to the Amazons and abducted Antiope* or Hippolyta*, by whom he had a son, Hippolytus*. He later married Ariadne's* sister Phaedra*, who bore him Demophon* and Acamas*. He further helped his friend Pirithous* in his battle against the Centaurs*, and together they abducted Helen*. When the two of them also tried to remove Persephone* from the underworld, Hades had them chained to a rock. And although Heracles* managed to free Theseus, the Dioscuri* had meanwhile recovered their captured sister Helen and Menestheus had assumed power over Athens. Disillusioned, Theseus betook himself to Skyros, where King Lycomedes* received him hospitably but later treacherously murdered him. Athens built a temple and celebrated the festival of Thesea in honor of Theseus.

Iconography. Theseus is represented as a slender young man, usually beardless and, like Heracles, wearing a lion's skin and carrying a club. Occasionally he wears a cloak and cap. His feats are frequently illustrated on monuments of antiquity, the battle against the Centaurs, for example, being shown in relief on the temple of Apollo at Bassae-Phigaleia (5th century B.C.). The abduction of Helen by Theseus can be seen on an amphora by Euthymides (c. 500 B.C.), now at Munich. On a bowl by Euphronius and Panaetius (c. 480 B.C.) in Paris Theseus is shown with Amphitrite. His adventure with the Minotaur is painted on a vase by Aeson (c. 420 B.C.), now at Madrid, and on many other vases. On frescoes at Pompeii Theseus appears especially often in the company of Ariadne, e.g. in the Casa del Poeta Tragico, Casa di Marco Lucrezio Frontone, Casa della Caccia (now at Naples), etc. His encounter with the Minotaur is illustrated in the Casa del Centenario.

THESMOPHORIA. See DEMETER.

THESPIUS [Gr. Thespios]. Son of Erechtheus* and founder of Thespiae in Boeotia. He had fifty daughters, by whom Heracles* begot fifty sons.

THESSANDRUS [Gr. Thessandros]. One of the Greeks who entered Troy in the Wooden Horse* (Virg. ii, 261).

THESTIUS [Gr. Thestios]. King of Pleuron in Aetolia, father of Iphicles (2)*, Althaea*, Leda*, etc. (Ov. viii, 487).

THESTOR. Son of Idmon and Laothoë; father of the soothsayer Calchas*.

THETIS. Greek sea goddess, daughter of Nereus* and Doris*. Zeus* and Poseidon* aspired to her favors, but as any son that she might bear was fated to be greater than his father, the gods gave her in marriage to Peleus*. At their wedding Eris* threw the apple of discord into the banqueting hall, an action which had disastrous results. Thetis gave Dionysus* shelter when he was pursued by Lycurgus* and offered hospitality to Hephaestus* when he was cast out of heaven. She helped even Zeus when the other gods conspired against him. Achilles* was her son, and she supported him constantly

in the Trojan War. When Achilles was insulted by Agamemnon, she persuaded Zeus to make things so awkward for the Greeks that Achilles received full satisfaction (Hom. Il. 351f., 397f., 495f.; Ov. xi, 221f.).

Iconography. Thetis is represented as a Nereid, often in the company of Peleus, e.g. on a vase by Peithinus (c. 500 B.C.), now at Berlin. On a bellied amphora (c. 340 B.C.) at London Thetis is shown nude as a bathing Nereid, resisting the attempts of Peleus to seize her. One of the scenes on the famous François krater is the procession of the gods on their way to the wedding of Thetis and Peleus, a motif that first occurs at a very early date in vase painting, e.g. on an Attic jug by Sophilus (c. 560 B.C.), preserved at Athens. Other scenes from Thetis' life are also illustrated, such as dipping Achilles in the Styx and visiting Hephaestus to ask for new armor for her son (e.g. on a fresco in the Casa di Sirico at Pompeii).

THIASOS. The crowd of Bacchantes*, Satyrs*, and Sileni* which, under the leadership of Pan* and Silenus*, formed the retinue of Dionysus*.

THISBE. See PYRAMUS.

THOAS. 1. King of Tauris, at whose court Iphigenia* served as priestess of Artemis. 2. King of Lemnos and father of Hypsipyle*. When the men of Lemnos were killed by their wives, he was the only one to escape the blood bath. He fled to Cyprus (Ov. xiii, 399). 3. Son of Jason* and Hypsipyle. 4. A companion of Odysseus and one of those who entered Troy in the Wooden Horse* (Virg. ii, 262).

THOÖN. One of the Giants*.

THOÖSA. Daughter of Phorcys* and Ceto*; mother by Poseidon* of the Cyclops* Polyphemus*.

THOT. Egyptian god, identified by the Greeks with Hermes*. He was the god of writing and science.

Iconography. Thot is represented as a man with the head of an ibis, a bird that was sacred to him.

THRIAE [Gr. Thriai]. Winged female demons who lived on Parnassus*. It was they who taught Hermes* the art of prophecy.

THRINACIA. Mythical island somewhere in the west where herds of cattle owned by Helius, the sun god, were kept. An ancient tradition identifies Thrinacia with Sicily (Hom. Od. xi, 107; xii, 127, 135).

THYBRIS. Poetical name for the Tiber (see TIBERIS); in Virgil also a king of Latium from whom the river took its name (Virg. viii, 330).

THYELLA. One of the Harpies*.

THYESTES. Son of Pelops* and brother of Atreus*. The curse pronounced on Pelops' descendants weighed also upon him. Consumed by hatred for his brother, Atreus killed Thyestes' son and served him to Thyestes as food. Another son, Aegisthus*, later took revenge on Atreus.

THYIA. Daughter of Castalius, a priest of Dionysus. She is said to have introduced the orgies in the god's honor. Women who celebrated the Dionysiac festival with licentiousness and ecstasies were called Thyiads after her. (see BACCHANTES) (Virg. iv, 302f.).

THYIADS. See THYIA.

THYRSUS [Gr. Thursos]. A staff entwined with ivy and vine shoots. It was the particular attribute of Dionysus* and the Bacchantes*.

TIBERINUS. See TIBERIS.

TIBERIS or TIBERINUS. The god of the river of the same name (Tiber) at Rome. A.t.s. Tiberis was the father of Ocnus* by Manto*. When Aeneas and the other Trojan exiles landed in Latium and ascended the Tiber, the river god accorded them his support. He later appeared to Aeneas and gave him good advice (Virg. viii, 36, 86). In the earliest Roman times there was a cult of Tiberinus, of which, however, no more is known.

TIBURTUS. The god of the river Anio in Latium. He was reputed to have founded ancient Tibur (now Tivoli) (Virg. vii, 671).

TIMANDRA. Daughter of Tyndareus* and mother of Evander*.

TIPHYS. The steersman of the ship Argo*.

TIRESIAS or TEIRESIAS [Gr. Teiresias]. The famous blind soothsayer from Thebes, descendant of the Sparti*. Acting as judge of a dispute between Zeus* and Hera*, he declared Hera to be in the wrong. The goddess punished him with blindness, but Zeus gave him the gift of prophecy. Others say Athena punished him for peeping at her as she bathed. In the legend of Oedipus it is Tiresias who reveals the truth to Oedipus. When advanced in years he, together with his daughter Manto*, was banished to Delphi, but he died on the way. Even after death, however, he retained the gift of prophecy, and he was able to give Odysseus advice when the two met in the underworld (Hom. Od. x, 492f.; xi, 32f.; xii, 267f.).

TISAMENUS [Gr. Tisamenos]. Son of Orestes* and Hermione*. He died in the struggle against the Heraclids* and was buried at Sparta on the order of an oracle.

TISIPHONE. One of the Erinyes* or Greek goddesses of revenge. She was the avenger of murder (Ov. iv, 481f.; Virg. vi, 555, 571; x, 761).

TITANS. The twelve children of Uranus* and Gaea*, consisting of six sons —Oceanus, Coeus, Crius, Hyperion, Iapetus, and Cronus—and six daughters—Thea, Rhea, Themis, Mnemosyne, Phoebe, and Tethys. Their children and grandchildren are sometimes also called Titans, e.g. Atlas and Prometheus. The two most important of the Titans were Cronus* and Rhea*, who were the parents of Zeus*. When Uranus had cast the Centimani* and Cyclopes* into Tartarus*, Gaea incited her children against their father. Under the leadership of Cronus the Titans maimed Uranus and forced him to abdicate his power in their favor. To ensure his own continuing authority Cronus devoured his children, but Rhea, by a ruse, managed to save Zeus. The latter now joined the battle with the Titans, fetching the Centimani from Tartarus to help him. Zeus and his supporters fought from Olympus, the Titans from Mt. Othrys, and the battle was one of life and death. Zeus emerged victorious and hurled the intransigents into the underworld, while a number of Titans submitted to his rule. The war of the Titans is regarded as an attack by the rough, uncontrolled forces of nature against law and order, represented by Zeus' rule. *Iconography*. The Titans as such are seldom the subject of art. Some of them appear on the great altar of Zeus at Pergamum (c. 150 B.C.). Figures from the War of the Titans and that of the Giants are often found intermingled in ancient works of art.

TITHONUS [Gr. Tithonos]. Son of Laomedon* and brother of Priam*. His wife Eos* obtained the gift of immortality for him but forgot to have it accompanied by eternal youth. At an advanced age Tithonus shrank to a little old man, finally changing into a grasshopper (Virg. iv, 585).

TITYUS [Gr. Tituos]. Powerful giant who tried to violate Leto*. Apollo* killed him with his arrows or Zeus* with his lightning, and in the underworld he was pegged to the ground, where two vultures ate his liver, which kept growing again (Hom. Od. vii, 324; Virg. vi, 595; Ov. iv, 457). *Iconography*. Tityus can be seen on some Greek vases as a bearded giant succumbing under attacks from Apollo and Artemis, e.g. on a krater at Paris (c. 465 B.C.) and on a vase by the so-called Penthesilea painter (c. 455 B.C.) at Munich.

TLEPOLEMUS [Gr. Tlepolemos]. Son of Heracles*. Having killed his uncle Licymnius, he fled to Rhodes, where he became king. In the battle for Troy, in which he later took part, he was slain by Sarpedon (2)* (Hom. Il. v, 659). He was regarded as the founder of several cities on the island of Rhodes, e.g. Lindos.

TRIOPAS. Thessalian king, father of Erysichthon*. He felled a wood sacred to Demeter* in order to build himself a palace on the site. In revenge the goddess caused him to be bitten by a poisonous serpent, whereupon he died.

A.t.o. his punishment consisted of an insatiable hunger.

TRIPTOLEMUS [Gr. Triptolemos]. A Greek hero, son of Celeus* and Metanira*. In gratitude for the hospitality that Demeter* received from Celeus, the goddess presented Triptolemus with several grains of corn and a chariot drawn by dragons. She also entrusted him with the task of teaching agriculture to mankind. He sometimes experienced difficulties on his travels, e.g. from Lyncus*, but Demeter stood by him. On his return home Triptolemus succeeded his father as king of Eleusis* and introduced the Thesmophoria (see DEMETER). *Iconography*. On older black-figured Greek vases Triptolemus is sometimes seen as an old king, dressed in a long robe, with a scepter in one hand and a sheaf of corn in the other. Later he is shown as a handsome, nude youth, and that is how he is represented, in the company of Demeter and Kore, in the famous relief at Eleusis (c. 450 B.C.).

TRITON. Greek sea god, son of Poseidon* and Amphitrite* or, according to the Romans, Salacia*. He rode on the water with horses and sea monsters and blew on his conch-shell horn to calm the seas (Ov. i, 333). Later several Tritons were known who belonged to Poseidon's retinue. *Iconography*. Triton is represented as a man whose body ends in a fishtail. He is also shown with the forelegs of a horse. He usually blows a shell, but sometimes plays the cithara, and is normally accompanied by Nereids*. Triton can be seen on many vases, reliefs, frescoes, and mosaics. Of a much later period is the Bernini Triton at Rome (Piazza Barberini).

TRIVIA. See HECATE.

TROILUS [Gr. Troilos]. Son of King Priam* of Troy. At the start of the siege of Troy he ventured from the city in order to water his horses but was captured and slain by Achilles* (Virg. i, 474). *Iconography*. In the Tomba degli Tori at Tarquinia the encounter of Achilles and Troilus is illustrated in an Etruscan wall painting: Troilus, mounted, is approaching a fountain behind which Achilles lies in wait. The same scene occurs on various Greek vases.

TROPHONIUS [Gr. Trophonios]. 1. Greek chthonic deity who dwelt in a cave near Levadia in Boeotia, where he had an oracle. After many kinds of ceremony the visitor went down into the cave and there received the oracular pronouncement of the god during sleep. 2. Brother of Agamedes* with whom he built the temple of Apollo at Delphi.

TROS. Son of Erichthonius*. He was one of the ancestors of Troy, and the city was named after him (Hom. Il. v, 265; xx, 230f.).

TROY [Gr. Troia or Ilion]. Very ancient city in the N.W. of Asia Minor, close to the Hellespont. The exact site of Troy long remained unknown; finally, in 1868, ruins of the city were found in Tell Hissarlik by Schliemann. Nine habitation layers can be distinguished, dating from 3000 B.C. to Imperial Roman times, and some have been further subdivided. It is thought that Homeric Troy is represented by level VIIa, which dates to Mycenaean times (15th-12th centuries B.C.). Tradition identifies the 12th century as the period when the Trojan War took place, and this is borne out by the results of excavations.

TURNUS. King of the Rutulians in Latium, son of Daunus* and Venilia*. He was betrothed to Lavinia*, but fate destined her for Aeneas*. He thus became the main opponent of the Trojans when they settled in Latium. He was finally slain in a duel with Aeneas (Virg. vii, 56, 641; ix, 728, 815; xii, 926).

TWELVE LABORS. See HERACLES.

TYCHE [Gr. = fate]. Greek personification of chance, first venerated as the tutelary deity of the state in Hellenistic times. The Roman goddess Fortuna* was identified with Tyche.
Iconography. Tyche is represented with a mural crown on her head. In her

hand she holds a horn of plenty or a ship's rudder. The most familiar likeness of Tyche is the statue by Eutyches (early 3rd century B.C.) in the Vatican Museum; it represents the city goddess of Antiochia: wearing the mural crown and

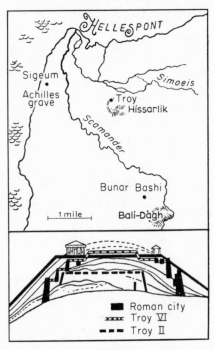

TROY

Troy lies to the south of the Hellespont in the plain of the Scamander and its numerous tributaries, chief of which is the Simoeis. In the 18th century a search was made for Troy in Tell Hissarlik, but German scholars identified the hill of Bali-Dagh, near Bunar Bashi, as the site of the city. Heinrich Schliemann began his excavations in 1870, again at Hissarlik, where he found many habitation layers, sometimes regularly arranged, sometimes confused. His successors identified nine layers, some of which were further subdivided, and compiled a chronology of the inhabited site stretching from 3200 B.C. to A.D. 400. The Troy of Priam was found in layer VI. A burial mound near Cape Sigeum was regarded in ancient times as the grave of Achilles.

clad in a loose-fitting mantle she is seated on a rock, with her right foot resting on the shoulder of the river god Orontes, who is emerging from the water. The statue was extremely popular, and in addition to being frequently copied it was also reproduced on coins.

TYDEUS. Son of King Oeneus* of Calydon; father of Diomedes*. He married Deipyle, daughter of Adrastus*, and took part with his father-in-law in the war of the Seven against Thebes* (Hom. Il. iv, 372f.; v, 800f.).

TYNDAREUS [Gr. Tundareos]. King of Sparta, husband of Leda* and father of the Dioscuri*, Clytaemnestra*, and Helen*. His brother Hippocoön* drove him from Sparta, but he was restored to power by Heracles*. He had no heir, as his sons the Dioscuri had been given a place among the gods, so he gave his possessions to his son-in-law Menelaus*.

TYPHOEUS. See TYPHON.

TYPHON or **TYPHOEUS** [Gr. Tuphoeus, Tuphaon, Tuphon or Tuphos]. A giant and monster, son of Tartarus* and Gaea*. He had a hundred fire-breathing heads, a hundred arms and legs in the form of snakes, and was of enormous length. By Echidna* he became the father of a number of monsters such as Cerberus*, Chimaera*, etc. He joined battle against the gods and put them all to flight except Zeus*. Although he managed initially to wound even Zeus, he was finally overwhelmed by the latter's thunderbolts and was buried under a mountain in Cilicia, under Aetna* in Sicily, or under the island of Inarime off the coast of Campania (Ov. iii, 303; v, 321, 348f.; Virg. ix, 716).

Iconography. The struggle between Zeus and Typhon is often illustrated, particularly on older Greek pottery, e.g. a Chalcidian hydria (c. 550 B.C.), now at Munich. The giant is here shown with large wings and with serpents for legs, and Zeus is rushing at him with a shaft of lightning in his raised right hand.

TYRO. Daughter of Salmoneus* and mother by Poseidon* of Pelias* and Neleus* and by Cretheus* of Aeson*, Pheres*, and Amythaon (Hom. Od. ii, 120; ix, 235).

TYRRHENUS [Gr. Turrenos or Tursenos]. Son of King Atys of Lydia. He led a group of Pelasgian colonizers to Italy. They settled in the country between the Arno and the Tiber (now Tuscany). This was how an ancient tradition accounted for the presence of the Etruscans in Italy. The race was called the Tyrrheni (= Etruscans) after their leader; the Tyrrhenian Sea also took its name from him (Herod. i, 94).

U–V

ULYSSES or ULIXES. Latin form of Odysseus*.

URANIA [Gr. Ourania]. Muse* of astronomy.

Iconography. Urania is represented with a globe in her left hand and a stylus in her right; her gaze is directed at the sky.

URANUS [Gr. Ouranos]. Son and husband of Gaea*. Uranus and Gaea are the oldest pair of gods in the Greek pantheon. Uranus was the father of the Titans*, Cyclopes*, and Centimani*. Fearful of his own offspring, he threw the Cyclopes and Centimani into Tartarus*, but the Titans rebelled and dethroned him.

VACUNA. Sabine goddess of agriculture, worshiped in a sacred wood near Reate (now Rieti).

VEDIOVIS or VEIOVIS. Ancient Roman deity whose significance remains uncertain. Some explain his name as meaning "the avenging Jupiter." He was venerated at Rome and Bovillae in Latium. His temples at Rome stood on the Capitoline and the island in the Tiber. He was represented as a young man with a bundle of arrows in his hand and a goat beside him. He was sometimes identified with Apollo*.

VENERALIA. See VENUS.

VENILIA. 1. Mother of Turnus* (Virg. x, 76). 2. Roman nymph, wife of Janus* (Ov. xiv, 334).

VENUS. Old Italic goddess of vegetation, protectress of gardens and vineyards. Later, under Greek influence, she became the goddess of love and beauty and was wholly identified with Aphrodite*. The hero Aeneas* was born of her union with the mortal Anchises*. She watched continuously over her son during his wanderings from Troy to Italy (Virg. i, 411, 658; v, 779; viii, 370; x,

331). The god Mars, too, was her lover (Ov. iv, 169f.). Her cult originated at Ardea in Latium. From an early period there were two temples of Venus at Rome, the older of which dated from 293 B.C. (Liv. x, 31, 9). The foundation day of these sanctuaries was celebrated on August 18 with the festival of the Vinalia Rustica. After the defeat at Lake Trasimene and consultation in 215 B.C. of the Sibylline Books*, a temple to Venus Erycina was consecrated on the Capitol (Liv. xxii, 9, 10; xxiii, 30, 31). The cult of Aphrodite on Sicily was thus brought to Rome. The foundation day of this temple was celebrated on the festival of Vinalia Priora on April 23. Another festival, the Veneralia, was held in honor of Venus Verticordia and Fortuna Virilis on April 1. Venus Verticordia (= who changes hearts) was invoked as the protectress against debauchery and had a temple at Rome as early as 114 B.C. She was possibly identical with Aphrodite of Cyprus, whose festival also fell on April 1. The dictator Sulla (c. 80 B.C.) regarded Venus as his tutelary deity, and her status was greatly enhanced by the veneration paid to her by Julius Caesar and Augustus because, as the mother of Aeneas, she was the ancestress of the Julian family. Caesar dedicated a temple to Venus Genitrix in his forum, and Hadrian finally erected the great temple to Venus and Roma near the Colosseum in A.D. 135. Among the many titles under which Venus was honored was that of Venus Pompeiana, tutelary goddess of the city of Pompeii.

Iconography. See APHRODITE.

VERTUMNUS or VORTUMNUS. Roman deity who protected gardens and orchards. His name (*vertere* = to change) refers to the changing seasons. He possessed the power to assume any

147

form he pleased and made use of it in his attempts to win Pomona's* favor. There was a statue of Vertumnus on the Vicus Tuscus at Rome, and a temple was dedicated to him on the Aventine in 264 B.C. Sacrifice was offered to him annually on dedication day, August 13. Some say Vertumnus was the city god of Volsinii (now Bolsena) and was also venerated by the Etruscans. Nevertheless, Vertumnus was originally an ancient Italian deity (Ov. xiv, 621f.).

Iconography. In Roman art Vertumnus is represented as a handsome young man wearing a crown of ears of grain or foliage. Sometimes he is an older man with a beard. His attribute is a horn of plenty.

VESTA. Roman goddess of domestic life and of the fire burning on the hearth. Her cult goes back to the earliest Roman times. According to legend Romulus* and Remus were children of a vestal virgin* and King Numa Pompilius instituted the Vestal religion and built a primitive temple at the foot of the Palatine. The temple took the form of a circular hut with walls of reeds and clay. A fire was kept burning continuously there by special priestesses called vestal virgins. The cult was based on the ritual significance that fire had for primitive man, in whose hut the fire had to be kept burning, the job of tending it falling to the daughters of the family. The temple of Vesta at Rome contained no statue of the goddess but only the "hearth fire" of the Roman state, the Palladium*, and the Penates* that Aeneas* was supposed to have brought from Troy. The fire was renewed annually on March 1, and if it went out between times it was regarded as a particularly ominous sign. The temple of Vesta was repeatedly destroyed and rebuilt. The present temple in the Forum Romanum* dates from the beginning of the 3rd century A.D. and was erected by the wife of Septimius Severus. Perpetual fire burned in the sanctuary until A.D. 394. Apart from the one at Rome, there was a temple of Vesta at Lavinium where the consuls offered sacrifice on accepting office.

The festival of Vestalia was held from June 7 to 15. On the first day of the festival the "penus Vestae," the sacred inner part of the temple of Vesta that was always closed, was open to women, who, barefoot, brought offerings to the sanctuary. On the last day the temple was cleaned. In family life the worship of Vesta was very closely associated with that of the Penates.

Iconography. The best-known statue of the goddess is the Giustini Vesta at Rome, a stern figure clad in a long garment and with her head covered; her right hand rests by her side and in her left she probably held a scepter.

VESTAL VIRGIN. Roman priestess whose duty it was to maintain the worship of Vesta*. The Vestals were originally four in number, later becoming six. It was their task to tend the perpetual fire in the temple of Vesta on the Forum Romanum*. They were chosen, while still children, from patrician families by the Pontifex Maximus (high priest), and had to serve for thirty years, during which they were under a vow to lead an austere and chaste life. Apart from tending the fire the Vestals had also to offer prayers daily for the prosperity of the people, the state, and the emperor. They also prepared the flour with which sacrificial animals were sprinkled. Failure to keep the fire alive was severely punished. Death was the lot of those who broke their vow of chastity: they were walled up alive in a tomb. On the other hand, Vestals enjoyed special privileges and were held in high esteem. In public they were accompanied by a lictor (an attendant who carried the fasces) and if they chanced to meet a man condemned to death he was reprieved. At public festivals they occupied a place of honor. Their dwelling was the Atrium Vestae, beside the temple of Vesta.

Iconography. Several statues of Vestals have been preserved in the porticoes which surround the inner courtyard of the Atrium of the Vestals on the Forum Romanum. These were the leaders of the small community. Their dress consisted of a girdled garment with long sleeves. A loose cloak was thrown over the shoulders and head. In their hair they wore the "infula," a fillet consisting of coils of hair. The statues display great dignity, the features being austere and distinguished.

VESTALIA. See VESTA.

VETURIA. Mother of Coriolanus* (Liv. ii, 40, 1).

VICA POTA. Ancient Roman goddess of victory. A shrine dedicated to her stood at the foot of the Velia in Rome (Liv. ii, 7, 12).

VICTORIA. Roman personification of victory, venerated as a goddess, especially by conquering generals. There was a temple to her at Rome. Victoria was held in greater esteem by the war-loving Romans than was her counterpart Nike* by the Greeks.
Iconography. See NIKE.

VIDUUS. Roman god who separated men's souls from their bodies when they died.

VINALIA. See VENUS.

VIRBIUS. Old Roman deity whose function is uncertain. He was worshiped in the sacred wood of Egeria* near Aricia in Latium and identified with the resurrected Hippolytus* (Ov. xv, 544; Virg. vii, 762, 777).

VOLCANUS. See VULCAN.

VOLTUMNA [Etruscan: Veltha or Veltune]. Tutelary goddess of the Etruscan League, whose twelve member cities held their formal annual meeting at her famous sanctuary near Orvieto or Bolsena (see TARCHON) (Liv. iv, 23, 5).

VOLTURNUS. God of the river of the same name in Campania (now Volturno), or—more probably—another name for the Tiber. The festival called Volturnia was celebrated on August 27, and Volturnus had a priest of his own. Nothing is known of the nature of this very old cult.

VOLUMNIA. Wife of Coriolanus* (Liv. ii, 40, 4).

VORTUMNUS. See VERTUMNUS.

VULCAN [Lat. Vulcanus]. Old Roman god of fire and the blacksmith's art, son of Jupiter* and Juno*, husband of Venus*. Early identified with Hephaestus*. His smithy was under Etna, and there he and the Cyclopes forged weapons for Aeneas* and others (Virg. viii, 372, 416, 424, 439). Weapons taken from the enemy were among the offerings made to him (Liv. i, 37, 5). The worship of Vulcan was closely linked with that of Maia* or Bona Dea*, and the priest of Vulcan offered sacrifice to Maia on May 1. A temple near the Circus Flaminius was consecrated to Vulcan in 215 B.C., and the festival of Vulcanaeia in his honor was held on August 23.
Iconography. See HEPHAESTUS.

W–Z

WOODEN HORSE of Troy. When the Greek army had besieged Troy* in vain for ten years, they pretended to abandon the siege, leaving behind a huge wooden horse in which Odysseus* and a number of companions were concealed. Sinon* the spy managed to persuade the Trojans, despite Laocoön's warning, to haul the horse into the city as a trophy. During the night that followed, the Greeks climbed out of the horse and fell upon the unsuspecting, rejoicing Trojans (Virg. ii, 13f., 234f.).
Iconography. The Trojan horse is represented on various Greek vases, e.g. a Corinthian aryballus (c. 560 B.C.) now at Paris: warriors are swarming up and around the horse, which is the center of heavy fighting. It is also shown being dragged inside the walls of Troy on a Pompeian fresco now in the Museo Nazionale at Naples: in the background can be seen the walls and towers of the city. A group of people are pulling the horse along by a rope, while a crowd of soldiers stand by looking on.

XANTHUS [Gr. Xanthos = yellow]. Another name for Scamander*.
XUTHUS [Gr. Xouthos]. Son of Hellen* and husband of Erechtheus' * daughter Creusa (3)*. His sons Ion and Achaeus became the mythical ancestors of the Ionians and the Achaeans.

ZAGREUS. Greek god of the underworld, later an epithet for Dionysus* in the Orphic mysteries*.
ZEPHYRUS [Gr. Zephuros]. Greek personification of the west wind. For the Romans he was the harbinger of spring, and they therefore called him Favonius (= he who favors).
Iconography. On the Tower of the Winds at Athens (1st century B.C.) Zephyrus is shown in relief as a naked, winged youth, using both hands to carry a cloth filled with spring flowers.
ZETES. Son of Boreas*; see CALAIS.
ZETHUS [Gr. Zethos]. Twin brother of Amphion*. Together they avenged the ill-treatment accorded to their mother Antiope*. Unlike the artistic Amphion, Zethus was of a coarse nature and an inveterate hunter.
ZEUS. The supreme god of the Greeks, father of gods and mankind, lord of the universe. The name Zeus (= bright), like that of Jupiter (= bright father), suggests a connection with the worship of the bright firmament. All nature and its manifestations were subject to Zeus. He assembled the clouds and scattered them; rain and snow were caused by him. It was he who secured the harmony not only of nature but also of the social order. Kings and princes derived their power from him and were accountable to him. He was the counseling god, the protector of the people's assembly and the preserver of the oath. The family, too, was under his care, and guests and strangers in particular enjoyed his protection. Lightning was the fearsome instrument with which he punished evildoers. No god could match his power against that of Zeus; and when some gods, including his wife Hera*, opposed him, they were severely punished. Only to fate (Moira) was even Zeus subject. His worship was widespread throughout Greece. One of the oldest places where he was specially venerated was Dodona*; there he revealed his will in the rustling of the sacred oaks. Olympia* later became the most outstanding center of his cult. The famous Olympic Games* were held in honor of Zeus, and the Nemean Games* were also dedicated to him. Zeus, finally, was the object of special devotion in Crete, where he was said to have been born. Accord-

ing to legend he was kept hidden on that island because his father Cronus* had hitherto devoured his own offspring. Nymphs reared the young Zeus, and the goat Amalthea suckled him. The Curetes* ensured that his crying would not reveal his whereabouts. He had numerous affairs with goddesses, but Hera, his sister, was his first wife. The Greek imagination regarded most heroes as sons of Zeus and no god was the subject of more myths than he. Zeus' abode was on Mt. Olympus in Thessaly, but Mt. Ida on Crete and Mt. Lycaeus in Arcadia were particularly sacred to him. *Iconography.* Zeus is represented in ancient art as a majestic figure with long locks and beard. His attributes are light-ning and an eagle; also a globe, a Nike, and a scepter. In older art he is shown nude; later he is often draped. He is represented countless times in the most widely varying functions and in connection with almost all the principal Greek myths. The most famous statue of Zeus in antiquity was that by Phidias in front of his temple at Olympia; it was made of gold and ivory and showed the god seated. Among surviving statues of Zeus the best-known is the bust from Otricoli, now in the Vatican Museum; calm, majesty, and kindness radiate from his noble countenance.

ZEUXIPPE. Attic nymph, mother by Pandion* of Erechtheus (2)*, Butes*, Procne*, and Philomela*.

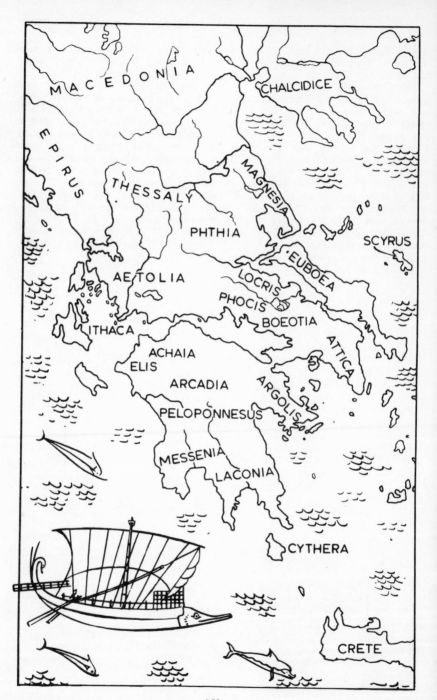

Dodona

Aegae

Delphi

Thebes

Megara Eleusis

Corinth Athens

Epidaurus

Nemea Mycenae

Argos

Olympia

Phigalia

Pylos

Sparta

CYTHERA

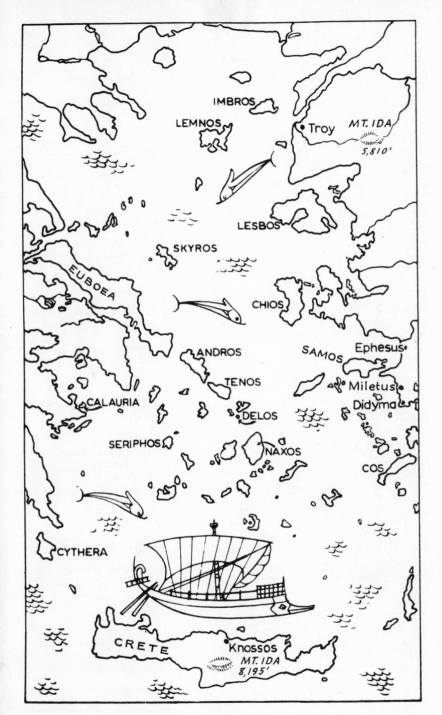

IMBROS

LEMNOS

Troy

MT. IDA
5,810'

LESBOS

SKYROS

EUBOEA

CHIOS

ANDROS

SAMOS

Ephesus

TENOS

Miletus

CALAURIA

Didyma

DELOS

SERIPHOS

NAXOS

COS

CYTHERA

CRETE

Knossos
MT. IDA
8,195'

THE ENCYCLOPEDIA OF THE CLASSICAL WORLD

J. H. Croon

This encyclopedia, companion to The ENCYCLOPEDIA OF CLASSICAL MYTHOLOGY, is a reference guide to Greco-Roman civilization and the ancient Mediterranean world which includes customs, religious practices, modes of warfare, laws and institutions, as well as cities, regions, mountains, rivers, and battle sites. Extended articles are devoted to the great personalities who shaped the ancient world and molded Western thought—men like Alexander the Great, Aristophanes, Aristotle, and Augustus.

Philosophy, literature, and the arts receive special emphasis. The plays of Aeschylus, Sophocles, and Euripides are treated individually as are the dialogues of Plato; literary genres and conventions are traced to their Greek or Latin origins. Broad artistic topics such as SCULPTURE and ARCHITECTURAL ORDERS are discussed, as well as specific styles and works of art such as CORINTHIAN COLUMNS and the LAOCOÖN.

This encyclopedia also presents in their classical context such varied subjects as METER, COINAGE, BOOKS, CHRONOLOGY, SHIPS, SLAVERY, EPIGRAPHY, PAPYROLOGY, and TEXTUAL CRITICISM. This original English translation of *Elseviers Encyclopedie van de Antieke Wereld* provides a *vade mecum* for English readers seeking knowledge of—and inspiration from—the world that fostered our civilization.

THE ENCYCLOPEDIA OF THE BIBLE

Edited by P. A. Marijnen

This complete reference work comprises thousands of persons and places, writings, institutions, and ideas associated with the Bible. Originally compiled by a team of leading Dutch experts on Biblical exegesis, including both Catholic and Protestant scholars, the Encyclopedia gives a complete listing of Biblical terms, together with the origins of many proper names (Jonah: "dove"; Methuselah: "spear bearer"); special articles on scriptural texts and sources (palimpsest . . . papyrus . . . Pastoral Epistles . . . Pentateuch); discussions of the meanings of theological concepts (Transformation . . . Tree of Life . . . Trinity); and articles that place in their scriptural context the most fundamental human ideas (life . . . light . . . love).

Noteworthy for scholarly completeness, yet lucid and readable, this new English edition of *Elseviers Encyclopedie van de Bijbel* will serve the scholar or theologian, as well as the layman.